RANDOM ISLAND PIONEERS

RANDOM ISLAND PIONEERS

Wilfred B.W. Martin

(with the assistance of Eileen Martin)

Creative Publishers
St. John's, Newfoundland
1990

Appreciation is expressed to the *Canada Council* for publication assistance.

The publisher acknowledges the financial contribution of the *Cultural Affairs Division of the Department of Municipal and Provincial Affairs, Government of Newfoundland and Labrador*, which has helped make this publication possible.

Printed in Canada by:

ROBINSON-BLACKMORE PRINTING & PUBLISHING LTD.
P.O. Box 8660, St. John's, Newfoundland A1B 3T7

Published by

CREATIVE PUBLISHERS
A Division of Robinson-Blackmore Printing & Publishing Ltd.
P.O. Box 8660, St. John's, Newfoundland A1B 3T7

Cover Photo
Rider's Harbour, the first permanent settlement on Random Island, was settled in the 1760s and abandoned in the 1860s. This picture of the harbour was taken in 1988.

1st Printing January 1990
2nd Printing April 1990

Canadian Cataloguing in Publication Data

Martin, Wilfred B. W., 1940 -

Random Island Pioneers

Includes bibliographical references.

ISBN 0-920021-72-7

1. Random Island (Nfld.) — Genealogy.

2. Random Island (Nfld.) — History.

I. Martin, Eileen II. Title.

FC2195.R36M37 1989 971.8 C90-0997507-5

F1124.R36M37 1989

TABLE OF CONTENTS

PREFACE

FOR MANY YEARS we have been interested in the sociocultural history of our home communities on Random Island. Three years ago we started researching the history of people and places on all parts of this island, with the aim of writing a book so that our findings could be shared with others. The first book, *Gleams in the Glooming* (Creative Publishers, 1988), from our research on the people and places on Random Island, contains a biographical sketch of Lillian May Martin and a collection of her poems. The present publication, *Random Island Pioneers,* is the second book developed from this research. The purposes of this book are (1) to offer an analysis of the origins of place names on Random Island, particularly the names which are suggestive of the identity of the early people on this island; (2) to give an overview of changes in the size of the population on Random Island from 1836 to 1981; (3) to review the nature and extent of the early industries of fishing, lumbering, shipbuilding, slate quarrying, brickmaking and farming on the island; (4) to identify and give background of the twenty-seven settlements which have existed on Random Island at one time or another; (5) to pinpoint the date when each place was permanently settled and (6) to identify the pioneers of each of the settlements on Random Island and provide genealogical notes on each family that settled on the island prior to 1900.

We have collected a considerable amount of information and a large number of pictures relating to all facets of the history of Random Island which we have not been able to incorporate in this book on *Random Island Pioneers*. However, we plan to continue our research on the people and places of Random Island and we will use some of this material in our next publication. It will focus on the history of the school and church in each of the settlements on the island.

Many Random Islanders have helped us in our endeavour to learn about our past and to make it known to others in book form. Acknowledgements for pictures used in the present publication are given throughout this book and a list of people who have been particularly helpful in sharing their knowledge about family origins and community histories is given in Appendix C. Since our research is ongoing, we would appreciate hearing of any material you have that might help us in this endeavour.

Wilfred B. W. Martin
Eileen Martin

CHAPTER 1

RESEARCHING RANDOM ISLAND PIONEERS

RANDOM ISLAND, the largest island on the coast of Newfoundland, is located on the north side of Trinity Bay. It is separated from the mainland by the river-like passages of Smith Sound and Northwest Arm of Random Sound. The protruding points of land and accompanying indentations of this rectangular shaped island suggest that the island would fit between the opposing sides of the Northwest Arm and Smith Sound, if it were closer to these shorelines. The high cliffs at the entrances to Smith and Random sounds, together with the steep hills on each side of Smith Sound and the Northwest side of Random Sound, give a fjord-like appearance to these waterways. As early people travelled in these waterways they went further away from the lucrative fishing grounds of the headlands. Hence, except for the establishment of settlements on the eastern end of Random Island, many of the early people were reluctant to settle on other parts of the island. But, over time, the lush forest, the availability of agricultural land and the many protected harbours and coves on the island attracted more than just winter people. People from other parts of Trinity Bay and from different communities in Conception Bay were joined by a few who came directly from England and Wales to make their homes on Random Island. The present research is designed to identify those who pioneered settlements on Random Island, to pinpoint when and why they came to the island, and to isolate where they came from to settle on it. Before addressing these questions, it is appropriate to describe the methods used to collect information relating to Random Island pioneers and to outline the plan for presenting our findings in this book.

Research Methods

The research process for this book was divided into two parts: (1) archival and library research and (2) field research. The bulk of the archival work was with vital statistics from church records. Newfoundland Government census, directories of people and places in Newfoundland during the 19th century, ship registry, land grant records and Colonial Papers were other primary sources studied. Secondary materials researched included newspapers, magazines and other published materials. Several interrelated approaches to data collection were combined during the field research. One approach was taped interviews with Random Islanders and former islanders. Thirty such interviews, ranging from one to five hours, were conducted with senior citizens who are, or were, long-time residents of Random Island. Another approach was to talk with Random Islanders concerning their genealogies and histories of their respective communities. In some cases, information on ancestors of island people was gathered from family Bibles. In addition, many people made available, for our perusal, private papers and family photo albums which relate to the history of people and places on Random Island. Finally, relevant information from tombstones in each of the twenty-four cemeteries found on Random Island was noted in compiling lists of the early settlers.

Certain problems were encountered in attempting to identify the adults on Random Island prior to 1900. This was especially the case when attempting to find the names of the women living on the island during those days. Since women did not have the right to vote their names were not included on early voters lists for Trinity Bay. This problem was exacerbated by the fact that women were not included in Newfoundland directories of those days. As expected, difficulties were encountered when attempts were made to pinpoint the place and date of birth of the adults, both male and female, living on Random Island during those early days. In many cases no records were found of the birth, marriage or death of those early people. Even when written records were located there were problems identifying exact dates. For example, church records relating to particular individuals were not always consistent, and those records were not always in line with other written documents. Nominal censuses were invaluable sources for identifying the previous places of abode of early settlers to Random Island, but they also contained contradictory information concerning the place of birth and age of many individuals. Given the earlier practice of expectant mothers moving to communities where a midwife lived, and sometimes spending extended periods of time awaiting the arrival of the newborn there, the recorded place of birth of the child was sometimes not the home of the parents. When comparing church records, one often finds that the date of birth as calculated from marriage records is different from that calculated from burial records. Undoubtedly, some of these are recording errors. But, it is speculated that false information was sometimes given at time of marriage to appear older or younger and thereby be more in line with the age of one's future spouse. Also, as seen when comparing inscriptions on tombstones with vital statistics as recorded in church records, errors were often made in recording the age of people and in the spelling of their names.

Book Plan

In order to set the stage concerning the geographical expanse, that is the coves, harbours and inland waters on Random Island, and simultaneously identify some of the early visitors to, and settlers on, this island, chapter 2 of this book is devoted to a discussion of the origins of place names on the island.

All settlements which have existed, at one time or another, on Random Island are identified in chapter 3. They are categorized as to whether they were the earliest settlements, whether they still exist, or whether they were outlying places on the island. In addition, chapter 3 includes an outline of the population growth and decline at different periods in the history of Random Island, and brief descriptions of the early industries of fishing, lumbering, shipbuilding, brickmaking, slate quarrying and farming on the island. Random Island pioneers are identified in Chapters 4, 5 and 6 as they became residents of the earliest settlements (Deer Harbour, Rider's Harbour, Silldown and Thoroughfare), of the present communities (Aspey Brook, Britannia/Lower Lance Cove, Elliott's Cove, Hickman's Harbour, Lady Cove, Middle Lance Cove, Petley/Aspen Cove, Snook's Harbour and Weybridge), and of the outlying places (Bar Point, Bluff Head Cove, Bound's Mead, East Random Head, George's Cove, Random Head Harbour, Robinson's Bight, Souley's Brook and Wake's Brook). Family names of those appearing as permanent settlers in each place on the island during each of the decades prior to 1900 are pinpointed. Also, the place and date of birth for some of the adults, that is those born during or before 1880 in each of the settlements on the island are presented in table form. Families that moved to the present settlements between 1900 and 1945 are noted. For the resettled communities of Deer Harbour, Thoroughfare and Middle Lance Cove, and where applicable for the outlying places, families taking up residence in them between 1900 and when they were phased out have also been identified. Given the difficulty in identifying all of the adults on Random Island prior to 1900, the tables presented in chapters 4, 5 and 6 do not claim to be complete listings. However, they are as complete as is possible from information unearthed in the present re-

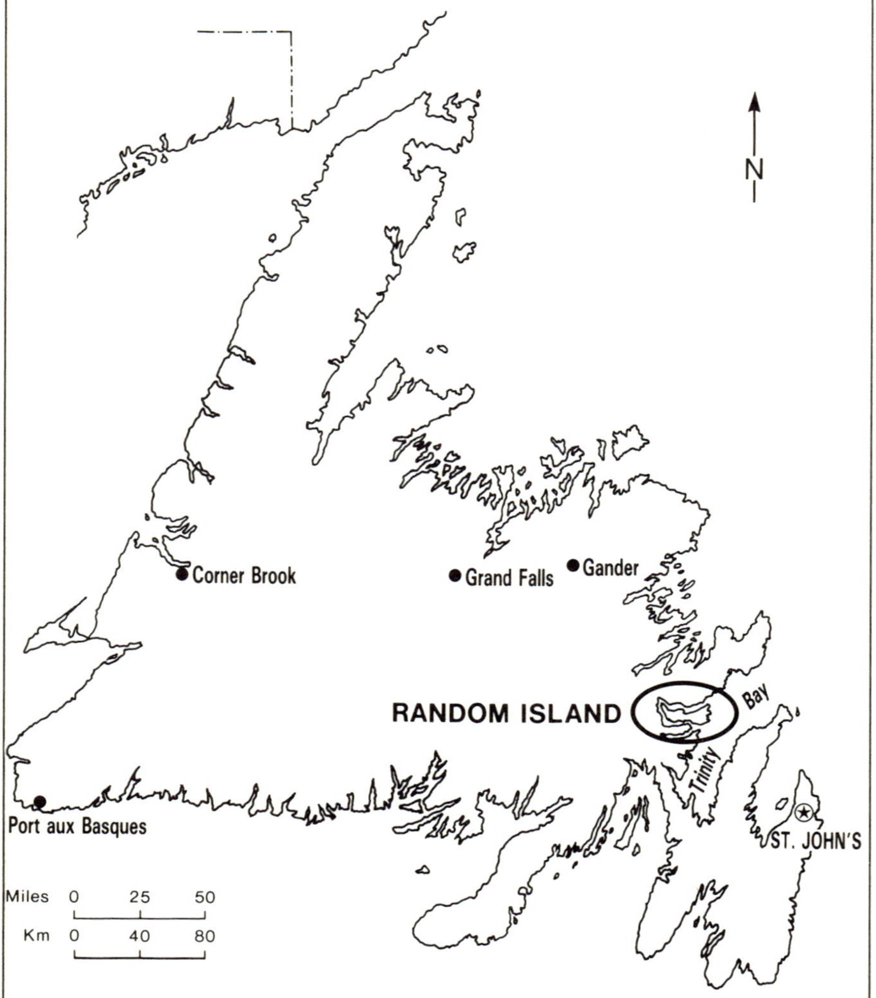

MAP 1-1 RANDOM ISLAND, NEWFOUNDLAND

search. These tables also have varying amounts of missing information about the place and date of birth, maiden names and number of marriages for certain individuals. Even with these shortcomings, this information may serve as a starting point for those interested in family trees and as a point of comparison for those with more complete genealogical information on specific families. Chapter 7, the final chapter of this book, is a collection of historical facts relating to different sociocultural features of island life and development.

Changes which have occurred in place names on Random Island over the years are listed in Appendix A. Some of the places where island people lived immediately prior to their settling on Random Island also underwent name changes. Appendix B is a listing of those changes as referred throughout this book. Appendix C contains acknowledgments to those who helped in different ways during the development of this book. It also contains a list of those who shared genealogical materials and information relating to the history of different places on Random Island. The primary data sources on which this book is based are identified in Appendix D, and the secondary material referred to in this book are listed in Appendix E. An index of family names of Random Island pioneers identified in this book is included.

CHAPTER 2

ORIGINS OF PLACE NAMES

AN EXPLANATION of the origin of the name of *Random Island* has eluded those interested for many decades. A Colonial paper of 1677 includes a map of Newfoundland which shows *Random Head*, but does not identify *Random Island* (Colonial Office, 199:18). A chart by Augustine Fitzhugh of Newfoundland and the fishing banks in 1693 identifies the headland of *Random* and a place named *Rantem* at the bottom of an inlet formed by this headland. According to the most Reverend M.F. Howley (1906:9), early maps labelled what is now *Random Island* as *Ireland*. The earliest reference to *Random Island*, so named as an island, as found in the present research is that on a 1784 map of Newfoundland. *Smith Sound*, the body of water separating the north shore of Random Island from the mainland of Newfoundland, is identified as such on Fitzhugh's 1693 chart of Newfoundland. It is likely that the sound got its name from a Captain John Smith, who is believed to have done naval duty in Newfoundland waters in the early 17th century. Like other parts of Newfoundland, most of the coves, inlets, tickles, harbours and points along the coastline of Random Island have been given names. Similarly, the ponds, gullies, steadies, cricks, rivers and brooks, as well as numerous hills, knobs, valleys, gulches, cliffs, rocks and other distinct geographical entities, including paths, lanes and roads have been named. While many of these names are known only through oral tradition, others have been included in written records for relatively long periods of time. Some of those found in early written documents have disappeared from the common usage and, in fact, are no longer known by any of the island residents. The focus of this chapter is the origins of places names, including existing and abandoned settlements, coves, points and ponds, as these names are seen to suggest the presence of early visitors, winter people and settlers to different parts of the island. By way of discussing the origins of place names on Random Island it is more convenient to divide the island into three parts than it is to deal with it in total. For this purpose, the three regions are: (1) the eastern, (2) the central and (3) the western.

Eastern Random Island

As indicated on Map 2-1, many geographical identities on the eastern part of Random Island have been named in honour of pioneers of this island. Before elaborating on these names it is interesting to note that while there are many such names in and around *Deer Harbour*, the origin of the name of *Deer Harbour* itself is not so easily established. In response to a request of a radio programme for histories of communities in Newfoundland, Lloyd King (1963) of Deer Harbour wrote that the harbour got its name because of the presence of deer in the forest surrounding the harbour when the first settlers came to it. The name of the former community of *Deer Harbour* is actually a shorten version of the first name of this place which, as identified in written records, was *John Brown's Deer Harbour*. This name was a reference to John Brown Marsh, who along with his brother Benjamin Marsh, was the first permanent settler in Deer Harbour. Newfoundland census of 1845 lists Deer Harbour on Random Island as *Deer Harbour Bounds*. As a carryover from this name, the flat land where the school and church were located in Deer Harbour is known as *the bound* by former residents of the harbour. While it is listed as Deer Harbour in subsequent censuses, the marine chart and certain maps refer to the Deer Harbour on Random Island as *Lower Deer Harbour* to distinguish it from *Upper Deer Harbour* which is also located on the north side of Trinity Bay, but to the southwest of Random Island along the shoreline to Bay Bulls Arm. In addition to the *Deer Harbour* on Random Island, there is a cove on the southern shore of the island which, in oral tradition, is known as *Deer Cove*. However, this cove is identified as *Salmon Cove* on the Government of Canada map of Random Island as well as on the marine chart of this area.

As is the case in other communities of Random Island, surnames of many of the early settlers have become associated with specific locations in and around Deer Harbour. But, unlike in other communities on Random Island, the residents of Deer Harbour generally referred to their land as *rooms*. For example, there were *Baileys' Room, Evelys' Room, Kings' Room, Marshes' Room* and rooms named after Newtons, Penneys, Purchases and Whelans in Deer Harbour. To refer to one's land as *a room* is probably an extension of a traditionally widespread practice in Newfoundland to refer to one's fishing stage and flakes in this manner. Certain locations in Deer Harbour are denoted by surnames of people who have long since gone from the area, and no one is exactly sure of who they were. For example, at the entrance to the north side of Deer Harbour there is *Bearns' Point*. While there are no written records of any Bearns ever living in Deer Harbour, it is likely that there were early visitors or winter people by this name in the harbour at one time. According to Seary (1976:26), there were Bearns in Newfoundland as early as 1681, with one George Bearns in Old Perlican in 1828. Near Bearns there is a *Thomas Cove*, and on the other side of harbour is *Jackson's Hill*. Presently, no one knows anything of the Thomas in Deer Harbour. It was, however, a Trinity Bay name as early as 1767 (Seary, 1976:477). Local tradition has it that the Jacksons came to Deer Harbour from Harbour Grace. They lived in Deer Harbour for only a short time before moving to Bell Island.

At the entrance to the south of Deer Harbour is *Gosse's Point*. Although no written records have been located concerning their presence in the harbour, the belief is that a family of Gosses lived on this point during early times. Near Gosse's Point there is an area known as *Sally Rowe*, and there is a fishing ground with this name. Records of the Methodist Church in Hant's Harbour show that a son was born to Edward and Sarah Rowe of Deer Harbour in 1844. Apparently they left the harbour shortly thereafter, but their name remained a part of oral tradition in association with where they lived and fished. To the south of Sally Rowe, there is *Mark's Cove*, also referred to as *Margot's Cove* and *Margaret's Cove*, The origins of these names are unknown. Nearby, there is a *Sibley's Cove*. While no written records have been found to indicate that anyone with the surname of Sibley lived in Deer Harbour, it is possible that someone with this surname inhabited this cove, or fished from it, or, as one story goes, was shipwrecked on the nearby point. As seen in Seary (1976:443), there were Sibleys and Cybleys on the south side of Trinity Bay during the 18th century. *Verge's Island*, a short distance from Sibley's Cove, was named in honour of the Verges who lived in Ireland's Eye, Bonaventure and Thoroughfare. Perhaps, they experienced some difficulties in the area, or fished near the island which now bears their name. Further south along the coast there is *Random Head Harbour* and *East Random Head*. *The Motion*, an island a few feet from East Random Head, rises to a considerable height above sea level and has a lighthouse on it. The sea is seldom calm around this area. If there is no swell or undertow as a result of easterly winds, one is likely to find sizeable lops from southern and southwest winds which can be very brisk in the area. Hence, the name *The Motion* has been given to this island.

In addition to names taken from points on the compass, for example, *Northwest Arm*, and other names which denote geographical

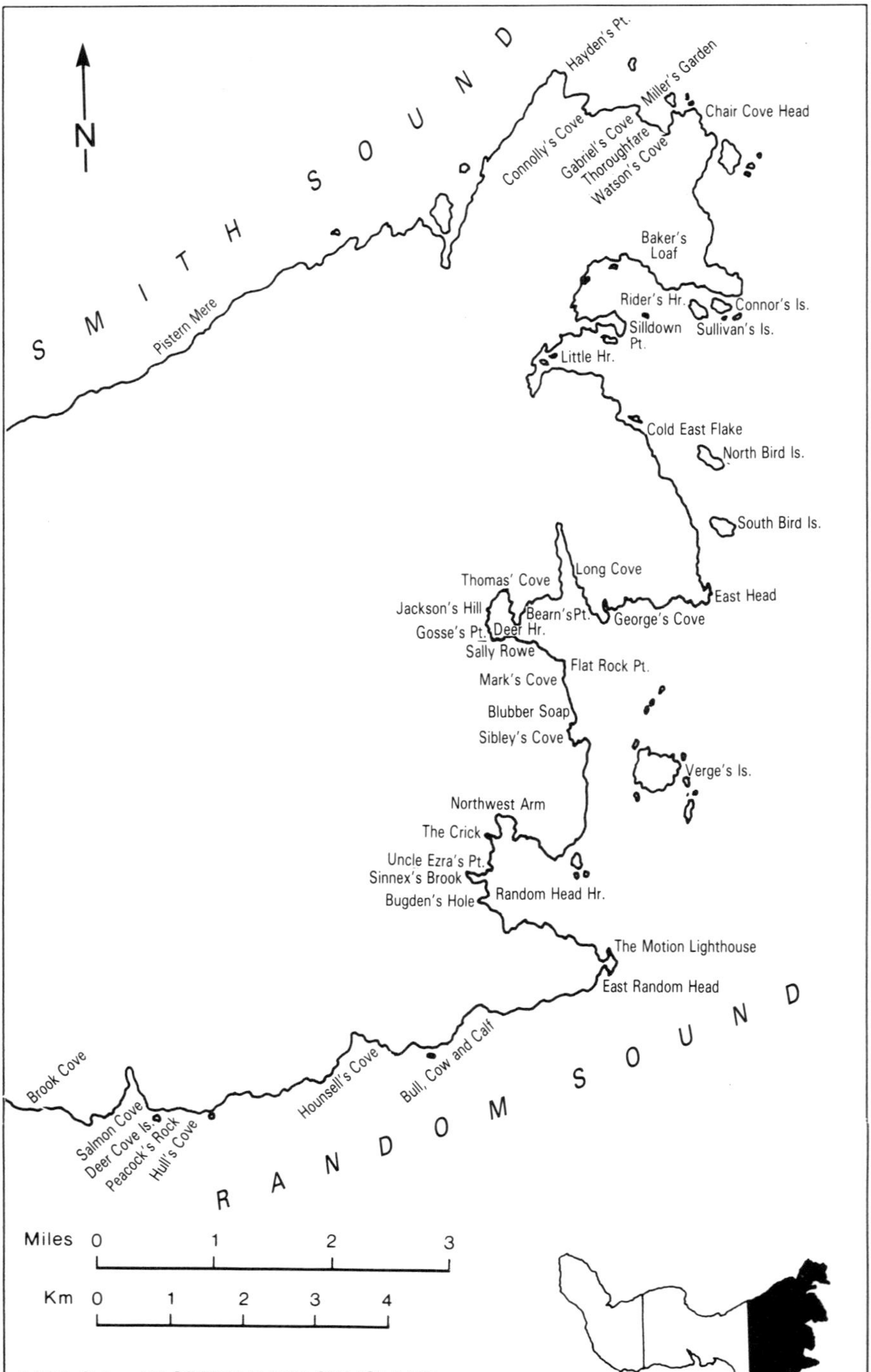

MAP 2-1 EASTERN RANDOM ISLAND

features such as *The Crick,* different locations in Random Head Harbour bear the names of early settlers. One such name is *Bugden's Hole,* a small cove overshadowed on each side with steep high hills which give way to lower hills and a narrow valley in the bottom. Another is *Uncle Ezra's Point,* located on the narrow waterway approaching the mouth of the main river emptying into Random Head Harbour and named after one Ezra Marsh who lived on this point during the early part of the present century. The gently sloping rock on Uncle Ezra's Point bear the markings, that is, letters, parts of words and compass points, from earlier visitors. Traditionally, it was widely believed that some of those early visitors were pirates who buried their wealth at Random Head Harbour. The main brook emptying into Random Head Harbour from Random Harbour Pond, especially that portion of the brook closest to the salt water, has been known in oral tradition as *Sinnex's Brook* for more than 100 years. One writer, and former resident of *The Motion Lighthouse,* has referred to this brook as "Cynics Brook" with the suggestion that the name is a curious one (Cooper, 1982:13). However, former residents of Deer Harbour report that two Sinnex brothers from Trinity lived in Random Head Harbour around 1840. While there is no written record of anyone with the surname Sinnex ever living this harbour, there were Sinnexes living in the Trinity area during that time and it is highly probably that *Sinnex's Brook* was named in reference to the people who spent time harvesting the forest nearby.

Place names along the southern shore of eastern Random Island include *Hounsell's Cove, Hull's Cove* and *Peacock's Rock.* It is believed that the naming of Hounsell's Cove was in association with this family name, but there is no evidence of this. Hull's Cove is said to have been named in honour of Uriah Hull of Heart's Content, who tilted on Random Island and, along with his wife and children, drowned off West Random Head in the early part of the 19th century. Peacock's Rock, an underwater rock in the tickle forming Deer Cove Island, got this name after Reverend Mr. Peacock, a United Church Minister, ran his boat on it while travelling from Hickman's Harbour to visit his parishioners at Deer Harbour in 1932.

To the northeast of Deer Harbour there is *Long Cove* which probably got its name because of its long narrow indraft, although there is a story that a family of Longs once lived in this cove. Between *Long Cove* and *East Head* (locally known as "Deer Harbour Head"), there is *George's Cove,* with *George's Cove Point* and *George's Cove Rocks* nearby. This cove, point and rocks were named in honour of a family of Georges that lived in George's Cove around 1870. Senior citizens, who are former residents of Deer Harbour, tell of reports they heard in their childhood some 90 years ago (around 1900) that lights were seen in George's Cove long after the settlement ceased to be. It was believed that the lights were spirits or ghosts of a young boy who is said to have drowned in George's Cove Pond.

Other early settlements on the eastern end of Random Island existed at *Rider's Harbour* (also spelt "Ridar's Harbour" and "Ryder's Harbour" in church records), and at *Silldown* (also spelt "Stilldown" and "Seldown" in different records). In oral tradition, Rider's Harbour has become known as *Rise's Harbour.* Although no written record has been found of any Riders (or Ryders) residing at Rider's Harbour, the name of this harbour could have derived from the presence of people with this surname as transient or winter people. There were Ryders in Scilly Cove (later renamed Winterton) in the early part of the 19th century. As noted in *Sailing Directions: Newfoundland* (1980:215), there is a *Rider Hill* dividing Trinity Harbour into two arms: *Northwest Arm* and *Southwest Arm. Sullivan's Island* and *Connor's Island,* which create Rider's Harbour, protecting it from the open bay, bear the names of early settlers, that is, the Sullivans and the O'Connors, in Rider's Harbour. In oral tradition, Sullivan's Island has also been known as *Toope's Island,* an apparent reference to the Toopes of Ireland's Eye who fished in this area, and, perhaps, had a fishing premise on the island. The name *Silldown* was not derived from a surname. It is speculated that it was so named because of the geographic features of the land in the area. At Silldown there appears to be one layer of rock over another, hence the reference to a sill. The different sills form a gentle slope from the landwash to low lying hills. Even though different spellings have been given for this place in written records, the present spelling of *Silldown* is the same as the original.

There is a natural passage way between Random Island and Ireland's Eye Island logically named *The Thoroughfare* for marine traffic to and from Smith Sound. The community of *Thoroughfare* was on the Random Island side of The Thoroughfare. There is a conspicuously high peak of some 546 feet (166 metres), known as *Baker's Loaf,* between Rider's Harbour and Thoroughfare. Whether this peak was named because of its resemblance of a loaf of bread, or whether there is connection between it and the people whose surname was Baker, who lived in Thoroughfare during the 1860s, is not known. The settlement of Thoroughfare was bound at the southeastern extreme by *Chair Cove Head,* so named because of chair-like shape of the land at one spot in this area. In oral tradition, this area is known as *Watson's Cove* which is in close proximity to *Miller's Garden.* To the northwest of Thoroughfare are *Connolly's Cove* (also spelt "Connley's Cove" on land grants) and *Gabriel's Cove* (also spelt "Gabol's Cove" in written records). The name of *Connelly's Cove* is an obvious reference to people of this name who visited this cove before it was permanently settled. To speculate, *Gabriel's*

Cove got its name because Thomas Gabriell, who resided in Trinity in 1675 and Heart's Content in 1681 (Seary,1976:191), visited this cove during his travels in the Trinity area. While no distinction was ever made between Connolly's Cove and Thoroughfare in any of the censuses, and they did share the same school and church, some of the former residents of this area claim that Connolly's Cove and Thoroughfare were two distinct identities. Travelling northwest from Connolly's Cove one comes to *Hayden's Point*, with *Hayden's Island* located near this point in the entrance to The Thoroughfare from Smith Sound. One story is that this point was the landing place of a schooner's crew after their schooner, which was skippered by a Captain Hayden, was wrecked on the rock between the point and the island.

Names of different ponds sometimes point to the surnames of winter people, some of whom became permanent settlers on Random Island. In many cases, such names are the only indication we have of the presence of those early people. For example, there are no written records of any Millers ever living in Deer Harbour, but there is a *Miller's Pond* in this area. The belief is that a Miller family had a winter tilt near this pond, perhaps in the 1830s. Similarly, one of the ponds in the Random Head Harbour area is known as *Hurdle's Pond*, because someone with that surname is thought to have spent winters in the area. *Hiscock's Pond* and *Churchill's Pond* bear the names of early settlers for whom there are written documents of a presence on this part of Random Island, but who have long since gone from the scene. Other ponds have been given the names of early settlers whose surnames were present in the settlements on the eastern end of the island until the settlements ceased to be. For example, in Deer Harbour area there are ponds named in honour of *Baileys*, *Kings* and *Penneys* (see Map 2-4).

Central Random Island

Many of the place names on the southern shore of central Random Island (Map 2-2) are in honour of visitors and winter people to this area before it was permanently settled. These names include *Robinson's Bight*, earlier called *Pistern Mere* but later renamed in honour of John and Cecilia Robinson of Trinity who are said to have spent several winters in this place before 1850. *Taylor's Cove* and the two points of land forming this cove are named after a family of Taylors who had a winter tilt in the cove around 1840. *Halfyard's Cove* may also bear the name of another visitor or temporary settler on Random Island. Seary (1976:209) records that there were Halfyards in Newfoundland in 18th century, and in Grates Cove in the 1830s. Many of the early settlers to Hickman's Harbour came from Grates Cove, and it is possible that a Halfyard from Grates Cove spent some time in the cove bearing this name. Transients or winter people with the surname of Strong, perhaps the Strongs who resided in Old Perlican during the early 19th century, visited or had winter tilts in the area to the east of the Hickman's Harbour quarries, hence the names of *Strong's Tickle, Strong's Island* and *West Strong Island*. One of the smaller islands near Strong's Tickle has become known, in oral tradition, as *Manuel's Island*, with an accompanying *Manuel's Rock* nearby. It is said that a schooner skipped by a person whose first name was Manuel ran aground on this rock while entering Strong's Tickle under sail, but it is unusual for a person's christian name, rather than one's surname, to be associated with a particular geographical identity. East of Strong's Tickle, there are other geographical identities such as *Canning's Head, Canning's Cove* and *Button's Gulch* which bear the names of pioneers of Random Island.

There is an interesting, but probably untrue, story written about the origin of the name of *Hickman's Harbour*. As reported in Smallwood (1984:937), Hickman's Harbour was named after one Jonathan Hickman of Grand Bank. It is suggested that Jonathan Hickman, who was born at sea in route from England to North America in 1747, was Captain James Cook's pilot when Cook was surveying the coast of Newfoundland in 1765. The idea is that upon entering Hickman's Harbour, Cook honoured his pilot by naming the harbour after him. There is considerable evidence to refute this story. First, Captain Cook did not chart Trinity Bay in 1765. Hence, it is very unlikely that he entered Hickman's Harbour at all. Trinity Bay was charted by Michael Lane in 1775, after Cook had left Newfoundland. Second, the story concerning any connection between Hickman's Harbour and Jonathan Hickman was based on speculation that was written and accepted as a fact (Fizzard, 1987:50). While the exact origin of the present name of Hickman's Harbour is still unknown, there is considerable evidence that it evolved from other names which were given to it at different times.

Hickman's Harbour was referred to as such by Jukes in describing his excursions in Newfoundland during 1839 (Jukes, 1842: 61-62). After sailing up Smith Sound, Jukes discovered that his vessel, the *Beaufort*, drew too much water to navigate the *Bar*, so he decided to take provisions for three days in a smaller boat and to travel the Northwest Arm of Random along with two of his men, leaving the rest of his crew to sail the *Beaufort* down Smith Sound and around the eastern end of Random Island to meet with them at *Hickman's Harbour*. However, Hickman's Harbour was, in written records, referred to by three other names even after it was permanently settled in the 1840s. Specifically, these names were *Reeke's Harbour, Rix Harbour* and *Rixis Harbour*. In addition, oral tradition which was still alive in the 1940s points out that this harbour was known by three other names as well. They were *Rixman's Harbour, Rexman's Harbour* and *Rickman's Harbour.*

To elaborate on the evidence for, and the origins of, the different names for Hickman's Harbour, it can be noted that during a visit to the Northwest Arm of Random in 1859, the Reverend Henry Petley, a Church of England Missionary, visited a Mr. Blundell of *Reeke's Harbour.* As documented in a later chapter of this book, the Blundells were the first permanent settlers of Hickman's Harbour and, from the description given by Reverend Mr. Petley, *Reeke's Harbour* is obviously *Hickman's Harbour.* He reported to have rowed about a mile from near the entrance of the harbour to Mr. Blundell's house. That is the approximate distance from the entrance to Hickman's Harbour, approaching it at the southeast point, to where the Blundells settled at the bottom end of the harbour. Petley also wrote that "from this harbour to Smith's Sound, across Random, the distance is only, in Eastern phrase, a couple of hours". This is another close estimation in that it is about two hours walking distance from the bottom of Hickman's Harbour where the early Blundells lived to Smith's Sound when walking in an eastern phase.

Marriage records in the Methodist Church at Hant's Harbour, Trinity Bay, for 1860 show that a George Green of Hant's Harbour and a Priscilla Blundon of *Rix Harbour, Random,* were married in that year by one Reverend Charles Comben. Blundells (sometimes referred to as "Blundons") were in Hickman's Harbour and Hatchet Cove at that time. However, given the references to Hickman's as *Rixis Harbour* and *Rickman's Harbour,* it is possible that the *Rix Harbour* referred to in those church records was *Hickman's Harbour.* Reverend Thomas Fox, a Methodist Missionary, at Old Perlican, reported that he baptized three children in *Rixis Harbour* on October 10, 1869. The three children were Henry Stephen, son of Charles and Emily Bryant; Harriett, daughter of Benjamin and Catherine Martin; and Eliza Jane, daughter of Samuel and Elizabeth Thistle. All three of those families had settled in Hickman's Harbour prior to 1869, and there is no evidence to suggest that they had moved to any other place. On the contrary, all evidence points to the fact they were permanent residents of Hickman's Harbour at the time of those baptisms. It is clear that Reverend Mr. Fox was referring to *Hickman's Harbour* as *Rixis Harbour;* a practice that continued in the oral tradition for many years by some of the early residents of Hickman's Harbour and surrounding communities.

Like many places on Random Island, it is probable that the early names for Hickman's Harbour (*Reeke's, Rix, Rixis, Rixman's, Rexman's* and *Rickman's*) were adopted from people who visited the harbour in order to get firewood and materials to build boats, in some cases spending a winter or more in the harbour building their boats before returning to their home base. Although the surname Reek is not included in Seary's (1976) book on family names in Newfoundland, it is possible that this surname was in Random Sound during earlier times. Reek was a family name in Christ Church, England and several families from Christ Church settled in Random Sound prior to 1850. Family names in Trinity in the late 18th century included *Ricks, Rex* and *Rix*. There was one family which, according to the birth records of the Church of England, may have been referred to by all three of these surnames. More specifically, John and Elizabeth Ricks had a child baptized in 1793, while John and Elizabeth Rex had one child baptized in 1790, and another in 1796, and John and Elizabeth Rix had a child baptized in 1798 and another baptized in 1803. There was also a George and Elizabeth Rex living in the Trinity area in 1832. The similarities between these surnames (Ricks, Rix and Rex) and the early references to Hickman's Harbour are too close to be coincidental.

There is an interesting parallel between the early names for what is now *Hickman's Harbour*, Random Island, and similar references to a place on the Northwest side of Smith Sound. Presently, on the government maps and marine charts of this area there is a place called *Hickman Harbour*, with *Hickman Islands* close by in Smith Sound. In oral tradition, references to Hickman's Harbour, Smith Sound, have included *Reekes, Rixis Harbour, Rickman's Harbour* and *Rexman's Harbour*. There are also written records showing variations in the name of *Hickman Harbour*, Smith Sound. This place is referred to as *Rexman's Harbour* in the 1901 and 1911 censuses of Newfoundland. McAlpine's (1904) refers to it as *Rickman's Harbour*.

Surnames of some of the Hickman's Harbour pioneers are associated with different geographical locations within the harbour. These place names, as identified in Map 2-2, include *Blundon's Point, Penney's Point, Adey's Point, Benson's Point* and *Martin's Cove*. All of these names were among the permanent settlers in the harbour. *Dean's Cove*, on the other hand, and the two ponds bearing this name (Map 2-4) were named in honour of one James Dean of Old Perlican who had a winter tilt in Hickman's Harbour during the early part of the 19th century, but he never settled permanently in the harbour. Incidentally, these ponds do not empty into the *Dean's Cove* part Hickman's Harbour. More than one hundred years after James Dean had left Dean's Cove, Alexander Dean of Southport, one of his descendants, made his home in the cove bearing his name. Rather than using a surname to identify *Matthew's Point*, this point was given a christian name. It was named after Matthew Hiscock who settled in Hickman's Harbour in the 1880s. In oral tradition, there is a *Beckford's Hill* in Hickman's Harbour where, according to senior citizens of the community, an old man named Beckford lived long before

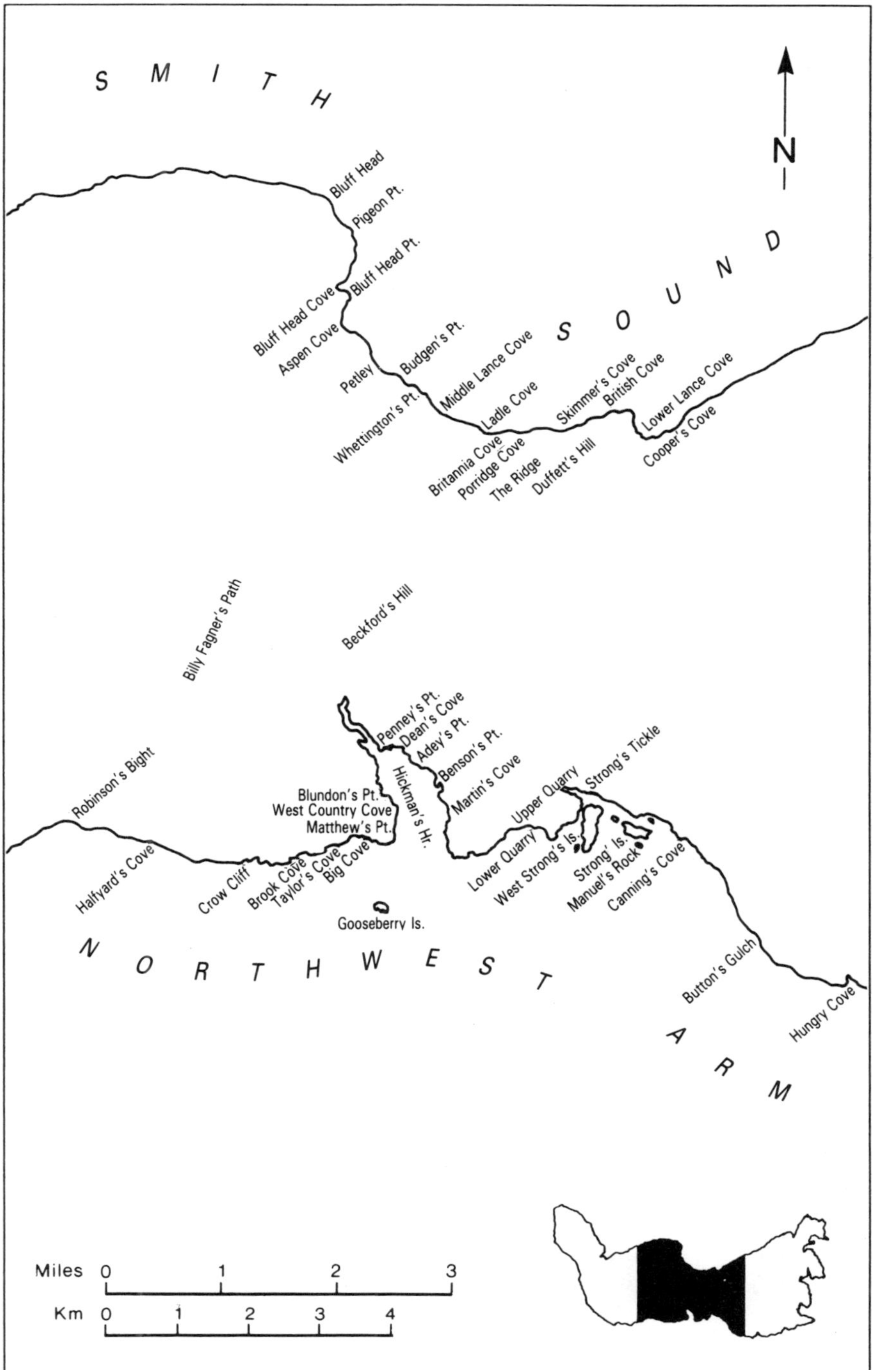

MAP 2-2 CENTRAL RANDOM ISLAND

their time. Since Seary's (1976) research into family names of Newfoundland did not find any early instances of Beckfords in Trinity Bay, the identity of this person is a mystery.

Some people believe that the name of *West Country Cove* in Hickman's Harbour originated because some of the settlers to this harbour came there from the West Country in England. While some of the pioneers of Hickman's Harbour were descendants of West Country emigrants, they did not come directly to the harbour from England. It could be that *West Country Cove* was named as such because it was on the west side of Hickman's Harbour and not for any connection with England.

Although there is no written record of any Dwyers ever living on Random Island, there is a *Dwyer's Pond* in the central part of the island. The name of *Billy Goudy's Pond* is an obvious reference to one William Goudy who was included on a voters list for Hickman's Harbour during the 1870s. Other ponds named in honour of Random Island pioneers are identified on Map 2-4. Among the names associated with logging locations, in oral tradition, are *Critch's Dam Gully,* named because the Critches of Hickman's Harbour had a sawmill near it, and *Butt's Steadies* where people of this name harvested the forest. *Billy Fagnar's Path* was named in honour of William Fagnar who was killed there in 1895 by a falling tree.

A study of the place names on the northern shore of central Random Island as presented on Map 2-2 reveals that at one time there were three *Lance Coves* on the Random Island shoreline in Smith Sound which were distinguished from each other by the prefixes "lower", "middle" and "upper". In fact, a recent Government of Canada map of Random Island labels another cove in the area as *Lance Cove*. Traditionally, however, this Lance Cove has been known as Ladle Cove (also spelt "Leadel Cove" in some records). The origin of the name *Lance Cove* for each of the coves so named in this area is likely tied to the earlier presence of a small slender fish known as "lance" in those coves. In fact, during earlier times lance were frequently found along the coast of Newfoundland and were often used as bait in the codfishery. Reverend Rhodes Disher, the Congregational Minister in Middle Lance Cove in 1908, referred to this cove as *Caplin Cove* (Disher 1954:29). This reference leads one to ask if caplin were sometimes known as lance by some of the early people.

The first name of what is now *Petley* was *Lance Cove,* but by the early 1900s it became known as *Upper Lance Cove.* Around 1915 it was renamed *Petley* in honour of a Church of England minister, Reverend Henry Petley. There were two Reverend Henry Petleys, who were father and son, and each served his Church on Random Island. The father came from England as a missionary with The Society for the Propagation of the Gospel in Foreign Parts, and as noted in the above discussion of the origin of the name of Hickman's Harbour, he visited different places on Random Island in 1859.

According to land grant maps, there is a *Whettington's Point* and a *Bugdon's Point* [sic] between *Middle Lance Cove* and *Upper Lance Cove (Petley)*. Bugden's Point is an obvious reference to the Bugdens who settled in Upper Lance Cove around 1850, and, maybe more specifically to James Bugden who received a land grant for this area. The name of Whettington's Point is somewhat of a mystery. There is no indication of anyone named Whettington ever living in this area. In fact, Seary (1976) did not find the surname Whettington in his search of family names of Newfoundland. However, according to Seary, the surnames of Whittle, Whitty and Whity were in the Trinity area during the 18th century. Could it be that the name of Whettington Point was derived from one of these surnames? It is also possible that this point was named in honour of a Captain Whittington who is believed to have attempted to make friends with the Indians in Smith Sound in the 17th century. A Sir Richard Whittington was Lord Mayor of London, England, in the late 14th and early 15th centuries. He is the hero in the once popular legend of Whittington and his cat.

Aspen Cove got its name because of the unusually large number of aspen trees found in the forest surrounding the cove in earlier times. While it is a separate geographical entity, generally considered as a settlement unto itself in Newfoundland Government censuses, many local people have often considered Aspen Cove as a part of Petley. In recent years, this cove has sometimes been referred to as *Little Deer Harbour* in local conversation. Prior to, and accompanying, the resettlement of Deer Harbour in 1967, several Deer Harbour families made their homes in Aspen Cove. One of those families floated a house from Deer Harbour to Aspen Cove, and another Deer Harbour family floated a house from Thoroughfare to Aspen Cove. Only a short distance from Aspen Cove is *Bluff Head Point, Bluff Head* and *Bluff Head Cove,* all of which were so named because of the topographic structure of the head. It is a large high land mass which rises steeply from the sea as it protrudes into the sound. In fact, this perpendicular broad face headland fits a dictionary definition of a "bluff". As labelled on the federal government of Random Island, *Pigeon Point* is between Bluff Head and Bluff Head Cove.

A widely held view is that *Britannia Cove* was once called *Porridge Cove.* While not incorrect, this is not the complete story, because what became known as *Britannia Cove* also included *Skimmer's Cove* and *Ladle Cove* (sometimes called *Lance Cove*). The exact origins of the names of

Skimmer's Cove and *Porridge Cove* are not known. However, it is speculated that Skimmer's Cove was derived from the surname Skinner found in Trinity during the early 19th century. Perhaps, the name *Porridge Cove* came about in reference to a certain type of food served in the cove in early times. With the neighbouring cove named *Ladle Cove*, and with a *Hungry Cove* on eastern Random Island (Map 2-1), one is reminded that food, or lack thereof, cooking utensils and cutlery were among the sources used in naming early places in Newfoundland. The change from those early names to that of *Britannia Cove* is said to have come about after a visit from a British Navy Ship by this name. *British Cove*, located to the east of Porridge and Skimmer's coves, was also named because of the British presence in Smith Sound at an earlier time.

The hill between Porridge Cove and Skimmer's Cove has, in oral tradition, been known as *The Ridge*. One wonders if there is any connection between the origin of this reference to *The Ridge* and the name *Porridge* in Porridge Cove, or whether *The Ridge* was named in reference to the steep hill separating Porridge Cove from Skimmer's Cove. While the name of *Duffett's Hill* is in honour of the pioneering Duffetts of Britannia Cove, the origin of the name of *Cooper's Cove*, a cove to the east of Lower Lance Cove, is less obvious. It is doubtful if anyone every lived at Coopers' Cove. Perhaps it was named in connection with transients or fishermen in the area.

A note on the recent change in reference to the names *Britannia* and *Lower Lance Cove* is in order. Prior to the closing of the post office in Britannia in the 1960s and the simultaneous establishment of a post office in Lower Lance Cove, the settlement of Lower Lance Cove was not widely known as such. The name *Lower Lance Cove* was generally reserved for the cove at the eastern end of the present settlement of Lower Lance Cove. In fact, many people, middle aged and older, who grew up in what is now Lower Lance Cove but are no longer residing on Random Island, consider themselves as former residents of Britannia rather than of Lower Lance Cove.

Western Random Island

There are several puzzling names along the coastline of western Random Island (Map 2-3). The name of *Lady Cove* is a case in point. One story is that a woman was the first person to go ashore in Lady Cove, hence the reference to *lady* in the naming of the cove. The suggestion of one former resident of Lady Cove is that the name came from the presence of brightly coloured beetles, also known as ladybugs, in the cove during early days. Another possibility is that the name of this cove came from the presence of the kittiwake, a bird locally referred to as the ticklace, but early called the ladybird. However, early records show *Lady*

Cove as *Lally Cove*, giving rise to the suggestion that the cove was first known as Lally Cove. In earlier times, the term *lally* (also spelt "lolly"), was used to describe loose ice floating on the water. More specifically, it referred to ice that had been crushed by the action of wind and wave to make it look like froth along the shoreline (Story, Kirwin and Widdowson, 1982:311). Howley (1901) noted that Lally Cove (Lolly Cove) on Newfoundland's south coast, got its name from the "slob, that is soft ground-up ice, broken into pulp mass by contact with rocks and shores". Because western and southwest winds often create slob ice in the Northwest Arm and pack it on the shores of Random Island in the Lady Cove area, one can easily see why it was named *Lally Cove*.

A 1988 Government of Canada map of Random Island labels the most easterly point of the Lady Cove area as *Lady Cove Point*. However, in oral tradition, this point is known as *March's Point*, an obvious reference to pioneers of this name. As recorded on an 1870s voters list, *March's Cove*, a cove to the west of March's Point later known as *London*, was settled before the actual cove of Lady Cove was settled. Even though there is no one presently living in London, the expression "down to London" is still a part of the local vernacular when referring to this cove. East of Lady Cove Point is *Oil Jar Cove*, so named around 1900 when someone travelling from Robinson's Bight to Lady Cove dropped and broke an jar losing all its contents in the cove.

To the west of Lady Cove is *Bald Nap Cove* and *Bald Nap Point*, both of which were obviously named with reference to an outcropping of bare rock that looms high on the nearby hill, locally called *Bald Nap*. *Nap* (also spelt "knap") is a Newfoundland word meaning "a raised portion of land, often with a round top" (Story, Kirwin and Widdowson, 1982:287). Hence, the term *Bald Nap* is an apt description of the hill in question. Prior to 1900, *Bald Nap* was considered as a settlement unto itself. It later became part of the community of Foster's Point. *Foster's Point* (later renamed *Weybridge*) was named in honour of winter people. According to Church of England records at Trinity, there were several Fosters living in the Trinity area in the 1780s and 1790s. Actually, there were two families of Fosters living at Rider's Harbour on Random Island around 1800. Perhaps, those people visited or settled briefly at the point which bears their name. The fact that there were other settlements named *Foster's Point* in Newfoundland, including one in Smith Sound, caused confusion, especially in mail delivery to Foster's Point, Random Island and to Foster's Point, Smith Sound. At the suggestion of Dorothy Gwillam, who was originally from a place near Weybridge, England, but had moved to Newfoundland and made frequent visits to *Foster's Point* with her friend Florence Adey, the name of the settlement of *Foster's Point* on Random Island was changed to *Weybridge* in 1953. Given the completion

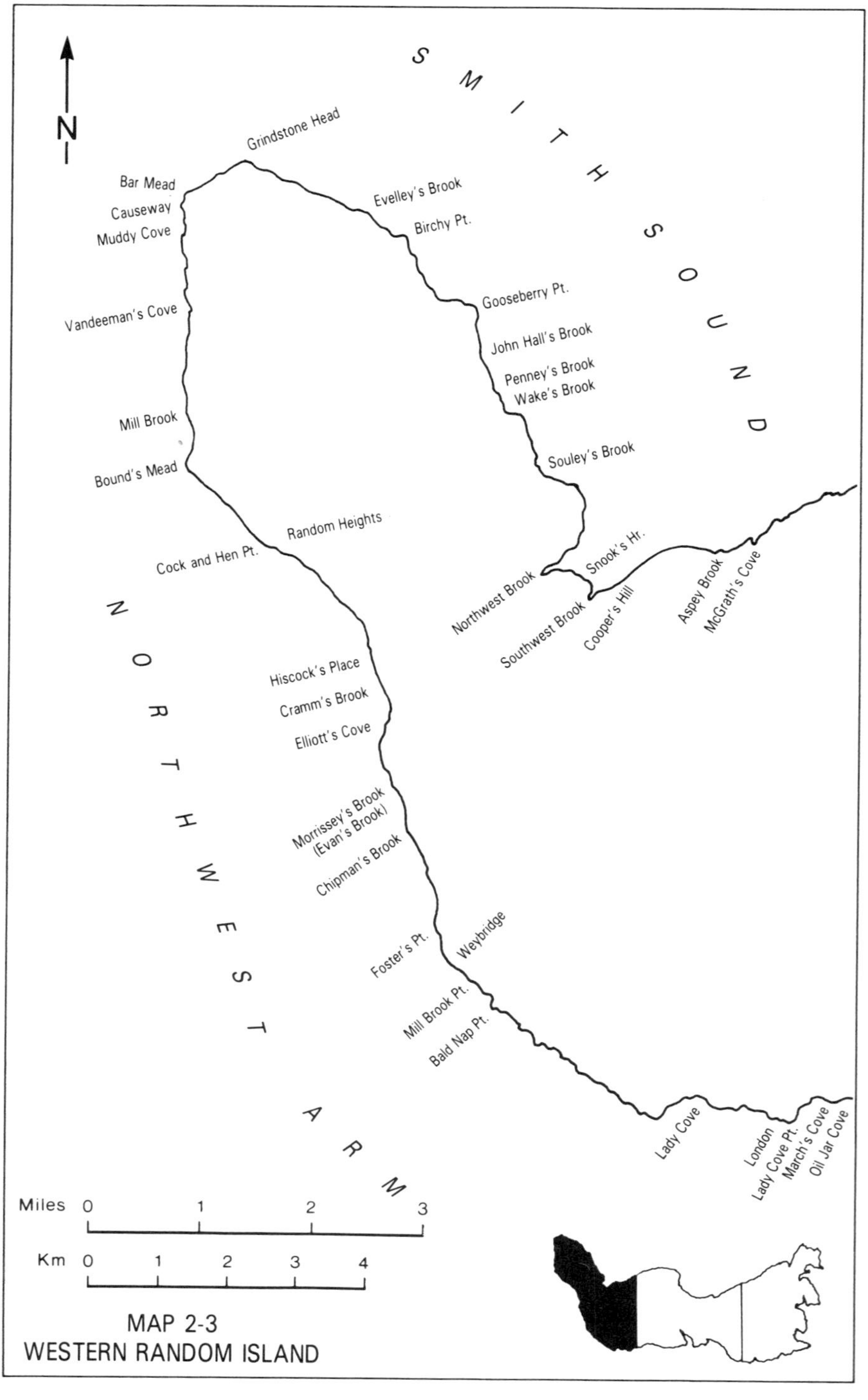

MAP 2-3
WESTERN RANDOM ISLAND

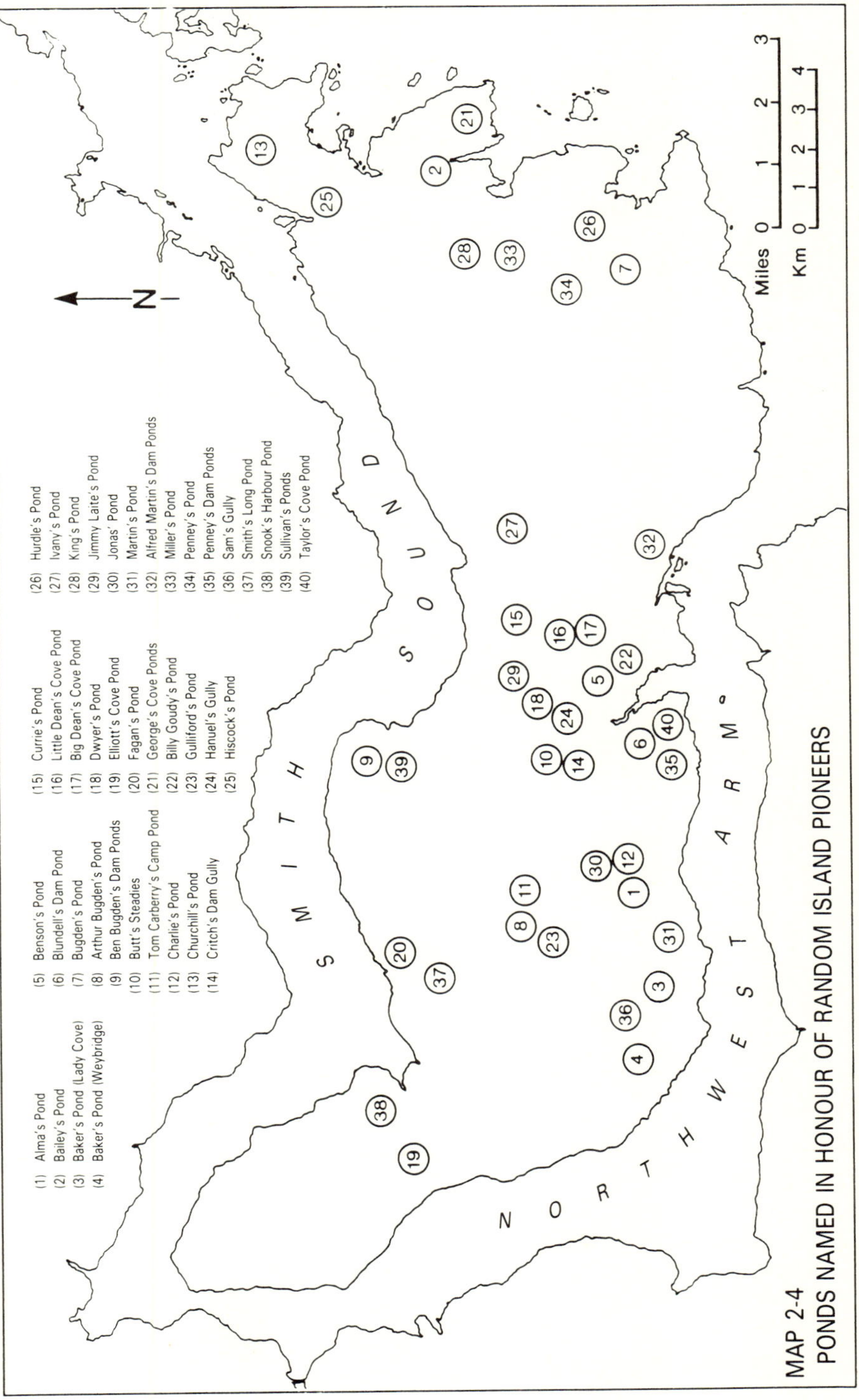

MAP 2-4
PONDS NAMED IN HONOUR OF RANDOM ISLAND PIONEERS

of the bridge linking Random Island to the mainland in 1952, this name change was readily accepted.

Even though there are no written records of any Elliotts ever living in *Elliott's Cove,* local tradition has it that it was named in honour of winter people who were in the cove prior to permanent settlers. Elliott (also spelt "Ellett") was a common surname in Newfoundland in the 18th and 19th centuries. Methodist Church records show that John Elliott was a planter at Hant's Harbour in 1812. Given the tendency for people from Hant's Harbour to winter on Random Island during those times, it is likely that *Elliott's Cove* got its name from the Hant's Harbour Elliotts. Similarly, *Cramm's Brook,* located to the north of Elliott's Cove and once considered a settlement unto itself but now a part of Elliott's Cove, *Morrissey's Brook,* sometimes referred to as *Evan's Brook,* and *Chipman's Brook,* both located to the south of Elliott's Cove, were named for winter people on Random Island. To elaborate, Cramm's Brook was named in honour of a family of Cramms from Old Perlican who had a winter tilt near this brook in the 1850s. Morrissey men from Trinity and Evans from Hant's Harbour worked the forest near the brook which bears both of these family names. Chipman's Brook was said to have been haunted by the spirit of a woman who died in a winter tilt there before the arrival of permanent settlers. The story is that her body was preserved with salt, as described locally she was "salted in", until the Spring came and she was taken to Spaniard's Bay for burial.

While it is not surprising to find the names of early settlers in Trinity Bay attached to different places on Random Island, the reason for the name of *Vandeeman's Cove* (see Map 2-3) is not so obvious. To speculate, since this Dutch-like surname is recorded only on land grant charts of the area it may have been named by the land surveyors with no reference to anything local.

On early maps of Random Island, several *Mill Brooks* are identified. This name is a reminder of the importance of forestry related activities to early settlers to Random Island.One of the most plausible explanations for the name of *Cock and Hen Point,* which is located to the north of Elliott's Cove, is the presence of mussel-like shell fish locally referred to as "cocks and hens". They were commonly used for bait for codfishing and are occasionally used for this purpose today. The low lying point of sand, mud and grass extending out into the Northwest Arm which is now named *Bound's Mead* was once called *Brown's Mead*. The origins of those names are not known. A brief analysis of the name *Bar Mead* is of interest here. In nautical language, the term *bar* is short for *barrier,* and refers to an obstacle such as a sandbank across a harbour. The present reference is to a sand bar across the narrow channel connecting the Northwest Arm of Random Sound to Smith Sound. In oral tradition, and in poetry, the term *mead* is sometimes used as a short for *meadow*. Given the growth of grass and seaweed on the shoreline of this shallow, sand and mud channel, there is an appearance of a meadow especially during low tide. By combining the presence of a barrier (bar) with the meadow (mead) appearance, the name *Bar Mead* was a natural for this area.

It is generally believed that the name of the community of *Aspey Brook*, like that of *Aspen Cove*, came about because the forest around the brook flowing through this place in early days was dominated by aspen trees. In fact, *Aspey Brook* was, commonly known as *Aspen Brook*, but due to mispronunciation and misspelling it got changed. Random Islanders sometimes refer to it *Apsey Brook*, and on occasions it is even spelt as such in church records. It is presently known as both *Aspey Brook* and Aspen Brook. One of the highway signs leading to this community in 1989 identified it as *Aspey Brook* while the sign at the beginning of the settlement referred to it as *Aspen Brook*. Reminders of early visitors to the Aspey Brook area are seen in the names of *McGraths Cove* (Map 2-3) and *Fagan's Pond* (Map 2-4).

Although no written record exists of anyone by the name of Snook having lived in *Snook's Harbour*, it is likely that the harbour got its name from that surname. There were many early instances of Snooks in different parts of Trinity Bay. For example, Church of England records at Trinity include one James Snook, a fisherman of that community in 1759. According to the census of Trinity Bay for 1800/01, William and Elijah Snook were proprietors and occupiers of a fishing room at New Perlican in that year. Later, as recorded in Methodist Church records at Bonavista, John Snook was a planter in Catalina in 1818. *Cooper's Hill* in Snook's Harbour was named after William Cooper moved there from Elliott's Cove during the 1880s.

A study of earlier maps of the coastline from *Aspey Brook* to the *Hefferton Causeway* reveals that the area includes many names of what were probably early settlers to this part of the Random Island. For example, there is a *Penney's Bight*, which suggest that Penney was a surname in this area at one time. As indicated by the names of *Souley's Brook* (also spelt "Sooley's Brook" "Suley's Brook"), *John Hall's Brook* and *Evelley's Brook*, there were also settlers in this area of Random Island whose surnames are no longer found among island residents. The origin of the name *Wake's Brook* is more puzzling than is the case for Souley's, John Hall's and Evelley's brooks. Rather than being associated with a surname, it is suspected that the name of Wake's Brook has another origin.

It might seem logical to assume that *Birchy Point* and *Gooseberry Point* were named because of the presence of birch trees and gooseberries on the respective points, but one must be cautious about speculating on the origins of these place names. There are many place names in Newfoundland containing references to *gooseberry* which have no trace of the berry known as such in contemporary Newfoundland. *Grindstone Head*, also located on the Smith Sound of the Hefferton Causeway, was so named because of its physical features. The head itself is composed mostly of shale cliffs, but the shoreline has many large rocks whose colour and texture resemble the grindstones once used for sharpening tools. These rocks are conspicuous in the mud and silt which cover the shoreline and sea bottom around Grindstone Head.

The *Hefferton Causeway* and bridge connecting Random Island to the mainland of Newfoundland were completed in 1952. At the official opening by the then Premier, Joseph R. Smallwood, this causeway was named in honour of the Honourable Samuel J. Hefferton, member of the House of Assembly for Trinity North and Minister of Education at the time. Locally, the causeway and bridge is generally referred to as *The Bar* or *The Bar Bridge.Random Heights*, a settlement started in the 1970s, is located on the highway between Elliott's Cove and the Causeway. It was named by its founding families of Deans, Simmons and Walters.

CHAPTER 3

SETTLEMENTS AND EARLY INDUSTRIES

OVER THE YEARS at least twenty-seven settlements were started on Random Island. Several of them, including Bar Point, Bluff Head Cove and Random Head Harbour remained small and existed for short periods, in some cases only three or four decades. Other settlements became relatively large and existed for much longer. For example, Rider's Harbour was the largest settlement on Random Island at one time and people lived there for about one hundred years before it was abandoned in the 1870s. Deer Harbour and Thoroughfare became well established and were remarkably prosperous communities for 130 years before socioeconomic and political processes dictated their demise. Presently, there are twelve settlements on Random Island with populations ranging from about 30 to 600 inhabitants. While most of these settlements have relatively long histories, two of them were started recently: Random Heights and a new Robinson's Bight. Random Heights was not previously settled, but Robinson's Bight was settled during the 1840s and abandoned in the 1920s. The purposes of the this chapter are (1) to identify the settlements which existed at different times in the island's history, (2) to point out the reasons why these settlements began, (3) to outline population changes in these settlements over the years and (4) to give an overview of the occupational pursuits of island residences during earlier days.

Earliest Settlements

The four earliest settlements on Random Island were Deer Harbour, Rider's Harbour, Silldown and Thoroughfare. As indicated by

Handcock (1985:25), Rider's Harbour was visited by fishermen from Trinity during the early 18th century. According to Church records, people from Ireland and England were among those who got married at Rider's Harbour between 1770 and the 1830s. Transient people visited different coves and harbours on the eastern end of Random Island during those days, although Deer Harbour and Thoroughfare were not permanently settled until around 1830. There are several reasons why the earliest communities on Random Island were on its eastern shores. First, these shores are closer than any part of Random Island to Trinity, a major fishing community and business centre in Newfoundland during the 17th and 18th centuries. Second, when travelling by water one has to bypass the eastern side of Random Island in order to enter Smith Sound or the Northwest Arm of Random; hence, the coves and harbours on this part of the island were logical landing points for early visitors and settlers to this area. Third, these harbours, especially Deer Harbour and, to some extent, Rider's Harbour, are excellent harbours protecting those who enter from storms and rough seas of the open bay. Fourth, these coves and harbours were close to good fishing grounds. Fifth, this part of Random Island was well forested at the time of arrival of those early settlers. Given these factors, it was natural for the eastern end of Random Island to be settled earlier than were the Northwest Arm and Smith Sound portions of this island.

With a population of 68 in 1845, Deer Harbour was the largest settlement on Random Island at that time, and, with only two exceptions, Deer Harbour experienced a population increase in each of the census periods from 1845 to 1961 (Table 3-1). It experienced a population decline between 1845 and 1869, but from 1884 to 1961 there was a small but steady population growth, the number of residents going from 81 to 203 people.

Fishing was the mainstay of Deer Harbour throughout its 130 year history. In the beginning the local inshore codfishery was the backbone of the community's economy. Later, in addition to this local fishery, many Deer Harbour fishermen prosecuted the Labrador fishery, and at different times, depending on the availability of fish, they fished from St. John's Harbour. To give an example of the importance of the fishery to Deer Harbour, of the total population of 117 in 1911, 41 men and 28 women were engaged in curing fish at that time. Over the years, a few fishermen from Deer Harbour joined sealing vessels and participated in the annual seal hunt off the coasts of Newfoundland and Labrador.

With the operation of water driven sawmills, the people of Deer Harbour broadened their economic base during the 1890s. Nine men were employed in two such sawmills in this harbour in 1911. Also during that time, each family in this community had "a potato garden" and "a small seed garden" which made them self-sufficient in the staple crops: potatoes, turnips and cabbage. Some 311 bushels of potatoes and 1800 heads of cabbage were grown in Deer Harbour in 1911. Most families had animals and poultry to supply them with meat and dairy products during those days.

The question of whether a road was to be constructed to link Deer Harbour to the road network on the island created much heated debate from the 1950s until the people left the harbour. For a time during the early 1960s it looked as if a road would be built to this community. In addition to constructing a large concrete public wharf in the community, the Provincial Government cut a right of way through the woods for a proposed road between Lower Lance Cove and Deer Harbour. Both projects were taken as signs of a long life for this fishing community, so much so that Green's Thoroughfare business was relocated to Deer Harbour where a building was constructed to accommodate it in 1962. However, a road was not to be. The resettlement policy of the Provincial Government persisted. As seen in Table 3-1, there was a decline in Deer Harbour's population, going from 203 people in 1961 to 171 people by 1966. Having lost all hope of getting a road, other people left this community in 1966. After learning that their Post Office was to be closed and that they would not be getting a school teacher for September 1967, the remaining population of about 150 left Deer Harbour during the late summer and early fall of 1967. Fourteen families settled in Hickman's Harbour, a few families moved to other communities on Random Island, four families went to Little Heart's Ease, two families selected Sunnyside, one family moved to Hant's Harbour and another one took up residence in Southport.

Rider's Harbour was not only the first permanent settlement on Random Island, it was for many years the largest settlement on the island. Its population of 69 people in 1836 made it the largest settlement on Random Island at that time, bigger in fact, than any other place in Random or Smith Sounds. Seven boats fished out of Rider's Harbour in 1836, and by 1845 there were fifteen such boats in this harbour. The people there grew 236 bushels of potatoes in 1836 and 175 bushels in 1845.

As seen from Table 3-1, Silldown had only a few inhabitants during its relatively short time as a settlement. While the terrain at Silldown may have been acceptable to those early settlers, it is likely that they were discouraged by the fact that it is open to the bay, and hence it was not a safe place to moor fishing boats or to construct fishing stages.

Rider's Harbour and Silldown were the only Roman Catholic settlements to ever exist on Random Island. According to the census of 1836 and that of 1845, most of the inhabitants of Rider's Harbour were

Roman Catholic and about 75% of those in Silldown were of this faith. However, by 1857, there were no Roman Catholics in Rider's Harbour, and the 18 inhabitants of Silldown were evenly divided between Roman Catholic and Church of England people. The change in religious affiliation of the people of Rider's Harbour was accompanied by a remarkable decline in the population of this settlement. It went from 60 Roman Catholic people in 1845 to 13 Church of England people in 1857. Combining these changes, as recorded in censuses, with vital statistics from the Roman Catholic Church at King's Cove and the Church of England Church at Trinity, it is concluded that the 60 people in Rider's Harbour in 1845 abandoned the harbour sometime between 1845 and 1857.

One explanation as to why the entire population of Rider's Harbour moved during that time is found in a story of oral tradition as recalled by former residents of Deer Harbour. It is said that two young men in Rider's Harbour got into a dispute over a young woman who had arrived in the harbour to become a servant to one of the families there. Each of the men claimed to have the favour of this young woman, and since neither was willing to have her love taken away from him a fight broke out between them with the rest of the people in Rider's Harbour taking sides in the dispute. As one version of the story goes, one man got killed in the ensuing battle over this woman. Another version is that one fellow was thrown overboard during the brawl and drowned off the main fishing premise in the harbour. Whatever the cause of death, the disturbance created severe divisions and conflicts among the people in this place. Apparently the people could not resolve these problems, nor could they live together in the same harbour after this happening, thus their sudden departure from this place to settle elsewhere. They left Random Island altogether, with some returning to Trinity and others settling in different places in the Trinity Bay. After this mass exodus from Rider's Harbour, a few other people, including a family of Marshes and one of Baileys from the Bonaventure, moved to Rider's Harbour and lived there for a few years before they settled in Deer Harbour. Similarly, a family of Langers from Trinity lived in Rider's Harbour during the 1840s before they became permanent residents of Thoroughfare.

The population of Thoroughfare was always considerably smaller than that of Deer Harbour. In fact, at different times there was only about half as many people in Thoroughfare as in Deer Harbour. Thoroughfare's population peaked at 74 in 1921. By 1951 it had dropped to 52, less than one-third the number of people living in Deer Harbour at the time (Table 3-1). During its early days, the economic base of Thoroughfare was similar to that of Deer Harbour in that each relied heavily on fishing and subsistence gardening. But, unlike Deer Harbour, Thoroughfare had no sawmills. Also, the location of Thoroughfare in relation to Smith Sound, Ireland's Eye and Deer Harbour meant that it became an important service centre for the area during the 1920s, and it continued this role until the mid 1950s. Beginning with Monroe Export Company Ltd. of St. John's, and later with E.J. Green of Winterton, there was a fish factory and general store at Thoroughfare for a number of years which served fishermen of Ireland's Eye Island, Deer Harbour and, to some extent, communities in Smith Sound. In addition, they served the woodsmen in communities at the mouth of Smith Sound, thereby creating a beehive of activity in Thoroughfare during the period in question. However, changing circumstances led to the decline of Thoroughfare in the late 1950s.

One of those changes was that people in all parts of Newfoundland, including Thoroughfare, were moving away from the fishing industry in the 1950s. Another change which had an impact on Thoroughfare was the disappearance of the sawmill industry located at the mouth of Smith Sound. In addition, during those days there was a strong desire among many Newfoundlanders in isolated communities to move to communities which were connected to the main road networks in the province. Thoroughfare was not only isolated but was a very small community with only 52 people in 1951, many of whom were at least middle age at that time. Unlike the resettling of most of the people of Deer Harbour to other communities on Random Island, none of the people of Thoroughfare resettled on Random Island when they left their community in 1960, even though some of the Thoroughfare people had settled in Petley and Lower Lance Cove several years before the community was officially resettled. The demise of Rider's Harbour and Silldown around 1870, and the resettling of the people of Deer Harbour and Thoroughfare in the 1960s, meant that four of the earliest communities on the island ceased to be.

Present Communities

After some people settled on the eastern end of Random Island, others chose to live in the coves and harbours on the Northwest Arm and Smith Sound shorelines of the island. In order to take advantage of the forest available on those parts of the island, the early people would spend the winter on the island cutting firewood and materials for house and boat building, and then return to their homes in other parts of Trinity Bay and on the north shore of Conception Bay for the summer fishery. However, many of them soon decided to settle permanently on the Random Island. But for these first permanent settlers to the Northwest Arm and Smith Sound portions of the Random Island there was a price to be paid in that they were moving away from rich fishing grounds. Stories have been told of how early settlers, even after they had established permanent homes on the island, would row back and forth from their new homes to their earlier fishing grounds. It is also known that after settling several of coves and harbours in the Smith Sound and Northwest Arm parts of Random Island to take advantage of the forest, many of the earlier settlers were faced with the situation of having to seek other forest areas. They found convenient locations in Smith Sound and the Northwest Arm to construct watermills for sawing. In many cases they used their island houses as their permanent place of abode while constructing dwelling houses at the sites of their sawmills which were not on Random Island at all, but on the mainland sides of the Sound and Arm. More specifically, some of the early settlers to the Britannia Cove/Lower Lance Cove area built sawmills at Nut Cove and Rixman's Harbour, both places on the mainland side and close to the entrance to Smith Sound. Similarly, early settlers to Hickman's Harbour and Lady Cove built sawmills on the mainland side of the Northwest Arm in locations such as Dartmouth, The Tolt, Sandy Beach, Passenger's Cove and places which now bear their names such as Hart's Mill, George's Mill and Sam Day's Pond.

During those times of constructing sawmills and working the forest in the other parts of Smith Sound and the Northwest Arm of Random, many of the earlier fishermen, depending on the availability of fish locally, were sometimes leaving the island during the summer months to prosecute the codfishery out of St. John's Harbour as well as on the coast of Labrador. Even though there was sometimes a need to travel far afield in search of codfish, it should be pointed out that the waters of Smith Sound, the Northwest Arm and neighbouring fishing grounds often yielded substantial quantities of codfish, salmon, herring and caplin.

Given the long, somewhat narrow waterways of Smith Sound and the Northwest Arm of Random, the portion of Random Island in these inlets is relatively well protected from rough seas. Hickman's Harbour, for example, is an excellent deep water harbour, well protected from the open sea and large enough to accommodate many fishing premises and boats. In fact, except for certain winds which give problems in particular locations, many coves and harbours along these shorelines of Random Island provide calm seas and good anchorage. These characteristics were obviously viewed with delight by the early settlers to the Northwest Arm and Smith Sound portions of Random Island.

Other features attracting the early settlers to the Smith Sound and Northwest Arm areas of Random Island were the availability of land and good growing soil. This is particularly true of places like Britannia Cove, Lady Cove, Lower and Middle Lance Coves, Petley and Weybridge, where considerable efforts were put into farming at different periods in

TABLE 3-1

POPULATION OF EARLIEST SETTLEMENTS ON RANDOM ISLAND FROM 1836 to 1966

	Years													
Settlements	**1836**	**1845**	**1857**	**1869**	**1884**	**1891**	**1901**	**1911**	**1921**	**1935**	**1945**	**1951**	**1961**	**1966**
	(number)													
Deer Harbour		68		53	81	96	90	117	123	153	160	186	203	171
Rider's Harbour	69	60	13	13										
SillDown	11	18	18											
Thoroughfare		18		40	42	57	67	62	74	62		52		
Totals	80	164	31	106	123	153	157	179	197	215	160	238	203	171

Source:Compiled from Census Returns for Newfoundland 1836 to 1945, and from Dominion Bureau of Statistics and Statistics Canada, 1951 to 1966.

the history of the island. The suitability of a vein of shale near Hickman's Harbour for making slate attracted certain early settlers to this harbour and created employment for others who settled there. Britannia Cove became the home of the Curries who developed the slate quarries in Nut Cove, Smith Sound. Later Britannia Cove and Hickman's Harbour grew into commercial and service centres in their own rights.

When placing the settlements on Random Island into the three groupings of earliest, present and outlying settlements, there is some question about the exact fit of each place in these groupings. Middle Lance Cove is a case in point. While it is probably one of the oldest settlements on the Smith Sound part of Random Island, it is not one of the four earliest settlements on the island. Given the fact that it had one of the first church/schools on the island, it cannot be described as an outlying settlement. It is not officially considered as an existing settlement on Random Island, although a descendant of the earliest settlers to this place has returned, after many years of absence, to live in Middle Lance Cove. Given this situation, it was decided to include Middle Lance Cove in the grouping of present communities on Random Island. Aside from Middle Lance Cove, there are twelve settlements on Random Island: Aspey Brook, Aspen Cove, Britannia Cove, Elliott's Cove, Hickman's Harbour, Lady Cove, Lower Lance Cove, Petley, Random Heights, Robinson's Bight, Snook's Harbour, and Weybridge. The populations of these communities for each of the census years from 1884 to 1981 are presented in Table 3-2. There are no statistics available on Robinson's Bight as a separate settlement after 1901. In fact, for many years after the original settlers had left it was uninhabited. The first inhabitants of the new Robinson's Bight settled there in the late 1970s, and the Department of Highways first erected road signs indicating the presence of this settlement in 1987.

Rather than give detailed attention to the compositions and changes in the populations of each of the settlements listed in Table 3-2, the present aim is to give an overview of the changes in the sizes of these communities over the years. By 1884, the first date for which a breakdown of the population in each of the present communities on Random Island is available, there were relatively large numbers of people in several of them. As shown in Table 3-2, there were 177 people in Britannia Cove (perhaps, including Lower Lance Cove and parts of Middle Lance Cove), 172 in Lance Cove (perhaps, including Aspen Cove and parts of Middle Lance Cove), and 141 in Hickman's Harbour.

Since Britannia Cove, Lower Lance Cove and part of Middle Lance Cove were sometimes considered as one settlement, precise numbers for each of these places in certain census years are impossible to ascertain. This makes it difficult to comment on population changes in each settlement. For example, the decline recorded for Britannia Cove between 1901 and 1911, that is, going from 180 to 105 people, was not an actual decline in the population in the area, but was in part a result of listing Lower Lance Cove separately. Taken together in 1911, Britannia Cove and Lower Lance Cove had a population of 212, which is larger than the population recorded for Britannia Cove (including Lower Lance Cove) in 1901. Similarly, the approximately 280% increase in the population reported for Britannia Cove from 1935 to 1945 was not really an increase at all, but only a result of combining Britannia Cove and Lower Lance Cove in the 1945 census. Also, while there was likely a considerable drop in number of people in Britannia Cove between 1951 and 1961, the decline was not as drastic as suggested by the figures of 308 for 1951 and 89 for 1961. The 1951 figure apparently includes Britannia Cove and Lower Lance Cove, while the 1961 figure does not include Lower Lance Cove (Table 3-2).

What was called Lance Cove in 1884 was referred to as Upper Lance Cove in 1911, and it has had its present name of Petley since around 1915. The 172 people listed for Lance Cove in 1884 undoubtedly included those in the neighbouring settlements of Aspen Cove, Bluff Head Cove and part of Middle Lance Cove. Aspen Cove was not listed as a separate place until 1891 and Middle Lance Cove was not listed as such until 1901 (Table 3-2), which is the same year that Bluff Head Cove appeared in the census (Table 3-3), but, all three places were settled before 1880. In noting that the population of Petley in 1971 was only 5 more than that given for Lance Cove in 1884, that is, 177 compared to 172, one must realize that the 1884 census included neighbouring communities while the 1971 census is for Petley only. Also, the decline in Petley's population from 177 in 1971 to 147 in 1981, as recorded in census for those years, is misleading because Aspen Cove was included as part of Petley in 1971, but it was given as a separate until in 1981. Taken together this area actually had a slight increase in population during that decade.

Hickman's Harbour, the largest community on Random Island since 1900, experienced a dramatic population growth from 1884 to 1911. During that time the population of this community actually increased by 146%, going from 141 in 1884 to 347 by 1911. It then declined slightly, but rebounded and grew substantially to reach 432 by 1945. Like most places on Random Island, Hickman's Harbour experienced a population decline during the 1950s and 1960s. However, there was a 16% increase in its population during the 1970s, yielding a total of 479 people in 1981 (Table 3-2).

In terms of population size, certain of the present communities on Random Island have been relatively stable over the years. Aspey Brook

TABLE 3-2

POPULATION OF PRESENT SETTLEMENTS ON RANDOM ISLAND FROM 1884 TO 1981

Settlements	Years										
	1884	1891	1901	1911	1921	1935	1945	1951	1961	1971	1981
	(number)										
Aspey Brook			45	36	52	36	37	37	41	69	55
Aspen Cove		33	21	26	28	23				51	
Britannia Cove	177	168	180	105	229	101	282	308	89	133	112
Elliott's Cove	43	43	74	80	75	57	55	53	74	67	106
- Cramm's Brook		5									
Hickman's Harbour	141	159	232	347	322	382	432	405	419	414	479
Lady Cove		89	101	149	148	120	128	123	117	121	155
Lower Lance Cove			107	6	184			194	195	180	
Middle Lance Cove			69	98	46						
Petley					105	131	124	124	136	177	147
- Lance Cove	172	141	140								
- Upper Lance Cove				107							
Random Heights											25
Robinson's Bight	15	17	15								
Snook's Harbour	65	88	49	51	44	50	66	62	61	78	81
Weybridge									106	98	146
- Foster's Point	54	79	110	127	116	92	133	106			
- Bald Nap	12	20	27								
Totals	679	842	1,063	1,233	1,171	1,176	1,257	1,218	1,237	1,352	1,537

Source: Compiled from Census Returns for Newfoundland 1884 to 1945, and from Dominion Bureau of Statistics and Statistics Canada 1951 to 1981.

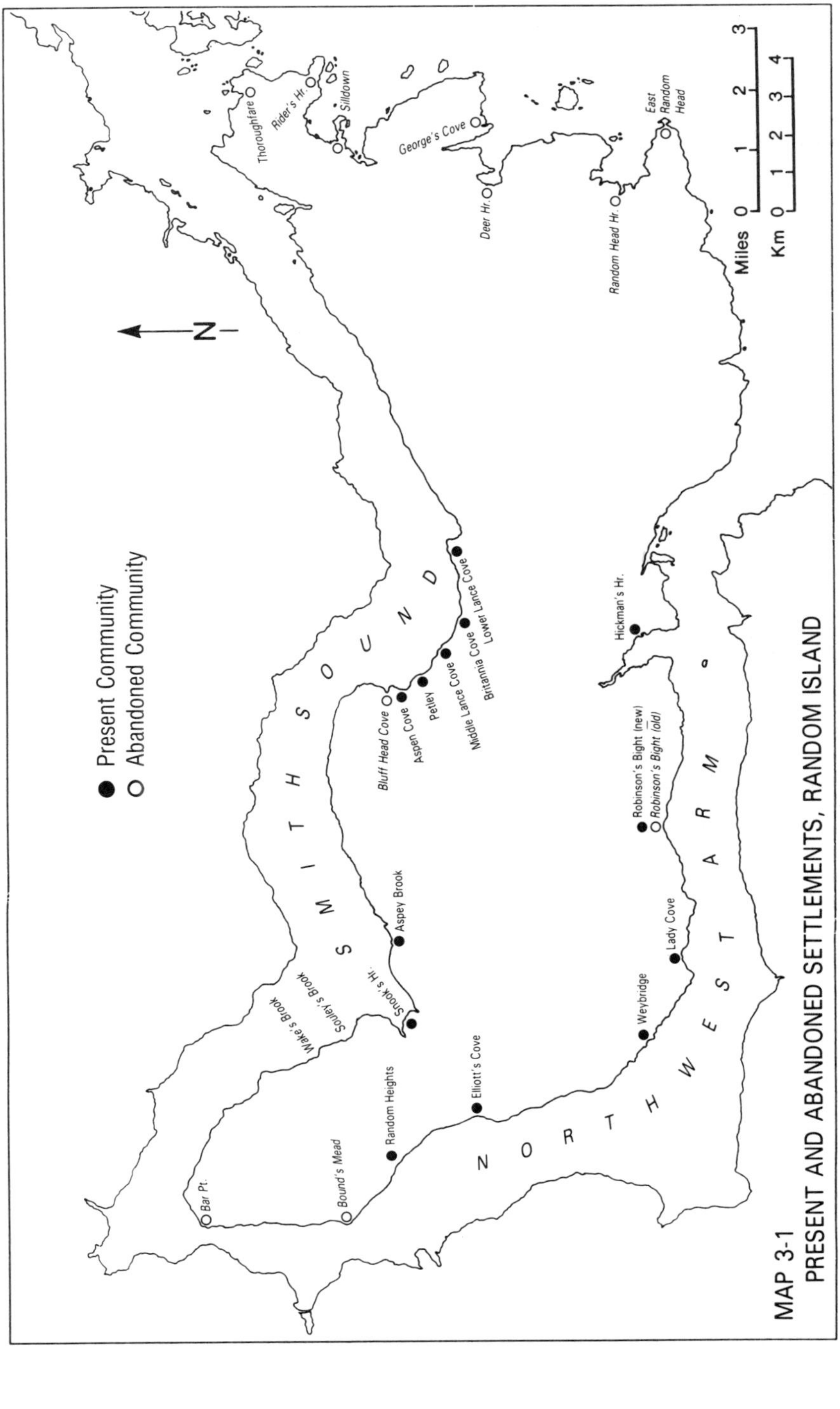

MAP 3-1
PRESENT AND ABANDONED SETTLEMENTS, RANDOM ISLAND

and Snook's Harbour are cases in point. Unfortunately, there are no census data available for Aspey Brook as a separate settlement prior to 1901. As seen from church records and other documents, there were people in Aspey Brook before that time. The population of Aspey Brook ranged from a low of 36 in 1945 to a high of 69 in 1971, with the 1981 population of 55 only 19 more than the 1945 count. Snook's Harbour's population peaked at 88 in 1891. It declined to 44 by 1921, and gradually increased to 81 by 1981 (Table 3-2). Part of the drop from 88 people in 1891 to only 49 by 1901 can be accounted for by the fact that in 1901, for the first time, and for the next two consecutive census years, Wake's Brook and Souley's Brook were considered as a separate settlement (Table 3-3). It should be noted that while many of the people in Wake's and Souley's brooks resettled in Snook's Harbour, many of them left Newfoundland altogether in the 1920s.

Elliott's Cove experienced a population growth of more than 50% between 1891 and 1901, going from 48 people, including the five at Cramm's Brook, to 74 people in 1901. The population of Elliott's Cove remained at 75 to 80 people for a couple of decades before dropping to 57 in 1935. The 1911 population of 80 was the highest this community had until 1981. There was a sharp increase of almost 70%, going from 67 people in 1971 to 106 by 1981.

The greatest population increase in Lady Cove came with a 50% increase between 1901 and 19ll, going from 101 to 149 inhabitants. There was little change in the size of this community during the next couple of decades. Although declining somewhat during the l930s, it increased slightly in the 1940s and 1950s only to decline to 117 in 1961, and then increase slightly to reach 155 by 1981.

Foster's Point and Bald Nap were considered separate settlements during the 19th century. From 1911 on they were considered as one place in the census records. Combining the populations in Bald Nap and Foster's Point, created a substantial increase in the population of what is now Weybridge between 1884 and 1901. During that time it went form 66 to 137 inhabitants. In fact, there were noticeable changes in the population of this community from any one census year to another. For example, there was a steady decline from 137 in 1901 to 127 by 1911, to 116 by 1921, to 92 by 1935. These declines were followed by an increase to 133 people by 1945. After two decades of little or no change, there was approximately a 50% increase between 1971 and 1981, the population reaching its highest point at 146 in that year (Table 3-2).

Outlying Settlements

In addition to the four earliest settlements which have since been vacated and the present thirteen settlements, including Middle Lance

TABLE 3-3

POPULATION OF OUTLYING SETTLEMENTS ON RANDOM ISLAND FROM 1874 TO 1935

	Years						
Settlements	**1874**	**1884**	**1891**	**1901**	**1911**	**1921**	**1935**
				(Number)			
Bar Point		12	32	25	11		
Bluff Head Cove				23	7		
Brown's Head				8			
East Random Head				6	7	5	
George's Cove	11						
Random Head Harbour				20		11	2
Souley's Brook				32	23	22	
Wake's Brook				14	17	26	
Totals	11	12	32	128	65	64	2

Source: Compiled from Census Returns for Newfoundland 1874 to 1935.

TABLE 3-4

SUMMARIES OF POPULATIONS IN RANDOM ISLAND SETTLEMENTS FROM 1836 TO 1981

	Years															
	1836	1845	1857	1869	1874	1884	1891	1901	1911	1921	1935	1945	1951	1961	1971	1981
								(number)								
Earliest Settlements	80	164	31	106		123	153	157	179	197	215	160	238	203		
Present Settlements						679	842	1,063	1,233	1,171	1,176	1,257	1,218	1,237	1,352	1,537
Outlying Settlements					11	12	32	128	65	64	2					
Totals	80	164	31	106	11	814	1,027	1,348	1,477	1,432	1,393	1,417	1,456	1,440	1,352	1,537

Source:Compiled from Totals presented in Tables 3-1, 3-2 and 3-3 above.

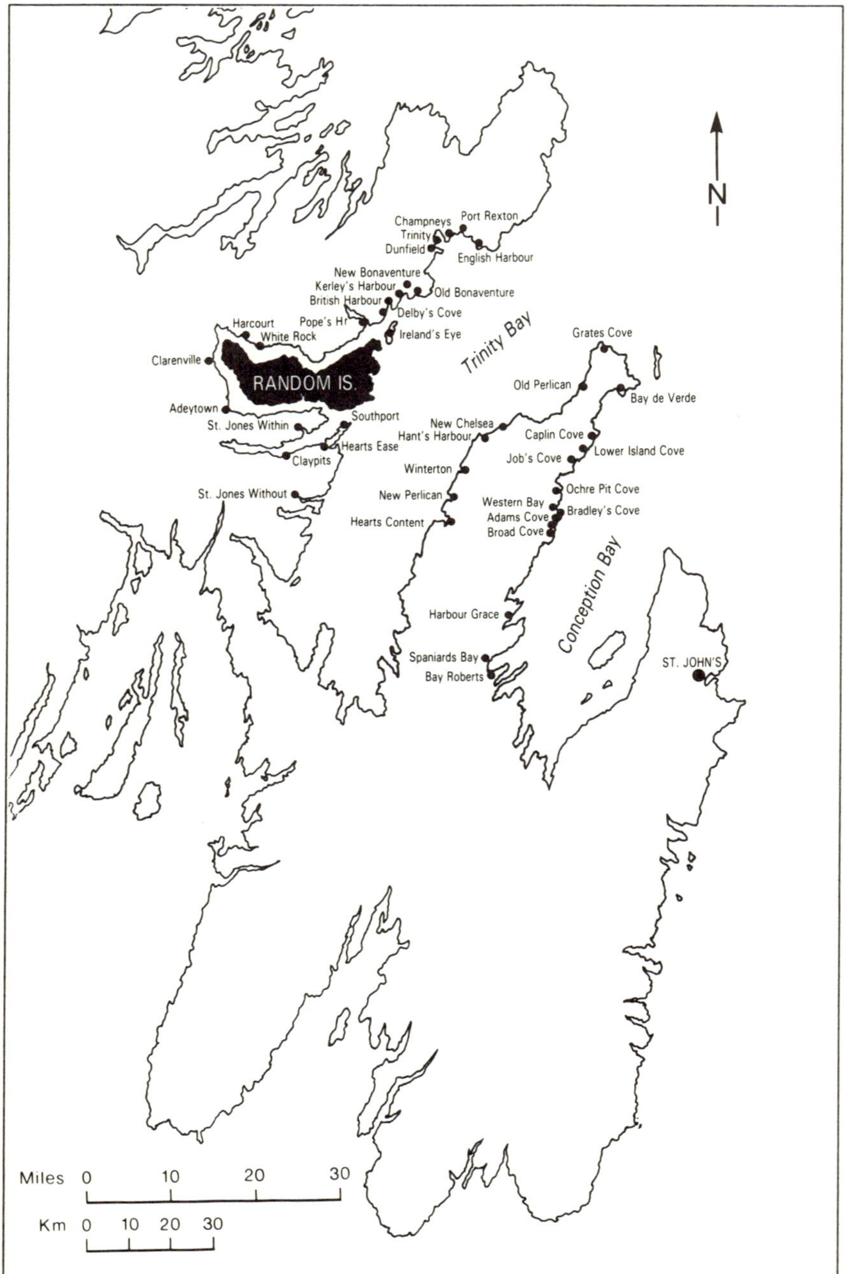

MAP 3-2 SETTLEMENTS WERE MANY RANDOM ISLAND PIONEERS PREVIOUSLY RESIDED

Cove, on Random Island, eight others existed at different times in the history of this island. They were Bar Point, Bluff Head Cove, Brown's Mead, East Random Head, George's Cove, Random Head Harbour, Souley's Brook and Wake's Brook. Each of these settlements has a history all its own. For example, the people on East Random Head were lighthouse keepers who left when the light became automated in the 1930s. Souley's Brook and Wake's Brook were later included in the Snook's Harbour census, even before the people at those brooks moved to Snook's Harbour.

Some of the outlying settlements on Random Island were small and existed for only short periods of time, while others were relatively large and vibrant places for several decades. One must be cautious about relying on censuses to draw conclusions concerning the length of time people lived in these outlying settlements on Random Island. For example, as seen in a later chapter on early settlers to those places, there were people in Bluff Head Cove in 1873, yet it did not appear in Newfoundland census as a settlement until 1901. It is also known that there were people in Random Head Harbour prior to 1901 and later than 1935, even though they are not shown in census to be there during those times. Similarly, church records and other documents show that people lived at Brown's Mead (Bound's Mead) prior to 1901, the only date for which a census is available for this place. Robinson's Bight was settled for at least thirty years before 1884, the first date for which census records are available for it as a separate settlement. As seen from Table 3-3, there were substantial numbers of people living in those outlying settlements. There were 128 people living in those places in 1901, but their populations had declined considerably by 1911. However, even though not shown in censuses, there were people living in some of those other settlements in the 1940s. For example, the people in Random Head Harbour at that time were included in the Deer Harbour census.

Map 3-1 shows where each of Random Island's abandoned settlements was located and identifies each of the present settlements on the island. Many of the pioneers of Random Island settled there from other Trinity Bay communities or from communities on the north side of Conception Bay (Map 3-2). The former place of residence of each of the families that settled on Random Island in the 19th century is identified later in this book.

Population: An Overview

In order to give an overview of the periods of growth and decline in the population of Random Island over the years, it is necessary to combine the numbers found in the earliest settlements, the present settlements and the outlying settlements for different times on the island.

These numbers are presented in Table 3-4, which shows the total population of Random Island for each of the census periods. The first census information available for any settlement on Random Island is for two of its earliest settlements: Rider's Harbour and Silldown. The combined population of these places in 1836 was given at 80 people. By 1845, there were 164 people in the four earliest settlements: Deer Harbour, Rider's Harbour, Silldown and Thoroughfare. The only count given for any specific settlement on Random Island in 1874 is the 11 people listed for George's Cove. In fact, this is the only time for which statistics are available on George's Cove, Random Island.

Since none of the present communities on Random Island was listed as such in the Newfoundland census prior to 1884, there is no way of knowing the exact size of these settlements during those early days. The 1857 census gives a population of 273 in Random Sound. One is not sure what places were included in the reference to Random Sound at that time. Obviously it did not include all of the Southwest Arm of Random Sound, because Fox Harbour (later renamed Southport) is listed separately in the 1857 census. However, both Smith Sound and Random Sound are included in the 1869 census, with 322 people in Smith Sound and 540 in Random Sound. Still, there is no way of knowing how many of the people in the two sounds were on Random Island at that time. A similar breakdown is given for 1874 when there were 417 inhabitants in the Northwest Arm of Random Sound and 378 in Smith Sound. The 417 in the Northwest Arm of Random would have included those in what are now Shoal Harbour and Clarenville, as well as other places in this arm. Similarly, the 378 in Smith Sound would have included settlements on both sides of the sound. Hence, contrary to the information given in Table 3-4, there were obviously more people on Random Island than are shown in the censuses periods prior to 1884. Indications of the general size of the settlements on Random Island during those years can be gleaned from the identification of early settlers in them as presented in chapters 4, 5 and 6 of this publication.

According to censuses of Newfoundland, the population of Random Island grew faster during the late part of the 19th century than it did at any other time. It went from 814 in 1884 to 1,348 by 1901, for an increase of almost 66%, whereas over the next fifty years it increased by only 8%, reaching 1,456 by 1951. There was a decline of 8% in the island's population between 1951 and 1971 so that the total of 1,352 people on Random Island in 1971 was about equal to the number there in 1901. Between 1971 and 1981, the population of the island increased by 14% to reach its highest level ever, that of 1,537 in 1981 (Table 3-4).

Early Industries

While the communities on Random Island had certain things in common with each other, there were particular differences with respect to the economic basis of specific places. While some of them emphasized the fishery, others developed around lumbering and many combined both of those activities with other economic pursuits. Over time, however, Random Islanders carved out a particular socioeconomic fabric which combined fishing, lumbering, shipbuilding, quarrying, brickmaking and subsistence farming. A brief look at the scope of these early industries will complement the preceding review of population, and will identify early economic bases of different settlements on Random Island.

Fishing

The inshore codfishery was the most important component of the fishing industry on Random Island throughout most of its history. However, two other fisheries should be noted as important contributors to the island's economy in early times. They were the Labrador and the lobster fisheries. As in many settlements around the Newfoundland coastline, the Labrador fishery made an important contribution to the

Kings' fishing premises with flakes (left), stages (centre) and twine store (right) in Deer Harbour in the 1960s. School and church are in the background.

economic base of most settlements on Random Island from the 1890s until the 1940s. In 1901, for example, there were 19 schooners directly engaged in the Labrador fishery from Random Island. In terms of home ports of these schooners, 3 were from each of the settlements of Bluff Head Cove, Britannia Cove and Hickman's Harbour, 2 each from Deer Harbour, Petley and Foster's Point, and 1 each from Snook's Harbour,

Curtis and Selby Kelly displaying codfish as taken from a "salt pound" in Deer Harbour in the mid 1950s. (Photo courtesy of Harvey Bailey)

Middle Lance Cove, Random Head Harbour and Thoroughfare. In 1911, the Labrador fishery was prosecuted by 6 schooners from Hickman's Harbour, 5 from Lady Cove, 4 from Petley, 2 from Deer Harbour and 1 each from Britannia Cove and Snook's Harbour. This fishery reached its peak for Random Island people in the mid 1930s. Forty schooners from the Island participated in the Labrador fishery in 1935.

As reported in Newfoundland census, the lobster fishery was an important component to the fishery on Random Island at the turn of the century. At that time there were lobster factories in Bald Nap, Britannia Cove, Deer Har-

Cutting, gutting and splitting codfish in the traditional way at Petley in the early 1950s. Note the "draw bucket" on the splitting table. (left to right), William Walters, James Walters Jr. and James Walters Sr. (Photo courtesy of Delilah and William Walters)

The *M. & J. Hayden* in Deer Harbour. This 33 ton fishing schooner was owned by William King and his sons, Cecil and Lloyd. (Photo courtesy of Lloyd and Myrtle King)

Azariah Thistle. Azariah, the first man to sail a schooner from Hickman's Harbour to participate in the Labrador fishery. He was burned to death in1905 while working on a coal boat at Sydney, Nova Scotia. (Photo courtesy of Ethel Thompson)

bour, Hickman's Harbour, Petley, Robinson's Bight and Thoroughfare. Some of these settlements, including Hickman's Harbour and Deer Harbour, had lobster factories until the 1940s. Certain settlements experienced booms with other types of fisheries during particular times. For example, there was the herring fishery in Britannia Cove, Deer Harbour, Hickman's Harbour, Petley, and Thoroughfare from the 1930s until the 1950s. There was also a prosperous caplin fishery in Hickman's Harbour during those decades.

Lumbering

Given the fact that the lush forest on Random Island was a major drawing card for people to settle the island in the first place, it is likely that considerable effort was given to harvesting the forest for firewood and building materials. Indeed, statistics available on the number of logs cut, the number of sawmills and the amount of lumber produced during early times give an indication of the importance of forest related industries to the economy of Random Island at that time. According to the Newfoundland census of 1901, the number of logs cut and the board feet of lumber produced in specific communities on Random Island in that year were as follows:

Community	*Number of Logs*	*Board feet of Lumber*
Aspey Brook	4,000	100,000
Elliott's Cove	4,000	80,000
Foster's Point	2,000	40,000
Bald Nap	6,000	150,000
Bluff Head Cove	9,000	144,000
Deer Harbour	6,000	100,000
Hickman's Harbour	20,000	600,000
Lady Cove	9,000	250,000
Middle Lance Cove	4,000	80,000
Robinson's Bight	3,000	80,000
Totals	67,000	1,624,000

Smith's water-driven sawmill which operated in Aspey Brook until the 1940s. Vincent Smith poses with a visitor on the bridge leading to the mill. (Photo courtesy of Leah and Colin Baker)

Another related set of statistics useful in getting an appreciation of the extent of forestry related activities on Random Island in earlier times is the number of sawmills that existed on the island. Newfoundland Census reported that in 1891 there were four sawmills in Hickman's Harbour, two in Elliott's Cove, and one each in Foster's Point, Bald Nap and Robinson's Bight. By 1901 there were thirty such mills on Random Island, and the number continued to grow, reaching fifty in 1911 and almost seventy by 1921. Except for Thoroughfare, each of the settlements on Random Island at that time had at least one sawmill, but most of the sawmills were concentrated in a few areas. To illustrate, thirty-seven, that is more than one-half, of the sawmills on the island in 1921 were in Hickman's Harbour, there were twelve in Britannia Cove, eleven in Petley, nine in Lady Cove and eight in Elliott's Cove.

Shipbuilding

Shipbuilding was an important industry from the very beginning on Random Island. In fact, some of the early winter people came to the island to get materials to build fishing boats, and they would often build their boats on the island before returning to their homes. Also, given the availability of wood for boat construction, punts and skiffs of various

The three-mast schooner named *Barbara Bar* nearing completion at Curries dockyard at Britannia Cove in 1917. (Photo courtesy of Leslie and Betty Ivany)

sizes were built in every settled cove and harbour on the island during early days. Most of the early fishermen built their own fishing boats. In addition to this type of boat building, many schooners were built on Random Island. Some of them were built for local use while others were built for people elsewhere.

Study of registry of ships suggests that shipbuilding was an important industry on Random Island as early as the 1850s. This registry shows that three schooners were built in Hickman's Harbour in 1857. One named *Margaret* was built for a John Phelan, another named *Racer* was built for John J. Blundon, and a third, the *Lucy Ann*, was built for Joseph Vivian. Shipbuilding continued to be a major industry on the island for many decades. According to registry of ships, Peter German Tessier of St. John's had three schooners built on Random Island between 1879 and 1881. Their names were *Verbena*, *Gladiola*, and *Sunflower*. John Steer of St.John's had the following schooners built on Random Island prior to 1890: *Brothers* in 1871, *Crocus* in 1878, *Pansy* in 1879, *Starlight* in 1881, *Lupin* in 1881, *Lillian* in 1876, *Poppy* in 1887 and *Energy* in 1887. There were eight schooners built on the island prior to 1900 for people in St. John's which were registered as follows:

United Brothers (1854) for Gustav Ehlers
Flora (1873) for Thomas Raffles Job
Jessie (1877 at Lance Cove) for Francis McDougall
Dreadnaught (1878) for Henry Goodridge
E.S.B. (1879) for Henry Goodridge
Steadfast (1879) for Walter Baine Grieve
William (1880) for William Duder
Lilly Joyce (1887) for Robert Thorburn.

James Hippesley of Harbour Grace had a schooner named *Try Again* built on Random Island in 1874. One year later, John Munn of Harbour Grace had the *Glance* built on the island. Also, during those days, several other schooners were built on Random Island for people living elsewhere in Trinity Bay. They include the following:

Dove (1859) for J.S. Clifford of Random
Zephyr (1870) for Benjamin Miller of Trinity
Active (1872) for Richard Gooby of Trinity Bay
Ranger (1872) for Mark Wells of English Harbour
North Star (1874) for William Smith of Random
Mary Ann (1877) for John Snelgrove of Trinity Bay
Lillian (1878) for J.H. Watson of Hants
Jessie (1879) for Alexander Bremmer of Trinity
Ella (1880) for J.H. Watson of Hants.

Many schooners were built on Random Island prior to 1900 for Islanders themselves. For example, Norman March of Lady Cove built a schooner named *Annie* for himself in Lady Cove in 1879. David Currie of Britannia Cove had at least four schooners built for use in the Currie business which operated out of that cove. They were named *Ocean Wave* (1880), *Primrose* (1881), *Arctic* (1882) and *Snowdrop* (1882). John Currie of Britannia Cove had the *Glance* built there in 1899. William Bugden of Lance Cove had the *Avenue* built for himself in Lance Cove in 1896.

In some cases the early records show schooners built on Random Island for people identified as island residents, but it is suspected that they were actually living elsewhere in Random Sound at the time. One such case is that of John Vey who had two schooners built on Random Island and he is said to have resided on the island at the time. His schooners were *Minnie*, built in 1877, and *Llewellyn* built in 1880. Another is the case of Nehemiah Frost who is recorded as living on the island and building a schooner named *Sparkling* there in 1878.

William Coish of Britannia Cove was a builder of fishing boats par excellence. (Photo courtesy of Hazel and Alfred Marsh)

From ships registry it is sometimes difficult to identify whether specific schooners were built on Random Island or elsewhere in Random and Smith sounds. For example, *Anne* was built in Smith Sound for Robert Beer of Middle Lance Cove in 1885, but it is not known if it was built in Middle Lance Cove or elsewhere in Smith Sound. Similarly, in 1898, the *United Brothers* was built in Smith Sound for Absalom Cooper of Bluff Head Cove.

There were many schooners built on Random Island prior to 1900 for which no registry has been found. For example, around 1870 James Penney King of Deer Harbour built a schooner which he called *Welfare*, although no record of her registry has been located. James Martin of Hickman's Harbour had three schooners built in that harbour prior to 1900 with Solomon Marsh of Deer Harbour as the master builder. They were the *Eclipse*, the *Lilly Maud* and the *Rosa Belle*. Solomon Marsh was a well known master builder and he built many schooners in different places on Random Island including four at Hickman's Harbour, two at Lady Cove and two at Random Head

Solomon Marsh of Deer Harbour, a master schooner builder, plyed his trade in different places on Random Island. (Photo courtesy of Wilfred Marsh)

Harbour. Several Marsh brothers of Deer Harbour had a schooner named *Little Joe* built in that harbour in the 1890s. Four Bugden brothers of Upper Lance Cove built a schooner for fishing and trading which they named *Four Brothers*. Also, before 1900, Abraham Martin of Hickman's Harbour had the *Hero* built in that harbour.

Shipbuilding continued to be an important industry on Random Island until 1940, with schooners being built in almost every community on the island at one time or another during those days. According to the registry of ships, the following schooners were built on Random Island between 1900 and 1936:

Sweet Home (1900 at Hickman's Harbour) for William Job
Lillian Joyce (1900 at Hickman's Harbour) for John Vardy
Lillian Grove (1900 at Britannia Cove) for Joseph Morris
Mistletoe (1900 at Snook's Harbour) for John Loder
Hawk (1900 at Lance Cove) for William Walters
Roving Sisters (1900 at Lance Cove) for John Bailey
Florence D (1901 at Bald Nap) for Willis Gulliford
Cactus (1904 at Deer Harbour) for Eli Toope
Effie B. (1904 at Lance Cove) for John Currie
Piney (1905 at Britannia Cove) for Martin Stone
Dreadnaught (1906 at Lance Cove) for Frederick, Charles Joseph and William Bugden
Alma B. (1906 at Lady Cove) for Hayward Burt
F.J. Morris (1906 at Deer Harbour) for Joseph Morris
Prospector (1907 at Britannia Cove) for John Currie
Alice C. (1907 at Britannia Cove) for John Currie
Inez G. (1911 at Foster's Point) for George Gulliford
Fannie Purchase (1914 at Deer Harbour) for George Purchase
Barbara Bar (1917 at Brtiannia Cove) for John Currie

Lilly Vardy (1918 at Deer Harbour) for James Vardy
E.F. Walters (1928 at Petley) for Japheth Walters
J.M. Bailey (1934 at Petley) for John Bailey
Gutha Percha (1935 at Hickman's Harbour) for Edmund Vardy
Monica B. Walters (1935 at Petley) for James T. Walters
Ivy and Muriel (1936 at Hickman's Harbour) for Edmund Vardy
H.V. Stone (1936 at Lower Lance Cove) for Mark Stone.

Slate Quarrying

Slate quarrying was an important industry for Random Islanders during the late 19th and early 20th centuries. The only slate quarries actually located on the island were at Hickman's Harbour, but islanders benefited from the presences of quarries on the neighbouring mainland. One of those quarries was located at Nut Cove in Smith Sound and another was at Dartmouth Cove, which is on the mainland side of Northwest Arm across from Hickman's Harbour.One of the Hickman's Harbour quarries was started in the 1860s by Charles Bryant, who settled in Hickman's at that time. The other quarry at Hickman's, as well as the one at Dartmouth, was operated by St. John's Merchants. According to Martin (1983:47), the original Nut quarry was operated by three Carberry brothers. Later Curries from Wales settled in Britannia Cove and developed the quarries at Nut Cove. Slate from the quarries on and near Random Island was said to be of the finest quality and was sold for roofing material in St. John's and England.

Pierce Currie, along with his brother, David, came from Wales to operate the slate quarry at Nut Cove in the 1850s. (Photo courtesy of Lucy Leawood)

Charles Bryant came to Hickman's Harbour around 1860 and started slate quarries near Strong's Tickle. (Photo courtesy of Ralph and Myra King)

Newfoundland census of 1869 reported that there were 173,000 slates produced in Smith Sound in the previous year. There were 40,000 slates quarried there in 1874. The Hickman's Harbour quarries were operating on a smaller scale at that time. One report is that those quarries produced 2,000 slates in 1884. The Nut Cove quarry closed in 1907 and some of the men laid off found work in the Hickman's Harbour and Dartmouth quarries. However, these quarries were soon to fall victims of market conditions. The last shipment

Hickman's Harbour slate quariries in 1904. Upper quarry is in foreground and lower quarry in background. Note the wharf, boom and shed at the upper quarry, and shed at lower quarry. (Photo courtesy of Provincial Archives of Newfoundland and Labrador)

of slate from Hickman's Harbour was in 1910. At that time the Hickman's Harbour quarry was operated by James Allison, a Yorkshire merchant. The story is told that the last ship to leave the Allison quarry at Hickman's Harbour was only half loaded with slate. It proceeded to St. John's, en route to England, and finished loading with barrels of cod liver oil. A fierce Atlantic storm caused the barrels to break loose and roll around in the hold of the ship. By time the ship arrived in England there was nothing left of its cargo except oil soaked slate dust and debris from the broken barrels (Martin, 1983:48).

Brickmaking

Historically, brickmaking was the core economic base of two communities on Random Island: Elliott's Cove and Snook's Harbour. There was a one kiln brickmaking operation in Elliott's Cove run by a 115 horsepower steam engine during the 1890s. In 1890 it employed more than 20 men and produced 700,000 bricks. By 1901 there were 37 men employed in this operation at Elliott's Cove. A brickyard was opened at Snook's Harbour in 1895 by Aaron Smith of Elliott's Cove. This brickyard was in operation for more than half a century. As Aaron got older and was no longer able to run the brickyard his sons, Attwood and Norman, continued to make bricks there until 1952. The Smith brickyard became well known in Newfoundland for its high quality bricks. It also

Smith's brickyard at Wake's Brook in the 1920s. Aaron Smith (centre), with St. John's brick buyers on left and brickyard workers Attwood Smith, Edwin Smith and Silas Smith on right, standing in front of bricks which were ready for market. (Photo courtesy of Alice and Shirley Smith)

produced popular clay pots for house plants. Over the years, Smith's brickyard provided employment for many men and broadened the economic bases of the surrounding communities. In 1920, for example, 14 men were employed at Smith's brickyard and they produced some 42,500 bricks.

Farming

To give an indication of the part subsistence farming played in the lives of Random Islanders as they attempted to eke out a living from their local environment, one can note the number of livestock, the amount of potatoes and cabbage grown, and the number of acres of land under cultivation on the island in earlier times. In 1884 there were 140 cows, about 200 swine and well over 300 sheep on Random Island. By 1891 there were 200 cows, more than 200 swine and 550 sheep on the island. The animal population increased to 340 cows, 250 swine and almost 1000 sheep by 1901. Even though the numbers of animals varied over the years, most families always had sheep to supply mutton and wool, swine for pork, and cows for dairy products and meat until the early 1950s when the island became more dependent on the outside for these products. During early days cows were also used to haul wood and do other work which was later assigned to horses.

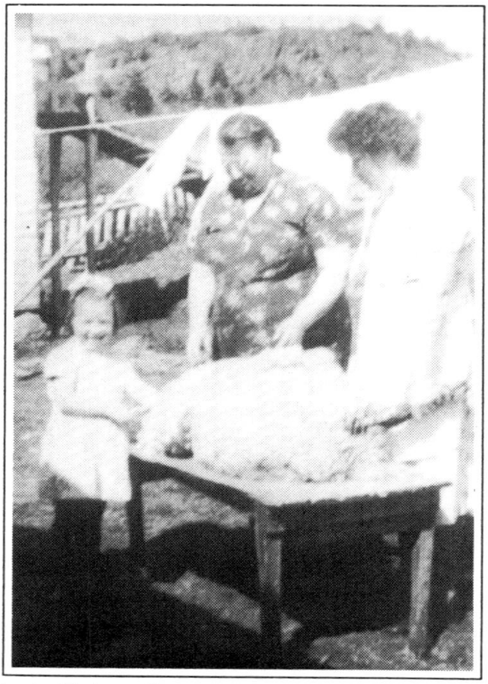

Louise Whelan and her daughter, Lydia, shearing sheep in Deer Harbour during the early 1950s, while Inez King looks on. (Photo courtesy of Lydia and Reginald Penney)

As in all rural Newfoundland communities during early times, potato was a staple in the diet of Random Islanders. Newfoundland census for 1884 gives the number of bushels of potatoes grown in each of the communities on Random Island as follows: Bald Nap 65, Bar Point 29, Britannia Cove 339, Deer Harbour 286, Elliott's Cove 117, Foster's Point 144, Hickman's Harbour 333, Lady Cove 170, Lance Cove 259, Robinson's Bight 37, Snook's Harbour 82, and Thoroughfare 48. Statistics on the harvest of potatoes and cabbage on Random Island in 1934 illustrate the extent of farming on the island at that time.

Community	*Bushels of Potatoes*	*Pounds of Cabbage*
Aspen Cove	162	400
Aspey Brook	405	650
Britannia Cove	1,120	850
Deer Harbour	960	3,700
Elliott's Cove	760	1,800
Foster's Point	1,297	4,300
Hickman's Harbour	4,314	39,900
Lady Cove	1,175	5,100
Lower Lance Cove	1,380	3,570
Petley	1,236	2,330
Random Head Harbour	45	
Snook's Harbour	705	1,710
Thoroughfare	408	5,200
Totals	13,967	68,660

Another view of the place of agriculture in the pursuits of Random Islanders is available in terms of the number of acres under cultivation at different times on the island. To illustrate, the acreage used for growing

Hay-making in Elliott's Cove in the 1920s. Cutting, drying and storing hay for their animals was a family effort in those days. (Photo courtesy of Hazel Brown)

potatoes on Random Island during the 1940s was as follows: Aspey Brook 2, Britannia Cove 35, Deer Harbour 12, Elliott's Cove 4, Foster's Point 12, Hickman's Harbour 29, Lady Cove 9, Petley 7, Snook's Harbour 1 and Thoroughfare 4.

CHAPTER 4

PIONEERS OF EARLIEST SETTLEMENTS

THE FIRST ARRIVALS on Random Island were transients and winter people. They came to the island, built tilts, and spent their winters on the island where they could take advantage of the forest for fuel and materials to built boats, wharfs, stages and flakes. Many of the winter people, especially those on the eastern part of the island, were sent there to cut wood for the fish merchants of Trinity. Hence, most of those first people to the island were men. Even those who brought their families from other places in Trinity Bay, or from the north shore of Conception Bay, would stay only for the winter and return to their previous residences to fish during the summer. The earliest settlements on Random Island were located at its eastern end. They were at Deer Harbour, Rider's Harbour, Silldown and Thoroughfare. Also in the this part of the island were the settlements of George's Cove in the 1870s, and of East Random Head and Random Head Harbour from the 1890s until the 1920s. Three of the seven settlements on the eastern end of Random Island became well established communities: Deer Harbour, Rider's Harbour and Thoroughfare. While there were winter people from Trinity in different parts of Random Island during the late 17th and early 18th centuries, Rider's Harbour was the first permanent settlement on the island, having been settled around 1770. It existed for about one hundred years before it was abandoned around 1870. Permanent settlers were a little later coming to Deer Harbour and Thoroughfare than they were to Rider's Harbour. However, Deer Harbour and Thoroughfare developed into thriving fishing/logging communities with all the facilities (schools, churches, lodges, post offices) of Newfoundland outports in those days. These two communities existed for 130 years or more before they were resettled in the 1960s. The aim of this chapter is to identify the early settlers to each of the four earliest settlements on Random Island: Deer Harbour, Rider's Harbour, Silldown and Thoroughfare.

Deer Harbour

Evidence that people lived in Deer Harbour earlier than revealed by available church records is found in a government census which shows it to be a relatively large settlement of some 68 people in the mid 1840s. More information on these people is found in the names of geographical locations in the area which have been passed on by oral tradition. As noted in chapter 2 on the origin of place names, there are many such names, including Bearns' Room, Gosses' Point, Jackson's Hill, Miller's Pond, Sally Rowe, Sibley's Cove and Thomas' Cove in the Deer Harbour. Some of these family names are of people who spent winters in and around the harbour taking advantage of the forest. Others are of people who were most likely permanent settlers in the sense that they came with the intention of staying, and perhaps inhabited the harbour all year around for several years before moving on. In addition to the attractive forest surrounding Deer Harbour, this naturally enclosed harbour provided protection from the bay while giving easy access to lucrative fishing grounds. Therefore, it is not surprising that early fishermen were attracted to this place. While there were winter people in and around Deer Harbour around 1800, it was not settled permanently until the 1830s or early 1840s. In viewing the family names of early people to Deer Harbour, a couple of points emerge. One is that all but one of the family names found there in the 1840s and 1850s were not there after that time. Another observation on the arrival of early people in Deer Harbour is that while there was an influx of new family names to that harbour during the 1860s, only one family name was added to the place between the end of that decade and 1900. The chronological order of people settling in Deer Harbour is as follows:

1830s - Bearns, Gosse, Jackson, Miller, Penney and others
1840s - Critch and Rowe
1850s - Marsh
1860s - Crocker, Evely, King, Penney, Purchase and others
1880s - Bailey.

1830s - Bearns, Gosse, Jackson, Miller, Penney and others

Given the population of 68 people in Deer Harbour in 1845, and given the fact that certain family names have been assigned to specific geographical locations, it is suggested that some of the earlier settlers, perhaps, the Bearns, Gosses, Jacksons, Millers, Sibleys and Thomas, were living in this harbour as early as the 1830s. According to oral tradition, there was a major forest fire that started at Smith Sound and burned across the eastern end of Random Island, consuming several dwellings and fishing premises at Deer Harbour during the 1830s. The story is that one Elijah Penney died from exhaustion in attempting to get the women and children into boats so they could row to safety from the fire.

1840s - Critch and Rowe

In addition to those people whom it is suspected were in Deer Harbour during the 1830s, Methodist Church records in Hant's Harbour show a family of Critches and one of Rowes living in Deer Harbour in the 1840s, namely, James and Mary Critch, and Edward and Sarah Rowe. Those records also report that John and Elizabeth Critch had children baptized in Deer Harbour in the 1850s. One might question whether the Deer Harbour referred to in these records is Upper Deer Harbour which is located at the entrance to Bay Bulls Arm, or the Deer Harbour, sometimes referred to as Lower Deer Harbour, on Random Island. Since the name Sally (Sarah) Rowe has been traditionally associated with a specific geographical location in Deer Harbour, Random Island, and because there is Critch's Rock in this area it is fairly certain that the Deer Harbour referred to in the Hant's Harbour records is Deer Harbour on the Random Island.

Benjamin Marsh. Benjamin was one of eight sons of the original Benjamin and Abigail Marsh who were Deer Harbour pioneers in the 1850s. Note the homemade buck saw which was a widely used tool when this picture was taken in 1931. His granddaughter, Daphne, offers a helping hand. (Photo courtesy of Minnie C. Marsh)

1850s - Marsh

The first permanent settlers in Deer Harbour to remain there and become an integral part of the community throughout its life, that is, until it was resettled in 1967, were Marshes. Two brothers, Benjamin and John Brown Marsh (spelt "Mesh" in early records) were the

Elizabeth Marsh (nee Marsh) and her son Otto at his christening in 1914. A historian in her own right, Elizabeth was of great assistance to the present writers in their research on Random Island pioneers. (Photo courtesy of Elizabeth Marsh)

first Marshes to settle in Deer Harbour. They were the sons of one Joseph Marsh, who, along with a James Toope, jumped ship in Trinity around 1810. It is said that Joseph Marsh and James Toope came to Trinity from Somerset, England, as sailors on a cargo ship. They decided, against the wishes of the ship's Captain, to remain in Newfoundland. In order to hide and not be forced to go back to England, they left Trinity and went to the Bonaventure area. It is said that they spent their first winter in Newfoundland in a tilt they constructed in a cove near Bonaventure Head. The next spring Joseph Marsh went to Bonaventure to live while James Toope made his way to Ireland's Eye, perhaps via Rider's Harbour (Seary, 1976:482). They subsequently married and started the Marsh and Toope families in these places, respectively. Joseph's wife was Elizabeth, and church records show Joseph as a planter in Bonaventure in 1825. One of the sons of Joseph and Elizabeth Marsh, Benjamin, left Bonaventure, and along with his wife, Abigail, lived in Rider's Harbour for few years before settling in Deer Harbour in the mid 1850s. Benjamin and Abigail had eight sons: Alexander, Arthur, Benjamin, Ezra, James, Job, Joseph and Solomon. One of these sons, Arthur, was born in Rider's Harbour in 1853. At least four of them were born in Deer Harbour: James in 1857, Ezra in 1860, Job in 1863 and Benjamin in

James Marsh, son of Benjamin and Abigail Marsh, drowned February 17, 1902, while attempting to deliver medical supplies to the lighthouse keepers at East Random Head. (Photo courtesy of John and Ivy Marsh)

1866. John Brown Marsh, another son of Joseph Marsh, left Bonaventure and later lived in Deer Harbour, perhaps before Benjamin went to Deer Harbour. While John Brown Marsh soon returned to Bonaventure, Benjamin stayed in Deer Harbour to become the patriarch of the Marsh family in this community. However, in those days, this harbour was known as John Brown's Deer Harbour, a possible reference to John Brown Marsh who lived here during the 1850s.

1860s - Crocker, Evely, King, Penney, Purchase and others

The 1860s saw several new families settle in Deer Harbour. Some of them remained for relatively short periods of time, while descendants of others were there throughout the life of the community. Kings were among the early settlers in Deer Harbour and they were an integral part of this community until it was resettled in 1967. Of English descent, James Penney King, the original King in Deer Harbour, is said to have been an offspring of the James King who lived at Bradley's Cove in 1773, and of the James King who lived in Western Bay in 1800. Perhaps the James King in Western Bay was a son of the James King in Bradley's Cove. Whatever the connection, James Penney King, his wife, Elizabeth, and their children were probably the first family to settle in Deer Harbour during the 1860s. Church documents show that William J. King, a son of James P. and Elizabeth King, was born in Bradley's Cove in 1857. It has been said that he was five or six years old when his parents moved to Deer Harbour. Hence, the suggestion that they did not settle in Deer Harbour from Western Bay until the 1860s.

William J. King. William was only a child when his parents, James P. and Elizabeth King, settled in Deer Harbour in the 1860s. Using his own schooners, he became a well-known fisherman in the area. He also had a water-driven sawmill in Deer Harbour. (Photo courtesy of Naomi King)

About the same time as James P. and Elizabeth King moved to Deer Harbour their daughter, Melina, married Edward Whelan (sometimes spelt "Whealon" in early

Amelia King (nee Hogarth of Trinity), wife of William King, and their granddaughter, Jemima in 1918. Along with her husband, Amelia was instrumental in convincing the government to open a post office in Deer Harbour. (Photo courtesy of Naomi King)

records) of Bradley's Cove. Edward and Melina also settled in Deer Harbour, thereby starting the first Whelan family in this community. Edward Whelan was of Irish descent, and probably an offspring of one William Whealon who lived in Bradley's Cove in 1756.

A third family to take up residence in Deer Harbour during the 1860s was that of Crockers from Bradley's Cove. Of English origin, the Crockers settled in Bradley's Cove in the 18th century. The Deer Harbour Crockers were most likely descendants of one William Crocker who lived in Bradley's Cove in 1796. Jesse Crocker of Bradley's Cove married Julia Ann King, a daughter of James P. King, who had settled in Deer Har-

James and Tobias Whelan were sons of Edward and Melina Whelan, the original Whelan couple in Deer Harbour. (Photos courtesy of Reginald and Lydia Penney and Baxter and Marilyn Marsh)

John Penney and his wife, Jemima (nee King), were among the pioneers of Deer Harbour. John was a son of George and Emily (nee Evely) Penney while his wife's parents were James P. and Elizabeth King. (Photo courtesy of Wilfred Marsh)

bour in the earlier 1860s. Jesse and Julia Crocker joined her parents in Deer Harbour around 1865. One of their daughters, Elizabeth, was born in Bradley's Cove in 1863, while another, Keziah, was born in Deer Harbour in 1867. Keziah married Benjamin Marsh, a son of the Benjamin Marsh who had settled in the harbour earlier. By 1912 the family name of Crocker had died out in Deer Harbour, but their offspring lived on through the Marshes in the community.

George Penney, son of George and Emily Penney, a longtime fisherman of Deer Harbour. (Photo courtesy of Reginald and Lydia Penney)

From written records, it is deduced that William Penney of English Harbour, along with his wife, Sarah (nee Hodder) of Ireland's Eye, were the first Penneys to settle in Deer Harbour. Taking up residence there in the 1860s, William was joined by his brothers George and Isaac, both of whom married women from this harbour. A Purchase family, Joseph and Fanny, also settled in Deer Harbour during the 1860s. It is speculated that Joseph came from Ship Cove (later became part of Port Rexton) where a

Priscilla Penney (nee Blundell of Hickman's Harbour) married Elijah Penney of Deer Harbour. They lived at Hickman's Harbour and Robinson's Bight before returning to Deer Harbour. (Photo courtesy of Minnie C. Marsh)

Joseph Purchase, maybe the father of the Joseph Purchase who settled in Deer Harbour, was a planter.

The first Evelys (sometimes spelt "Evelly" and "Evelley") in Deer Harbour were William and Patience Evely. Their son, John, was born in Trinity in 1864. Since William Evely is listed in Lovell's Newfoundland directory for 1871, it is likely that he moved to Deer Harbour in the 1860s. There were never many Evelys in this settlement, and with the passing of John Evely in 1929 and his wife, Naomi, in 1945, this name disappeared.

Baptismal records of the Roman Catholic Church in King's Cove, Bonavista Bay, show that three people were baptized in Deer Harbour in 1866: Ellen Hogan, Patrick Sullivan and Mary Ellen Newton. No other evidence has been found to substantiate the presence of Hogans and Sullivans in this community. However, there were Newtons in Deer Harbour for many years. Mary Ellen Newton was probably the daughter of Frederick Newton, who is said to have been the first Newton to have settled here. Apparently, Newton was a common name in Deer Harbour in the late 1880s. Five Newtons were identified as fishermen at Deer Harbour by McAlpine in 1894. It is said that the Newtons occupied three dwelling houses there, which suggests that there were at least three primary families of Newtons in the harbour at that time. But shortly thereafter they left this community.

Lovell's 1871 directory of Newfoundland gives the population of Deer Harbour as 53 people, including the following fisherman: William Evely, James King, Benjamin Mesh, John Mesh, Frederick Newton, George Penney, Joseph Purchase and Edward Whealon. There were no new families settling in Deer Harbour during the 1870s.

1880s - Bailey

Although the original Baileys in Deer Harbour came there from Ireland's Eye, as far as can be ascertained, they were from the same Bailey (also spelt "Bayly", "Baily" and "Bayley") family that lived in Bonaven-

Julia Bailey (nee Hyde of Bonaventure). Her husband, Jordan was one of the original Bailey brothers to settle in Deer Harbour in the 1890s. She was a midwife in Deer Harbour for about sixty years, attending to the delivery of more than 90 babies during that time. (Photo courtesy of Harvey Bailey)

ture in the 18th century, some members of which lived in Rider's Harbour during the 1850. A cove in Rider's Harbour still bears the name of this family. More specific to the Baileys settling in Deer Harbour, James Bailey of Ireland's Eye married Elizabeth Crocker of Deer Harbour in 1883 and started the first Bailey family in the harbour. Apparently, James' mother, whose name was Catherine (nee Mesh), accompanied her son to the harbour. She died in Deer Harbour in 1885 at the age of 56. Shortly after James Bailey settled in the harbour, he was joined by his brother, Jordan, who married a Julia Hyde of Bonaventure. Their sister, Phoebe, married George Penney of Deer Harbour.

By way of summarizing and adding to the foregoing review of early settlers to Deer Harbour, Table 4-1 includes date and place of birth of adults in this harbour prior to 1900. Also, where known, husband and wife have been grouped together here and maiden names are included for those interested in genealogical pursuits. It is seen that the early settlers to Deer Harbour were, for the most part, an even mixture of people from the Trinity area and from two communities (Bradley's Cove and Western Bay) on the north side of Conception Bay.

Kenneth Bailey, son of Jordan and Julia Bailey, a longtime fisherman of Deer Harbour, who was admired for his craftsmanship in building fishing boats. (Photo courtesy of Harvey Bailey)

TABLE 4-1

DATE AND PLACE OF BIRTH OF SOME OF THE ADULTS IN DEER HARBOUR PRIOR TO 1900

NAME	DATE OF BIRTH	PLACE OF BIRTH
Benjamin Bailey Catherine Bailey (nee Mesh)	 1830	 Bonaventure
James Bailey Elizabeth Bailey (nee Crocker)	1856 1863	Rider's Harbour Bradley's Cove
Jordan Bailey Julia Bailey (nee Hyde)	1870	Ireland's Eye Bonaventure
James Critch Mary Critch		
John Critch Elizabeth Critch		
Jesse Crocker Julia Ann Crocker (nee King)	1836 1842	Bradley's Cove Western Bay
John Crocker	1874	Deer Harbour
Sarah Jane Crocker	1866	Deer Harbour
Walter Crocker *1st Wife*	1875	Deer Harbour
Mary Crocker (nee Penney) *2nd Wife*	1880	Deer Harbour
Mary Ann Crocker (nee Marsh)	1886	Deer Harbour
James Evely		
John Evely Naomi Evely (nee Penney)	1864 1874	Trinity
William Evely Patience Evely (nee Hogarth)	 1829	 Trinity

NAME	DATE OF BIRTH	PLACE OF BIRTH
William Evely	1866	Deer Harbour
Ellen Hogan		
James P. King	1814	Western Bay
Elizabeth King	1816	Western Bay
Jemima King	1851	Western Bay
William J. King	1857	Bradley's Cove
Amelia King (nee Hogarth)	1856	Trinity
Abigail Marsh	1852	Rider's Harbour?
Alexander Marsh		
1st Wife		
Jane Marsh (nee Purchase)		Deer Harbour
2nd Wife		
Emma Jane Marsh (nee King)		St. Jones Within
Alexander Marsh	1881	Deer Harbour
Elizabeth Marsh (nee Marsh)	1892	Deer Harbour
Arthur Marsh	1853	Rider's Harbour
1st Wife		
Isabella Marsh (nee Hodder)		Ireland's Eye
2nd Wife		
Sarah Marsh (nee Noseworthy)	1869	Shoal Harbour
Benjamin Marsh	1827	Bonaventure
Abigail Marsh (nee Dalton)	1822	
Benjamin Marsh	1866	Deer Harbour
Keziah Marsh (nee Crocker)	1868	Deer Harbour
Benjamin Marsh	1885	Deer Harbour
Eliza Marsh	1875	Deer Harbour
Ezra Marsh	1860	Deer Harbour
Caroline Marsh (nee Seaward)	1865	Gooseberry Cove
Henrietta Marsh	1882	Deer Harbour

NAME	DATE OF BIRTH	PLACE OF BIRTH
James Marsh	1857	Deer Harbour
Elizabeth Marsh (nee Adey)	1849	Lee Bight
Job Marsh (senior)	1863	Deer Harbour
1st Wife		
Susan Marsh (nee Purchase)	1865	Deer Harbour
2nd Wife		
Julia Marsh (nee Baker)	1874	Hatchet Cove
Job Marsh (junior)	883	Deer Harbour
1st Wife		
Jane Marsh (nee Penney)	1880	Deer Harbour
2nd Wife		
Maggie Marsh (nee Butt)	1901	Hickman's Harbour
John Brown Marsh	1825	Bonaventure
Joseph Marsh		
1st wife		
Sarah Marsh (nee Noseworthy)		Lee Bight
2nd wife		
Jane Marsh (nee Hyde)		Bonaventure
Solomon Marsh	1856	
Mary Jane Marsh (nee Critch)	1873	Hickman's Harbour
Robert Miller		
Edwin Newton		
Frederick Newton		
Ellen Newton (nee Furey)		
John Newton		
Mary Ellen Newton	1866	Deer Harbour
Peter Newton		
Thomas Newton		
Helen Newton (nee Baker)		Granny's Cove

NAME	DATE OF BIRTH	PLACE OF BIRTH
Elijah Penney		
Elijah Penney	1872	Deer Harbour
Priscilla Penney (nee Blundell)	1880	Hickman's Harbour
George Penney (senior)		English Harbour
1st Wife		
Emily Penney (nee Evely)		Deer Harbour
2nd Wife		
Pheobe Penney (nee Bailey)	1859	Ireland's Eye
George Penney (junior)	1885	Deer Harbour
1st Wife		
Clara Penney (nee Brown)	1889	Thoroughfare
2nd Wife		
Eliza Jane Penney (nee Dodge)	1896	Little Heart's Ease
Isaac Penney	1853	English Harbour
1st Wife		
Martha Penney	1853	
2nd Wife		
Annie Penney		
John Penney		Deer Harbour
1st Wife		
Jemima Penney (nee King)	1879	Deer Harbour
2nd Wife		
Elizabeth Penney (nee Avery/Peddle)	1868	Southwest Arm
Margaret Penney	1850 (circa)	English Harbour
Margaret Penney	1878	Deer Harbour
Rachel Penney	1882	Deer Harbour
Rebecca Penney	1850 (circa)	English Harbour
Rebecca Penney	1877	Deer Harbour
Samuel Penney		
Sarah Penney (nee King)	1852	Western Bay

NAME	DATE OF BIRTH	PLACE OF BIRTH
William Penney	1841	English Harbour
Sarah Penney (nee Hodder)		Ireland's Eye
William Penney	1874	Deer Harbour
Diannah Penney (nee Whelan)	1875	Deer Harbour
Fanny Purchase	1851	Ship Cove
George Purchase	1867	Deer Harbour
1st Wife		
Rhoda Purchase (nee Whelan)		Deer Harbour
2nd Wife		
Emma Jane Purchase (nee King/Marsh)	1866	St. Jones Within
Joseph Purchase	1831	Ship Cove
Fanny Purchase	1825	
Philip Purchase	1859	Freshwater
Mary Jane Purchase (nee Evely)	1866	Freshwater
Edward Rowe		
Sarah Rowe		
Patrick Sullivan		
Edward Whelan	1837	Bradley's Cove
Melina Whelan (nee King)	1840	Western Bay
Elias James Whelan	1869	Deer Harbour
Lucy Ann Whelan (nee Hodder)	1872	Ireland's Eye
Tobias Whelan	1879	Deer Harbour
Dorcas Selina Whelan (nee Critch)	1880	Hickman's Harbour

Source: This Table was developed from vital statistics from the Methodist Church at Bay de Verde, Blackhead, Britannia Cove and Carbonear; vital statistics from the Church of England at Trinity and Trinity East; vital statistics from the Roman Catholic Church at King's Cove; Trinity Bay Census of 1800-01; 19th century lists of voters as recorded in *White's Papers* at Trinity; nominal census for Deer Harbour in 1935 and 1945; *Lovell's Province of Newfoundland Directory for 1871*; *McAlpine's Newfoundland Directory 1894 to 1897*; *McAlpine's Newfoundland Directory for 1898*; tombstones on Random Island; and interviews with Islanders.

1900/67 - Avery, Ivany, Kelly, Poole and Watton

Five family names were added to the list of permanent settlers in Deer Harbour from 1900 until it was resettled in 1967. They were Avery, Ivany, Kelly, Poole and Watton. After the death of his father, Elias Avery as a teenager of Long Beach accompanied his mother, Elizabeth, to Deer Harbour where she married John Penney. Later, Elias married Jemima King of Deer Harbour, thereby starting the Avery family in this community in the 1930s. Alonzo Ivany of Ivanhoe and Thoroughfare married Neta Marsh of Deer Harbour and created the Ivany family in this community in the 1940s. The Kellys of Deer Harbour are of Irish descent. Two brothers, David and James, offspring of one David Kelly from Ireland who had settled on Ireland's Eye Island prior to 1850, married two Marsh sisters of Deer Harbour, Sarah and Lillian, respectively, and made their homes in Deer Harbour in the early 1900s. The family name of Poole became a part of the Deer Harbour population when Lawrence Poole of Harcourt moved to Deer Harbour in 1940. The Watton family of Deer Harbour began when William Watton of this harbour, but formerly of Old Tilt (renamed Ivanhoe), married Elsie Jacobs from Little Heart's Ease and settled in the harbour. William grew up in Deer Harbour, having gone there as a young boy to live with Naomi Evely after his mother died.

Rider's Harbour

It is impossible to ascertain the exact time of arrival of each of the families to Rider's Harbour and their lengths of stay there. However, as far as can be gathered from written records the following were the family names in Rider's Harbour and the decades in which they first appeared in this place:

1770s - Hodder, Rogers, Sevier and Spurrell
1780s - Foster, Quinn and Purset
1800/09 - Archibald, Britt, Dewley, Sullivan and others
1810/19 - Aspell, Bartlett, Barron, Bugden and others
1820s - Abbott, Borders, Connors, Maloney and others
1830s - Davis, Devine, Finnley, Hearne and others
1840s - Langer
1850s - Bailey, Churchill, McGrath and Mesh
1860s - Baker, Hodder and Toope.

1770s - Hodder, Rogers, Sevier and Spurrell

Records of people living in Rider's Harbour suggest that Hodders, Rogers, Seviers and Spurrells were the first people to settle there. Church of England records at Trinity include the marriage of William Sevier of Ringwood, Hants, England, to Rachel Haddow [sic] of Rider's Harbour in 1770. These records also show that they had children born in Rider's Harbour in the 1780s. Sevier (also spelt "Civier" and "Seviour" in Rider's Harbour) and Hodder were among the enduring names in this settlement. While the Seviers lived there continuously from 1770 until the 1830s, Hodders were absent from Rider's Harbour for several years to return to the harbour in the 1860s. Joseph Rogers married Elizabeth Spurral (later spelt "Spurrell") in Rider's Harbour in 1773. Their previous places of abode are not known. Elizabeth probably lived in the Trinity area and may have been related to the Thomas Spurrell of Trinity who married Jane Sevier of Rider's Harbour in 1808.

1780s - Foster, Quinn and Purset

Two Irishmen married Rider's Harbour women in Rider's Harbour during the 1780s. One was Darby Quinn of Ross, Ireland, who married a Sarah Foster in 1786. The next year John Purset, a sailor, from Ireland, married Mary Sevier. Both of these couples made Rider's Harbour their home for a number of years.

1800/09 - Archibald, Britt, Dewley, Sullivan and others

Census for Trinity Bay shows that each of the following men was a proprietor and an occupier of a fishing room in Rider's Harbour in 1800/01: John Archibald, John Dewley and Sons, Richard Hodder, Thomas Hiscock, Michael Malone(y), William Mealey [sic] and William Sevier. This census is the first reference to the family names of Archibald, Dewley, Hiscock, Malone(y) and Meagher in Rider's Harbour. Later records show that John Archibald of Rider's Harbour married Bridgett Brennick of White Rock. The family name of Dewley (also spelt "Dawley") was a familiar one in Rider's Harbour for a number of years. It is known that Patrick and Mary Dawley had children born there in the 1820s. Except for the reference to Michael Malone(y) as an occupier of a fishing room in Rider's Harbour during 1800/01, no reference is found to any Malone(y)s in this place. The listing of Mealey in Rider's Harbour at that time may have been meant to read Meagher. The Roman Catholic Church records at King's Cove, Bonavista Bay, show that William and Flora Meagher had a son baptized in Rider's Harbour in 1826.

Family names appearing in Rider's Harbour during the first decade of the 19th century, other than those listed on the 1800/01 census, were Britt, Roberts and Sullivan. Thomas and Mary Britt had a son born in Rider's Harbour in 1803. However, it is suspected that this family stayed in this harbour for only a short period of time. John Roberts of Tingleton, England, married Amelia Sevier of Rider's Harbour in 1800. Since this is the only reference found to this family name in Rider's Harbour, it is not known if they lived in this harbour after their marriage. James Sullivan of Youghall, Ireland, married Eleanor Quinn of Rider's

Rider's Harbour, the first permanent settlement on Random Island, was settled in the 1760s and later abandoned. More than 100 years after their ancestors, Benjamin and Abigail Marsh left Rider's Harbour to make their home in Deer Harbour, Rider's Harbour became the fishing station and summer home of John and Ivy Marsh of Lower Lance Cove.

Harbour in 1804, and they settled in Rider's Harbour. Other Sullivans in this settlement included the families of John and Elinor Sullivan and Jessy and Mary Sullivan. The fact that one of the islands which form Rider's Harbour has been named Sullivan's Island has meant that this family name has been associated with this harbour over the years. In addition to Sullivan, the family name of Hiscock, which was added to Rider's Harbour in the early 1800s, has also become associated with Rider's Harbour in that there is a pond in the area which bears this family name to this day. As noted later in this chapter, there were Hiscocks in Thoroughfare in the 1850s.

1810/19 - Aspell, Bartlett, Barron, Bugden and others

During the second decade of the 19th century several families settled in Rider's Harbour for the first time. They included the names of Aspell, Bartlett, Barron, Brennick, Bugden, Butler, Cornel, Curran, Duggan, Fowlow, Mackey, Mahoney, O'Donnal, Ryan, Strickland, Tobin and Toope. Records of the Roman Catholic Church in King's Cove show that there were at least four families of Aspells (sometimes spelt "Asbell", "Asbil", "Aspelle" and "Aspill") in Rider's Harbour between 1815 and 1830. For example, John Aspell and Bridgette Brennick had five children there during that time. There were also the families of John and Catherine Aspell, John and Mary Aspell, and Patrick and Mary Aspell in Rider's Harbour in those days. In addition to Bridgette Brennick, who married John Aspell, there was a Richard Brennick (also spelt "Brennock", "Bronnick" and "Brinnock") in Rider's Harbour. A child of Richard Brennick and Catherine Hart was baptized in Rider's Harbour in 1832. Records of the Roman Catholic Church in King's Cove show that each of the following couples had a child baptized in Rider's Harbour in 1817: James and Mary Cornel, John Duggan and Anne Daley and James Fowlow and Elinor Foster. Sponsors at those and other baptismal ceremonies at Rider's Harbour between 1810 and 1819 included some people whose family names were not recorded in Rider's Harbour prior to those days, and, in fact, no other reference to their names have been found. Those names include Thomas Barron, Edward Curran, S. Mackey, William O'Donnal, Jeremiah Ryan, and Thomas Tobin. There were also Stricklands in Rider's Harbour between 1810 and 1819. Joseph Strickland was a sponsor at a baptismal ceremony in the harbour in 1811. Eighteen years later, John and Catherine Strickland had a daughter baptized in Rider's Harbour.

Thomas Bartlett of Dorset, England, married Mary Butler of County Kilkenny, Ireland in Rider's Harbour in 1819. They lived in Rider's Harbour for several years after their marriage. Also in that year, two Irishmen married Rider's Harbour women and started families in Rider's Harbour. One was Michael Mullaly, who married who married Elinor Flemming, and the other was Maurice Mahoney, who married Kitty Asbelle.

A family of Bugdens lived in Rider's Harbour in 1814. Joseph Bugden, probably of Scilly Cove (now Winterton) moved to Rider's Harbour prior to 1814 when he and Susannah Bugden had a daughter baptized in that harbour. As reported by Seary (1976:482), James Toope of Somerset, England, lived in Rider's Harbour in 1812. He later moved to Ireland's Eye.

1820s - Abbott, Borders, Connors, Maloney, and others

Study of written documents suggests that several family names appeared in Rider's Harbour for the first time during the 1820s. They were Abbott, Borders, Burry, Coleman, Connors, Grace, Mahoney, Mullaly, Murphy, O'Connell, O'Connor and Power. Three references have been found to Abbotts in Rider's Harbour. Catherine Abbott was a sponsor at the baptismal ceremony of a child of James O'Connor and Winney Rafters of Rider's Harbour in 1820s. King's Cove Roman Catholic Church records show a James Abbott living in Rider's Harbour around the same time, but there is no indication of his relationship to

Catherine Abbott. Later a William Abbott is given as a sponsor at a baptismal in this community. Also, according to the records of the Roman Catholic Church in King's Cove, there was a Michael Murphy, his wife, Betsy (nee "Peach" or "Push"), and a Michael Mullaly, his wife, Elizabeth (nee Cody) living in Rider's Harbour in the 1820s. During that decade, Bridget Power of County Kilkenny, Ireland, married at Rider's Harbour, but whom she married is not known.

There were Connors and O'Connors (probably the same family) living Rider's Harbour during the 1820s. Specifically, they were Patrick and Mary Connor, Michael Connor and Joseph O'Connor. Other family names found in Rider's Harbour for the first time during the 1820s are seen among the adults who were sponsors at baptismal ceremonies. However, it is not known if they were residents of Rider's Harbour at that time, or if they just happened to be there when the priest made his visit. Those people include Michael Borders, Mary Burry, John Coleman (perhaps, Colman), Simeon Cotter (perhaps, Connor), John Grace, John Mullaly and Thomas Tobin.

1830s - Davis, Devine, Finnley, Hearne and others

Except for the name of Hearne which appears in Rider's Harbour when a Patrick Hearne of County Cork, Ireland, married at Rider's Harbour in 1830, the only family names new to this settlement during the 1830s were those of people who were sponsors at baptismal ceremonies for children of families who had already settled in Rider's Harbour. The sponsors included Ellen Bryan, Johanna Cotters, John Davis, Nicholas Devine, John Finnley and John Miller. Since no other records have been found concerning the presence of any of those people in Rider's Harbour, it is possible that some of them were only visitors to Rider's Harbour at the time, while others may have lived there for a fishing season.

1840s - Langer

The only evidence of any new families settling in Rider's Harbour during the 1840s was that of Thomas and Mary Langer (sometimes spelt "Langhour", "Langor" and "Langhour"). It appears as if the Langers came to Rider's Harbour from Trinity, and were probably descendants of David Langer who lived in Trinity in 1730. It has also been suggested that the Langers of Rider's Harbour were also related to those in Heart's Content during that time. Thomas and Mary lived in Rider's Harbour for a few years before moving to Thoroughfare. In fact, church records suggest that between 1844 and 1862 they moved several times between Thoroughfare and Rider's Harbour.

The population of Rider's Harbour dropped from 60 people in 1845 to only 13 people in 1857. However, a study of church records show that the 60 people who were there in 1845 had all moved out by the early 1850s. They had abandoned the harbour and a new group of people had moved into it. In fact, those who moved out were mainly Roman Catholic people and those who moved in belonged to the Church of England. Thomas and Mary Langer were among the first to settle in Rider's Harbour after it was abandoned by the earlier people, but they were soon joined by others in the 1850.

1850s - Bailey, Churchill, McGrath and Mesh

Benjamin and Catherine Bailey of Bonaventure moved to Rider's Harbour during the 1850s. Their son, James, was born in Rider's Harbour in 1856. They lived in Rider's Harbour for a few years before moving to Ireland's Eye in the 1860s where they had another son, whom they named Jordan, in 1870. James and Jordan later settled in Deer Harbour and started the Bailey family in that community. Accompanying the Baileys to Rider's Harbour were Catherine's brother, Benjamin Mesh, and his wife Abigail. They had a son, Arthur, born in Rider's Harbour in 1853. Shortly thereafter they moved to Deer Harbour where they became known as Marshes. There is also written record of a Phillip McGrath fishing in Rider's Harbour for one season, that of 1859. Since no other reference has been found to him, it is suspected that he spent only one summer in this harbour.

1860s - Baker, Hodder and Toope

According to Church of England records at Trinity, James and Joanna Baker lived at Rider's Harbour in 1862. Shortly thereafter they moved to Thoroughfare. A high dominant hill between Rider's Harbour and Thoroughfare carries this family name, Baker's Loaf. Church of England records at Trinity also show that Harriett Bailey of Rider's Harbour married Reuben Toop(e) of Ireland's Eye in 1861. They lived in Rider's Harbour for a few years before moving to Ireland's Eye. The island that is officially known as Sullivan's Island in Rider's Harbour is often referred to as Toope's Island by local fishermen. Perhaps it was named in honour of Reuben Toope. While Hodders were among the first people to settle Rider's Harbour in that they settled there in the 1770s, this family name was absent from this place for many years. However, it returned to Rider's Harbour during the 1860s with Stephen and Rosanna Hodder having a son, whom they called John, born there in 1862.

Table 4-2 includes a list of adults living in Rider's Harbour prior to 1870 along with other information about them and their families as gathered from early records. It is noted that several people from Ireland and England were married in Rider's Harbour at that time. Given the number of surnames in Rider's Harbour, it is suggested that it had a transient and cosmopolitan population.

TABLE 4-2

SOME OF THE ADULTS IN RIDER'S HARBOUR PRIOR TO 1870

NAME	ADDITIONAL INFORMATION
Catherine Abbott	Catherine Abbott was a sponsor at a baptismal ceremony at Rider's Harbour in the 1820s.
James Abbott	
William Abbott	
John Archibald Bridgett Archibald (nee Brennick)	John Archibald and Bridget Brennick got married in Rider's Harbour in 1814.
Andrew Aspell	
John Aspell Catherine Asbelle	
John Aspell Bridgette Aspell (nee Brinneck)	John and Bridgette Aspell had five children in Rider's Harbour between 1815 and 1820.
John Aspell Mary Aspell	
Patrick Aspell Mary Aspell (nee Tannis or Quinn)	
Benjamin Bailey Catherine Bailey (nee Mesh)	Benjamin and Catherine Bailey left Bonaventure and lived in Rider's Harbour for a few years during the 1850s moving to Ireland's Eye. Their sons James and Jordan later settled in Deer Harbour.
Rosannah Bailey	
James Baker Joanna Baker	James and Joanna Baker had a son born in Rider's Harbour in 1862.
Thomas Bartlett Mary Butler (nee Butler)	Thomas Bartlett of Poole, Dorset, England, married Mary Butler of County Kilkenny, Ireland, at Rider's Harbour in 1819.
Thomas Barron	
Richard Brennock Catherine Brennock (nee Hart)	Richard Brennock and Catherine Hart were married at Rider's Harbour in 1832.

NAME	ADDITIONAL INFORMATION
Thomas Britt Mary Britt (nee Foster)	Thomas Britt from Ireland married Mary Foster of Rider's Harbour in in 1802.
Michael Broders	
Ellen Bryan	
Joseph Bugden Susannah Bugden	It is suspected that Joseph Budgen came from Scilly Cove (Winterton) to Rider's Harbour prior to 1814.
Mary Burry	
George Churchill Mary Churchill	George and Mary Churchill had children born in Rider's Harbour, Silldown and Thoroughfare during the 1850s.
Charles Civier Ellen Civier	Civiers and Seviers were likely of the same family in Rider's Harbour.
Emilia Civier	Emilia Civier was baptized as an adult Roman Catholic in Rider's Harbour in 1830.
Richard Civier	Richard Civier was baptized as an adult Roman Catholic in Rider's Harbour in 1830.
John Colman	John Colman (perhaps Coleman) was a sponsor at a baptismal ceremony in Rider's Harbour in 1826.
Michael Connors	
Patrick Connors Mary Connors (nee Butler)	
James Cornel Mary Cornel	
Johanna Cotters Simon Cotters Edward Curran	Given the nature of the handwriting in Church records, it is possible that "Cotters" and "Curran" were meant to read "Connors."
John Davis	
Nicholas Devine	
Patrick Dawley Mary Dawley (nee Tanner)	Perhaps, "Dawley" and "Dewley" were given in reference to the same surname.
John Dewley Mary Dewley	

NAME	ADDITIONAL INFORMATION
John Duggan Anne Duggan) (nee Daley	John and Anne Duggan had a child born in Rider's Harbour in 1817.
John Finnley	There is also reference to a John Finlan in Rider's Harbour at the same time as John Finnley. It is likely both names refer to the same person.
John Foster Sarah Foster (nee Baker)	John Foster of Rider's Harbour married Sarah Baker of Heart's Ease in 1807 and settled in Rider's Harbour.
Mary Foster	As recorded in Roman Catholic records at King's Cove, Mary Foster resided in Rider's Harbour in 1822.
William Foster Charity Foster (nee Hiscock)	William Foster of Rider's Harbour married Charity Hiscock of the same place in 1806.
James Fowlow Elinor Fowlow (nee Foster)	
James Fowlow Mary Fowlow (nee Quinn)	
Mary Fowlow	Mary Fowlow was baptized as an adult by a Roman Catholic Priest in Rider's Harbour in 1826.
John Grace	John Grace lived in Rider's Harbour in 1829.
Patrick Hearne	Patrick Hearne of County Cork, Ireland, was married in Rider's Harbour in 1830.
Henry Hiscock Maria Hiscock	Henry and Maria Hiscock moved between Rider's Harbour and Thoroughfare in the 1850s.
James Hiscock Julienna Hiscock (nee Brinnick)	James and Julienna Hiscock had four children in Rider's Harbour between 1822 and 1832.
Joseph Hiscock Catherine Hiscock (nee Brennock)	
Thomas Hiscock	
Talian Hiscock	
Charles Hodder Grace Hodder	Charles and Grace Hodder had four children in Rider's Harbour between 1795 and 1803.

NAME	ADDITIONAL INFORMATION
Richard Hodder Bridgette Hodder (nee Harnum)	
Stephen Hodder Rosanna Hodder	
William Hodder Jane Hodder (nee Bayly)	William Hodder of Ireland's Eye and Jane Bayly of Rider's Harbour were married in 1853 married in 1853.
Thomas Langer Mary Langer	From 1844 to 1862, Thomas and Mary Langer had at least six children. Some of whom were born in Rider's Harbour while others were born at Thoroughfare.
S. Mackey	
Catherine Mahoney	
Maurice Mahoney Kitty Mahoney (nee Aspell)	Maurice Mahoney of County Cork, Ireland, married Kitty Aspell of Rider's Harbour in 1819.
S. Mahoney Julianne Mahoney (nee Aspell)	
Michael Malone	
Philip McGrath	
Edward Meagher	
William Meagher Flora Meagher (nee Janes?)	William and Flora Meagher had a son baptized in Rider's Harbour in 1826.
Benjamin Mesh Abigail Mesh	Benjamin and Abigail Mesh (later became Marsh) lived in Rider's Harbour for a few years before settling in Deer Harbour where they were the first permanent settlers.
John Miller	
John Mullaly Elinor Mullaly	
Michael Mullaly Elinor Mullaly (nee Flemming)	Michael Mullaly of County Kilkenny, Ireland, married Elinor Flemming of Rider's Harbour in 1819.
Michael Mullaly Elizabeth Mullaly (nee Cody)	Michael and Elizabeth Mullaly were living in Rider's Harbour as early as the 1820s and had a child baptized baptized Rider's Harbour in 1833.

NAME	ADDITIONAL INFORMATION
Michael Murphy Betsy Murphy (nee Peach or Push?)	
James O'Connor Winnifred O'Connor (nee Rafters)	Winnifred Rafters appears in Church records several times with different spellings including Winney Rafters and Winnifred Rafteria.
Joseph O'Connor	
William O'Donnal	
Bridget Power	Bridget Power of County Kilkenny, Ireland, was married at Rider's Harbour in 1826.
John Purset Mary Purset (nee Sevier)	John Purset, a sailor from Ireland, married Mary Sevier of Rider's Harbour in 1787.
Darby Quinn Sarah Quinn (nee Foster)	Darby Quinn of Ross, Ireland, married Sarah Foster, a widow, of Rider's Harbour in 1786.
John Roberts Amelia Roberts (nee Sevier)	John Roberts of Tingleton, Dorset, England, married Amelia Sevier of Rider's Harbour in 1800.
Joseph Rogers Elizabeth Rogers (nee Spurral)	Joseph Rogers and Elizabeth Spurral were married in Rider's Harbour in 1773.
Jeremiah Ryan	
Charles Sevier Ellen Sevier	
Richard Sevier Eleanor Sevier (nee Delaney)	Richard Sevier of Rider's Harbour and Eleanor Delaney of Hearts Ease were married in Rider's Harbour in 1823.
Moses Sevier Sweet Sevier (nee Pinhorne)	Moses Sevier, a planter of Rider's Harbour, married Sweet Pinhorne of Scilly Cove in 1806. They had 9 children born in Rider's Harbour between 1807 and 1826.
William Sevier Hannah Sevier (nee Wiseman)	William Sevier of Rider's Harbour married Hannah Wiseman of Trinity in 1814.
William Sevier Rachel Sevier (nee Hodder)	William Sevier of Ringwood, Hants,England, married Rachel Hodder of Rider's Harbour in 1770. This is the first marriage recorded for Random Island.

NAME	ADDITIONAL INFORMATION
Thomas Spurrell Jane Spurrell (nee Sevier)	Thomas Spurrell of Trinity married Jane Sevier of Rider's Harbour in 1808. Apparently, they settled at Rider's Harbour.
John Strickland Catherine Strickland (nee Moors or Murs)	John and Catherine Strickland had a daughter baptized in Rider's Harbour in 1829.
Joseph Strickland	
James Sullivan Eleanor Sullivan (nee Quinn)	James Sullivan of Youghall, Ireland, married Eleanor Quinn of Rider's Harbour in 1804.
James Sullivan Mary Sullivan	
Jeremiah Sullivan Elinor Sullivan	
Jessy Sullivan Mary Sullivan (nee Fowlow)	In the Roman Catholic Church records at King'sCove, Jessy Sullivan's wife, Mary, is referred to as Mary Foley and as Mary Fowlow.
John Sullivan Elinor Sullivan	
Thomas Tobin	
James Toope	James Toope of Somerset, England, lived in Rider'si In 1812.
Reuben Toop Harriett Toop (nee Bailey)	Reuben Toop(e) of Ireland's Eye married Harriett Bailey of Rider's Harbour in 1861.
James Vail Sweet Vail (nee Pinhorne/Sevier	James Vail (perhaps, Veal), of Christ Church, England, married Sweet Sevier, a widow, of Rider's Harbour, in 1829.

Source: This Table was developed from vital statistics from the Church of England at Trinity and Trinity East; vital statistics from the Roman Catholic Church at King's Cove; Trinity Bay Census of 1800-01; and 19th century lists of voters as recorded in *White's Papers* at Trinity.

Silldown

Newfoundland census shows that there were eleven people in Silldown in 1836, with an increase to eighteen people in 1845, and the same number in 1857. A voters list for 1835 has two voters at Silldown, one was Richard Sevier (senior) and the other was Richard Sevier (junior). However, no church records have been found for people living in this place during the 1830s or 1840s. There is, however, a record of a child born to George and Mary Churchill in Silldown in 1856. This Churchill family also lived in Rider's Harbour and Thoroughfare during the 1850s. It is suspected that other inhabitants of Silldown lived at Rider's Harbour at one time or another. Even if they did not live in Rider's Harbour, it is likely that those in Silldown during the 19th century were listed in church records as residing in this harbour.

Thoroughfare

Since the area around Thoroughfare was well forested during early times, and since this part of Random Island is close to Trinity, it is likely that Thoroughfare and neighbouring coves on Random Island were used by Trinity merchants, who sent men there to cut logs and firewood throughout the 18th century. Also, because the tickle separating Random Island from Ireland's Eye was a main route, that is, "a thoroughfare", for boats travelling from Rider's Harbour and Trinity, it is very likely that the coves on the Random Island side of this tickle were stop-over points. As noted in the earlier chapter on the origin of place names on Random Island, it is suspected that Connelly's Cove and Gabriel's Cove bear the names of early visitors to this area. Based on written records, the chronological order in which people settled Thoroughfare is as follows:

1830s - Abbott and Piercey
1840s - Mills
1850s - Brown, Churchill, Eastman, Hiscock and Langer
1860s - Bailey, Baker, Hodder and Ivany
1880s - Bungay, Gray, Leonard and Verge
1890s - Maidment and Miller.

1830s - Abbott and Piercey

According to a voters list for 1835, there were 3 eligible voters in Thoroughfare at that time: Matthew Abbott, William Abbott and John Piercey. By 1837, the two Abbotts had left Thoroughfare to live in British Harbour. Apparently, the Pierceys stayed in Thoroughfare for only a short time as well. No church records have been found to show their presence in settlement.

Thomas and Jemima Mills. In 1885, they opened the first post office in Thoroughfare. (Photo courtesy of Clyde Tuck)

1840s - Mills

The Mills were the first permanent settlers to Thoroughfare in that they came early and stayed to become a part of this community for over 100 years. The present research suggests that they settled in Thoroughfare during the late 1840s. One story is that Thomas Mills came to Thoroughfare from Dorset, England, sometime during that decade. Later, perhaps not until the mid 1850s, a Thomas Mills from Old Perlican settled in Thoroughfare. Lovell's Newfoundland directory for 1871 includes a Thomas Mill, Planter, and a Thomas Mills, Planter of Perlican, living in Thoroughfare at that time. A voters list compiled during the 1870s refers to one of the Thomas Mills in Thoroughfare as "English Tom". Each of the original Thomas Mills in Thoroughfare had a son named Nathaniel. *McAlpine's Newfoundland Directory for 1904* distinguishes between the two Nathaniel Mills living there at that time as "Nathaniel Mills of Thos. of England" and "Nathaniel Mills of Thos. of Perlican". Marriage records in the Church of England at Trinity suggest that one Nathaniel Mills, who married Ann Loder in 1870, was born at Thoroughfare in 1846. The Methodist records at Hant's Harbour suggest that the other Nathaniel Mills in Thoroughfare in those days was born in Old Perlican in 1842. Hence, there were two distinct families of Mills in Thoroughfare from very early on in the life of this community. Together, the two Mills families established this surname as one of most common ones in Thoroughfare. In fact, the Mills were not only among the first permanent settlers to this place, but they had the greatest number of people in it during each of the decades from 1840 to 1940.

John and Sophia Mills. John, born in Thoroughfare in 1861, was a son of the original Thomas Mills to settle in this place. Sophia was a Bugden from English Harbour. (Photo courtesy of Clyde Tuck)

1850s - Brown, Churchill, Eastman, Hiscock and Langer

According to Reverend Henry Petley, there were only "four or five" houses in Thoroughfare when he visited there in 1859 (Tocque,

James Brown, his wife Leah (nee Cooper), and their children. James was a son of Moses and Rachel (nee Mills), the original Brown family in Thoroughfare. Front row (left tpo right) Delilah, Leah (mother), Blanche in mother's arms, Leah, James (father) and William. Back Row (left to right) Clara, Edward, Mary and Hannah. (Photo courtesy of Lloyd and Myrtle King)

1878:136). This information suggests that some of the early people in Thoroughfare were transients. The present research suggests that during the 1850s five families joined the Mills in Thoroughfare, but not all of them became permanent settlers. Of the five family names of Brown, Churchill, Eastman, Hiscock and Langer, only Brown and Langer continued in the community until it was resettled in 1960.

Moses Brown. Moses, grandson of the original Moses Brown inThoroughfare, was, along with his wife, Theodosia, the last couple to leaveThoroughfare when it was resettled. (Photo courtesy of Lillian Williams)

The Brown family began in Thoroughfare when Moses Brown, who was born in Spaniard's Bay, Conception Bay, in 1826, married a Rachel Mills of Thoroughfare in 1859. In his early days, Moses Brown was a cook on foreign going vessels, but he came to Thoroughfare on a local schooner. Whether he met the Mills before coming to Thoroughfare, as some suggest, is not known.

After Rachel died, Moses left Thoroughfare to live in the United States for a number of years before returning. He died in 1927 in Thoroughfare at the age of 102. His son, James, settled in Thoroughfare. In fact, James' son, Moses Brown, was the last man to leave Thoroughfare when it was resettled in 1960. Moses Brown and his wife, Theodosia, stayed in Thoroughfare for a winter after the community had been abandoned. While all the people had resettled, Green's business was still in operation during that winter. It was run by a family from Ireland's Eye Island to supply the needs of the people on that island and at Deer Harbour.

One of the families that went to Thoroughfare in the 1850s was that of George and Mary Eastman. They had a son, Joseph, born there in 1852. They resided in Thoroughfare for only a short time, probably moving to Ireland's Eye where church records show a George and Mary Eastman residing in 1855. There was also a family of Churchills in Thoroughfare during the 1850s. Like the Eastmans, the Churchills stayed in Thoroughfare for only two or three years. George and Mary Churchill had a child born in Thoroughfare in 1852; another of their children was born in Silldown in 1856, and a third was born in Rider's Harbour in 1858. Moving from one place to another every two or three years was typical of many families on Random Island in those days. Church of England records also show that Henry and Maria Hiscock had a son named Henry, who was born in Thoroughfare in 1852. Like the Churchills and Eastmans, the Hiscocks stayed in Thoroughfare for only a short time. It is suspected that they moved to Rider's Harbour, where Church of England records for Trinity show a Henry and Maria Hiscock had a son born in 1854. It is also possible that they lived in Rider's Harbour before moving to Thoroughfare, because there were Hiscocks in Rider's Harbour as early as 1800.

William James Langer. A grandson of the original Langers in Thoroughfare, William was the last person buried in Thoroughfare before it was resettled in 1960. (Photo courtesy of James Langer)

There is evidence that Thomas and Mary Langer of Rider's Harbour moved to Thoroughfare around 1850. They had a son, William, born in Thoroughfare in 1853 (one record suggests 1851). However, shortly thereafter the Langers returned to Rider's Harbour, where they had another son named Joseph born in 1858. Furthermore, it seems as if the William Langer who was born in Thoroughfare in 1853 later married Emily Clark of

Cuckold's Cove (later renamed Dunfield), and they settled in Thoroughfare. Most, if not all, of the Langers in this community over the years were the descendants of William and Emily Langer.

Diinah Langer with one of the few horses in Thoroughfare. (Photo courtesy of James Langer)

1860s - Bailey, Baker, Hodder and Ivany

According to written documents, four families took up residency in Thoroughfare during the 1860s. Their surnames were Bailey, Baker, Hodder and Ivany. While none of these four families stayed in Thoroughfare for very long in those early days, Hodders and Ivanys returned to this community after 1900.

Baptismal records of the Church of England in Trinity show that James and Joanna Baker had two children born in Thoroughfare during the 1860s and two born there in the 1870s. As noted above, James and Joanna Baker lived in Rider's Harbour in 1862. Methodist Church records at Hant's Harbour show that Stephen and Rosanna Hodder had a child baptized at Thoroughfare in 1869. Since no other information has been found concerning this family, it is suspected that they were in Thoroughfare for only a short period, perhaps not residents of Thoroughfare at all. Maybe they were visitors to Thoroughfare or had planned to be there when the Methodist minister arrived. There were Hodders in Rider's Harbour as early as the 1770s. Since many of the early settlers to this part of Random Island tended to move from one place to another, it is very likely that Hodders visited Thoroughfare and may have lived there at various times during 19th century. Indications are that there were Ivanys living in Thoroughfare during the late 1860s. James and Mark Ivamy [sic] were listed as fishermen of this community in 1871 (Lovell, 1871). Some years later in 1887, church records show that a George Henry Ivany of Thoroughfare married a Rachel Mills of the same place.

Several of the families living in Thoroughfare during the 1850s and 1860s had moved away from this place before 1870. Lovell lists the following fishermen of Thoroughfare in 1871: William Baily (later, Bailey), James Baker, Moses Brown, James Ivamy [sic] and Mark Ivamy [sic]. Lovell's directory also includes two men with the name Thomas Mills, while both are identified as planters one is referred to as Perlican Thomas Mills. It is likely that most of these family names were in Thoroughfare prior to 1871. In fact, as seen above, many of them were in Thoroughfare for some thirty to forty years prior that time. A list of voters in Thoroughfare compiled during the early 1870s is not consistent with Lovell's 1871 directory. Those voters were: Abraham Bailey, William Bailey, James Baker, Moses Brown, John Ivany, Nathaniel Mills and Thomas Mills. This Thomas Mills is further identified as "English Tom", even though Perlican Tom is not included. The inclusion of William Bailey in Lovell's directory for 1871 and the appearance of Abraham Bailey's name on a voters list for about the same time are the only references found to any Baileys living in this community. There were Baileys at Rider's Harbour in the 1850s, and it is also known that Baileys settled in Deer Harbour in the 1880s.

1880s - Bungay, Gray, Leonard and Verge

Written records suggest that four families, namely, Bungay, Gray, Leonard and Verge, appeared in Thoroughfare for the first time during the 1880s. Arthur Edward Bungay of Thoroughfare and Harriett Elizabeth Hollett of Ireland's Eye were married in Thoroughfare in 1888. No other record of this couple has been found. Since Bungay was not a family name in the area at that time, it is suspected that the Arthur Bungay in question was either a visitor to the area, or a transient person who came, perhaps, as a sailor and stayed for only a short time. Another family in Thoroughfare during the 1880s, which also seems to have been a transient one, was that of George and Rachel Gray (also spelt "Grey"). Methodist Church records show that they had a daughter born in Thoroughfare in 1887 and a son born there in 1889. Unlike the surname of Bungay, that of Gray was found in Trinity Bay during the mid 19th century. For example, there was a William Gray in Trinity in 1854. It is possible that the Grays of Thoroughfare in the 1880s were descendants of those in Trinity earlier. A family of Leonards came to Thoroughfare during the 1880s. Daniel, son of Stephen and Mary Leonard, was born in Thoroughfare in 1884. At the age of 22 years, Thomas Leonard died at Thoroughfare in 1901. It is believed that the Leonards went to Thoroughfare from British Harbour.

There is some evidence to suggest that a family of Verges lived in Thoroughfare in the 1880s, but it did not become an established family in this settlement. In earlier times there were Verges in Ireland's Eye and Bonaventure. Perhaps the James Verge who lived in Thoroughfare during the 1880s was from one of those places and spent a short period of time in Thoroughfare. Methodist Church records show that Patience Verge was buried in Thoroughfare in 1925. She was 85 years old at the time of her passing. However, there was no Verge family living at Thoroughfare at that time. Patience was the wife of Joseph Verge of Rixman's Harbour, a harbour on the north side of Smith Sound. Joseph and Patience were the only people living in Rixman's Harbour for a number of years. The story is told that when Patience died, Joseph, who was then alone in the harbour, lit a large fire on the highest hill in Rixman's Harbour to get assistance from outside. Thoroughfare people saw the fire and, suspecting there was trouble, immediately went to Rixman's Harbour. At the request of Joseph, they brought his wife's remains to Thoroughfare for burial.

1890s - Maidment and Miller

During the 1890s, Maidment and Miller were the only two family names added to those already in Thoroughfare. The story is told that a sailing schooner from the south side of Trinity Bay, perhaps from Hant's Harbour, was shipwrecked on Thoroughfare rock in the fall of 1897. All the crew members made it to safety and were given accommodations, food and clothing by the people of Thoroughfare while awaiting transportation back to their homes. One of the crew members named Heber Maidment, of Hant's Harbour, got such a warm welcome he decided to spend the winter in Thoroughfare. Within a few months he married Jessie Elizabeth Miller of Thoroughfare and they started the Maidment family which resided in this community for a number of years. As seen in the baptismal records of the Methodist Church, there was a married couple named William and Mary Miller in Thoroughfare in 1900. One Elisha Miller was granted land there in 1919. Oral tradition has it that at least one family of Millers went to Thoroughfare from Ireland's Eye Island during the 1890s, but returned to that island after a few years in Thoroughfare. Other than the Maidments and Millers, Thoroughfare had no new family in the 1890s. In fact, by that time many of the early families such as Bakers, Churchills, Grays, Hiscocks and Hodders had gone from the community. McAlpine's Newfoundland directories for the 1890s include only four family names among the fishermen in Thoroughfare: Brown, Langer, Leonard and Mills. More specifically, the fishermen in Thoroughfare in the 1890s were James Brown, William Langer, Stephen Leonard, George Mills, John Mills, Nathaniel Mills (senior), Nathaniel Mills (junior), Thomas Mills (senior) and Thomas Mills (junior).

Written records are such that it is impossible to identify the place and date of birth of many of the adults in Thoroughfare prior to 1900. It is obvious that many of those early people were transients, staying for relatively short periods of time. Thoroughfare was settled by people from three areas in Newfoundland: the Trinity area, Old Perlican and Hant's Harbour and Mint's Cove (Spaniard's Bay) in Conception Bay. There is a question as to whether one branch of the Mills in Thoroughfare came directly from England to this place or whether all the Mills came to Thoroughfare via Old Perlican. In terms of numbers, Mills was the dominant family name in Thoroughfare prior to 1900 (Table 4-3). Together with the Browns and the Langers, the Mills formed the continuity in families in Thoroughfare from its beginning in the 1840s until its resettlement in 1960.

1900/60 - Cooper, King, Loder, Parrott, Toope and others

There were less than twenty fishermen in Thoroughfare at the turn of 20th century. McAlpine lists the following fishermen in this place in 1904: James Brown, Phillip Leonard, Thomas Leonard, William Langer, Heber Maidment, Elisha Miller, George Miller, William Miller, George Mills, John Mills, Nathaniel Mills of Thos. of England, Nathaniel Mills of Thos. of Perlican, Silas Mills, Thomas Mills and Walter Mills. This directory also refers to a person by his surname only, that of Willis. He was then the manager of the Newfoundland Slate Quarry Company in Smith Sound.

While the population of Thoroughfare ranged from 50 to 70 people between 1900 to 1960, there were substantial changes during this period in terms of people leaving the community and others moving into it. During this period several new family names including Cooper, King, Loder, Parrott, Toope and Watton appeared in Thoroughfare for the first. Also during this time, two family names, those of Hodder and Ivany, which were among earlier settlers but had since disappeared from list of permanent residents of Thoroughfare, became part of this community again. Methodist Church records suggest that Walter and Patience King lived in Thoroughfare during 1916. It is believed that they came to Thoroughfare from Bonaventure and stayed for only a few years. There are no Kings included in any of the directories or censuses for Thoroughfare. Burial records for Thoroughfare show that Janet Adams died at the age of 56 and was buried there in 1916. Since no other record of the family name of Adams has been found for Thoroughfare, it is concluded that there were no Adams as permanent settlers there. Perhaps Janet moved there to live with a relative or friend shortly before her passing.

TABLE 4-3

DATE AND PLACE OF BIRTH OF SOME OF THE ADULTS IN THOROUGHFARE PRIOR TO 1900

NAME	DATE OF BIRTH	PLACE OF BIRTH
Matthew Abbott		
William Abbott		
Abraham Bailey		
William Bailey		
James Baker Joanna Baker		
James Brown Leah Brown (nee Cooper)	1860 1863	Thoroughfare Ireland's Eye
James Brown Sarah Brown (nee Baker)	1830 (circa)	Spaniard's Bay Fox Harbour
John Brown Mary Brown		
Moses Brown Rachel Brown (nee Mills)	1826 1830s	Spaniard's Bay Old Perlican
Moses Brown Theodosia Brown (nee Toope)	1885 1887	Thoroughfare Ireland's Eye
Arthur Edward Bungay Harriett Elizabeth Bungay (nee Hollett)		 Ireland's Eye
George Churchill Mary Churchill		
George Eastman Mary Eastman		
George Gray Rachel Gray		
Henry Hiscock Maria Hiscock		

NAME	DATE OF BIRTH	PLACE OF BIRTH
Stephen Hodder		
Rosanna Hodder		
George Henry Ivany		Thoroughfare
Rachel Ivany (nee Mills)		Thoroughfare
James Ivany		English Harbour?
John Ivany		English Harbour?
Mark Ivany		English Harbour?
Thomas Langer	1820 (circa)	Trinity?
Mary Langer		
William Langer	1851 or 1853	Thoroughfare
Emily Langer (nee Clark)	1861	Cuckold's Cove
William James Langer	1886	Thoroughfare
Dinah Ann Langer (nee Adey)	1891	Lee Bight
Stephen Leonard		British Harbour
Mary Leonard		
Thomas Leonard	1879	
Heber Maidment	1875	Hant's Harbour
1st wife		
Jessie Elizabeth Maidment (nee Miller)	1873	
2nd wife		
Lydia Maidment (nee Pelley)		
Elisha Miller		
Blanche Miller		
George Miller		
William Miller		
Mary Miller		
Alfred Mills	1880	Thoroughfare
Caroline Mills	1880	Thoroughfare
George Mills	1856	Thoroughfare
George Mills	1871	Thoroughfare
Fanny Mills		
James Mills	1878	Thoroughfare
John Mills	1861	Thoroughfare
Sophia Mills (nee Bugden)	1868	English Harbour

NAME	DATE OF BIRTH	PLACE OF BIRTH
Nathaniel Mills	1846	Thoroughfare
Ann Mills (nee Loder)	1850	Ireland's Eye
Nathaniel Mills	1842	Old Perlican?
Elizabeth Mills	1846	
Phillip Mills	1888	Thoroughfare
Harriett Mills (nee Loder)	1886	Ireland's Eye
Rachel Mills	1819	
Silas William Mills	1875	Thoroughfare
Sarah Jane Mills (nee Bugden)	1875	English Harbour
Thomas Mills		
Milley Mills		
Thomas Mills	1815 (circa)	
Jane Mills	1814	
Thomas Mills	1853	Thoroughfare
Sarah Mills	1857	
Thomas Mills	1854	Thoroughfare
Jemima Mills (nee Vokey)	1864	Little Harbour
Walter Mills	1879	Thoroughfare
Ann Mills		
William Mills		Thoroughfare
Violet Mills (nee Mercer)		Bay Roberts
William Mills		Thoroughfare
Mary A. Mills (nee Ivany)		
John Piercey		
James Verge		

Source: This Table was developed from vital statistics from the Methodist Church at Britannia Cove and Hant's Harbour; from vital statistics from the Church of England at Trinity and Trinity East; 19th century lists of voters as recorded in *White's Papers* at Trinity; *Geographical Index to Land Grants 1830-1930*; nominal census for Thoroughfare in 1935 and 1945; *Lovell's Province of Newfoundland Directory for 1871*; *McAlpine's Newfoundland Directory 1894 to 1897*; *McAlpine's Newfoundland Directory for 1898*; tombstones at Thoroughfare; and interviews with Random Islanders.

The Loders were among the first new families to settle in Thoroughfare after 1900. This family is of the same lineage as the Loders who settled Snook's Harbour in the 1880s. Their roots are in Devonshire, England, where their ancestors are said to have been proprietors of the Boer Head Inn. Charles Dickens often visited this Inn and he refers to it in his novels. It is said that Silas Loder who was born in Devonshire in 1819 became a planter at Ireland's Eye during the 1840s. One of his sons,

A 1927 Verge's Island picnic including Langers, Loders and Mills of Thoroughfare. Front row (left to right) George Langer, Thelma Langer, Irene Langer, Delilah Langer, Marion Loder, Sybil Loder, Max Loder and Nathaniel Mills. Back row (left to right) Lizzie Ellen Loder (nee King of Deer Harbour) and Bertha Loder. (Photo courtesy of Marion Davis)

named John, moved to Snook's Harbour in the 1880s and started the Loder family there. James, another of his sons, settled in Ireland's Eye where he had a son named Silas. This Silas Loder married Lizzie King of Deer Harbour and they settled in Thoroughfare in 1914. Silas taught day school and was a lay reader in the Methodist Church at Thoroughfare until 1942.

Gilbert and Rachel Toope and their children moved from Ireland's Eye to Thoroughfare in 1918. Around 1930, another family from Ireland's Eye moved to Thoroughfare. It was Edward and Monica Cooper and their children. At about the same time, John George Ivany, his wife, Hilda Jane (nee Bailey of Deer Harbour), and their five children moved across Thoroughfare Tickle from Ivanhoe on the Ireland's Eye side of the tickle to the community of Thoroughfare on the Random Island side of it.

After managing the Monroe Export business at Thoroughfare for several years in the 1930s, Raymond Parrott of Winterton moved his family to Thoroughfare in 1943 where he continued to work in the Thoroughfare business which was later taken over by E.J. Green of Winterton. His family stayed in Thoroughfare until 1957. Also around 1940, a family of Wattons, namely, Arthur, his wife, Clara Maud, and their children, moved from Ireland's Eye to Thoroughfare. Later, Frank and Patience Hodder and their family of Ireland's Island settled in Thoroughfare and lived there for a few years before the community was abandoned. During 1950s, Calvin and Eileen Green of Winterton lived in Thoroughfare, where Calvin managed Green's general store and fish business.

Unlike Deer Harbour where, except for a few families who had left earlier, the entire community left as a group, Thoroughfare had a slower death. Although fewer in number than at Deer Harbour, they moved over a longer period of time. The last family to move was that of Moses and Theodosia Brown. They are reported to have spent some time there after all others had left. Also, unlike the resettling of Deer Harbour where most of its people moved to other communities on Random Island, the people who left Thoroughfare during and after the 1950s moved from Random Island altogether.

CHAPTER 5

PIONEERS OF PRESENT COMMUNITIES

MANY OF THE PIONEERS of the present communities on Random Island came from other places in Trinity Bay and settlements on the north shore of Conception Bay. Except for Random Heights and the new Robinson's Bight, both of which began in the late 1970s, all the present communities on Random Island have existed for at least 130 years, with most of them permanently settled for about 150 years. This chapter identifies the pioneering families in each of the present communities prior to 1900 and the previous place of residence of each family. Those who moved to each community between 1900 and 1945 are also noted.

Aspey Brook

As suggested by the names of Fagan's Pond and McGrath's Cove, there were visitors, perhaps winter people, in the Aspey Brook area before it was permanently settled. Perhaps, they were in this area as early as the 1850s. The present research revealed that the family names of permanent settlers in Aspey Brook and the decades when they took up residence in this area are as follows:

1870s - Smith
1880s - Phillips
1890s - George and Janes.

1870s - Smith

Aspey Brook was founded in the early 1870s by William and Lydia Smith (nee Hopkins) of Hant's Harbour. As noted in the presentation on the early settlers to Elliott's Cove later in this chapter, William Smith, the founder of Aspey Brook, was one of six brothers who went to Elliott's

Silas, a son of William and Lydia Smith, and his wife Caroline (nee Hiscick of Champneys), and their children, Vernon (left), Ralph (right) and Leah (back). (Photo courtesy of Leah and Colin Baker)

William Smith and his wife Lydia (nee Hopkins). They were the first permanent settlers of Aspey Brook and William operated a sawmill in this place for many years. (Photo courtesy of Ross Martin and Alice Smith)

Cove from Hant's Harbour during the early 1860s. William and Lydia moved to Aspey Brook during the 1870s. According to one source, they had thirteen children, including two sets of twins. Several of their children were born before their parents moved to Aspey Brook. Their children included five daughters (Agnes, Emma, Leah, Lucy and Mary Ann) and five sons (Barzillai, John, Luther, Silas and Stephen). The five sons settled in Aspey Brook, thereby giving rise to the dominance of Smiths in this place over the years.

Roland, son of Barzillai Smith and, and his wife Emily (nee Blundell of Hickman's Harbour), and their children Jane and Gladys. (Photo courtesy of Gladys Hefford)

Henry Phillips and his sister-in-law, Fanny Phillips (nee Patey) in Aspey Brook in the early 1950s. (Photo courtesy of Alice and Earl George)

1880s - Phillips

Methodist Church records of 1888 reveal that David Phillips, then of Aspey Brook but formerly of British Harbour, married one Elizabeth Green, then of Britannia Cove but formerly of Scilly Cove (later renamed Winterton), and they made their home in what was sometimes called Lower Aspey Brook. Two of their sons (Alfred and John) also settled in Aspey Brook.

1890s - George and Janes

Robert George of Smith Sound married a Martha Elizabeth Phillips of Aspey Brook in 1893, and they made their home in the Aspey Brook area for a short time thereafter. As described in the section on Middle Lance Cove later in this chapter, this is the same Robert George who, along with his first wife, Sarah (nee Thorne), resided in Middle Lance Cove during the 1880s. Also during the 1890s, one Ambrose Janes from

TABLE 5-1

DATE AND PLACE OF BIRTH OF SOME OF THE ADULTS IN ASPEY BROOK PRIOR TO 1900

NAME	DATE OF BIRTH	PLACE OF BIRTH
Robert George	1854	Hearts Content
Martha E. George (nee Phillips/Green)	1859	Scilly Cove
Ambrose Janes	1873	Broad Cove
Mary Ann Janes (nee Clarke)	1872	Kerley's Harbour
David J. Phillips		British Harbour
Elizabeth Phillips (nee Green)	1859	Scilly Cove
Agnes Smith		
Barzillai Smith	1855	Hant's Harbour
Esther Ann Smith (nee Critch)		Hant's Harbour
Emma Smith		
John Smith	1863	Hant's Harbour
Elizabeth Mary Smith (nee Fifield)	1864	English Harbour
Leah Smith		
Luther Smith (senior)	1875	Elliott's Cove
Marion Smith (nee Verge)	1891	Old Bonaventure
Mary Ann Smith		
Roland Smith	1886	Aspey Brook
Emily Smith (nee Blundell)	1896	Hickman's Harbour
Silas Smith	1872	Elliott's Cove
Caroline Smith (nee Hiscock)	1874	Champney's West
Stephen Smith	1871	Elliott's Cove
Sarah Smith (nee Blundell)	1877	Hickman's Harbour

NAME	DATE OF BIRTH	PLACE OF BIRTH
William Smith	1834	Hant's Harbour
Lydia Smith (nee Hopkins)	1841	Hant's Harbour

Source: This Table was developed from vital statistics from the Methodist Church at Britannia Cove, Foster's Point, Hant's Harbour, Random North and Shoal Harbour; vital statistics from the Church of England at Trinity; *McAlpine's Newfoundland Directory 1894 to 1897*; *McAlpine's Newfoundland Directory for 1898*; nominal censuses for Aspey Brook in 1935 and 1945; tombstones in Aspey Brook, Britannia Cove and Elliott's Cove; and interviews with Random Islanders.

Broad Cove, Conception Bay and his wife, Mary Ann (nee Clarke) from Kerley's Harbour resided in Aspey Brook. The family names of George and Janes were among the residents of Aspey Brook for relatively short periods. *McAlpine's Newfoundland Directory for 1898* lists the following fishermen of Aspen Brook: Robert George, Ambrose Janes, and six Smiths (Barzillai, John, Luther, Silas, Stephen, and William).

Table 5-1 shows date and place of birth of some of the adults in Aspey Brook prior to 1900. When known, husband and wife are included together and maiden names of wives in this community during that time are given. As shown in this table, the population of Aspey Brook during the 19th century consisted mainly of descendants of William and Lydia Smith. Later there were two primary families of Phillips, descendants of David and Elizabeth, in this settlement.

1900/45 - Bowring

As reported in the 1935 nominal census, all of the family names in Aspey Brook in 1935 were there before 1900. By 1945 there was one additional surname among the residents of this community. It was that of Bowring, with Watson Bowring of Britannia Cove and his wife, Rosa (nee Adey) of Foster's Point living there.

Britannia and Lower Lance Cove

In attempting to use written documents to identify the earlysettlers to specific places along the Britannia/Lower Lance Cove/Middle Lance Cove/ Petley shoreline of Random Island, one meets with considerable difficulty. There are several reasons for this problem including the similarity in place names and the changes in those names over the years. To elaborate, what is now considered as Britannia includes early place names of Ladle Cove and Porridge Cove. For many years the whole area from Lower Lance Cove to Middle Lance Cove was considered to be Britannia. What is presently named Lower Lance Cove includes places earlier referred to as Skimmer's Cove and British Cove, as well as Lower Lance Cove itself. As noted elsewhere in this book, Petley was first called Lance Cove but on occasions was referred to as Upper Lance Cove to distinguish it from Middle Lance Cove and Lower Lance Cove. On some of the early voters lists, as well as in different Newfoundland directories, Middle Lance Cove and Lower Lance Cove have been referred as Lance Cove. Another reason for the difficulty in using written documents to pinpoint exact places of residence of early settlers along this stretch of Random Island in Smith Sound is the fact that people from each of these places have often been recorded to be residing in Britannia Cove. The fact that the Methodist Church in Britannia Cove served Methodists in each of the adjacent settlements resulted in many of the people being identified as residences of Britannia Cove when, in fact, they lived in one or another of the neighbouring coves. For example, some of the early Laites in Lance Cove (Upper Lance Cove/Petley) are recorded in the Methodist Church as residents of Britannia Cove. Similarly, some of the Bugdens who were actually residing in the Lance Coves (Upper and Middle) are also recorded as residents of Britannia Cove.

A similar situation exists, but not to any great extent, when viewing the Church of England records for the area. Early records in Trinity show people as living in Lance Cove without distinguishing between the three Lance Coves. On occasions these records indicate that certain people were residing in Smith Sound without specifying whether they were on Random Island or the other side of the sound. In viewing the Church of England records for Petley, it is seen that a few of the people in Lower Lance Cove, and some who once lived in Middle Lance Cove, are recorded as residents of Petley (Lance Cove and Upper Lance Cove). Given the nature of these records, the place of abode of some of the earlier settlers to this area of Random Island as identified in this research may not be exact. For the present purposes, it was decided to look at Britannia Cove and Lower Lance Cove as one unit and to identify the early settlers to both of these areas simultaneously. While Middle Lance Cove is considered as a settlement unto itself, Petley and Aspen Cove are taken together and focused on later in this chapter.

As with other places on Random Island, the Britannia Cove/Lower Lance Cove area, including British Cove, Ladle Cove, Porridge Cove, Skimmer's Cove, Lance Cove and all points in between, were frequented by early visitors from Trinity who came to take advantage of the forest during the 18th century. Perhaps even earlier than this, people came to this area to hide from the English authorities who forbade permanent settlement in Newfoundland. The name of British Cove, a small cove to the west of Lower Lance Cove Head, may well indicate the presence of British visitors long before the place was permanently settled. Similarly, Cooper's Cove, a beach just to the East of Lower Lance Cove, may bear the name of visitors to the area for which no written records are available. From written documents it is seen that the Britannia Cove\Lower Lance Cove area was permanently settled in the 1850s. During the second half of the 19th century a relatively large number of people settled in this area to harvest the forest, to fish Smith Sound, to work in the slate quarries which were established at Nut Cove on the North side of the sound, and to develop the commercial infrastructure associated with these activities. The present research indicates that the chronological order of families settling this area is as follows:

1850s - Bowring, Currie and Hiscock
1860s - Harris, Hart, Ivany, Pittman and others

1870s - Coish, Duffett, Eastman, Piercey and others
1880s - Butt, Hoskins, Janes, Squires and others
1890s - Blundon, Pelley, Stone, Verge and others.

Moses Currie and his wife Sadie (nee Whelan of Western Bay). Moses, a son of Pierce and Lucy Currie, was well known as a cobbler. Sadie was renowned in the area for her dress-making . (Photo courtesy of Mac and Audrey Burt)

1850s - Bowring, Currie and Hiscock

Among the first permanent settlers to Britannia Cove were Bowrings and Curries. Written documents show that the Curries arrived during the 1850s, and it is widely believed that the Bowrings arrived at about the same time. The early Bowrings in Britannia Cove included George, Henry, Joseph Richard and William George. During the early part of the 19th century, there were Bowrings at Coley's Point, St. John's and Trinity. Perhaps, the Britannia Cove Bowrings are descendants of some of those earlier Bowrings in Newfoundland, although some believe they came to Britannia Cove from England. Church of England records at Trinity show that Henry Bowering of Dorset, England, married Susanna Cook in 1831, thereby suggesting that the Bowrings lived at the entrance to Smith Sound before moving to Britannia Cove. The Methodist records of Britannia Cove show Bowrings among its first adherents. There are "Bowerings" interred at the Congregational cemetery in Middle Lance Cove. It is suspected that those listed in the Methodists records as "Bowrings" and those in recorded as "Bowerings" on the tombstones in the Congregational cemetery are of the same family.

The first Currie to live in Smith Sound was John Currie, a Welshman and a professional slate cutter, who came to the area in the late 1840s or early 1850s to start a slate quarry at Nut Cove. John later moved to St. John's, and his cousins, David and Pierce, who had come to Britannia Cove in the late 1850s, took over the operation of the slate

Joseph R. and Louisa Bowring. They were among the pioneering Bowrings to Britannia Cove, where Bowrings operated a sawmill. (Photo courtesy of Raymond Ivany)

quarry. According to the obituaries in *The Methodist Monthly Greeting* for David Currie, who died in 1906, and his wife, who died in 1914, David came to Smith Sound in 1858. They were married in 1859 and settled in

Martin Bowring of Britannia Cove and his wife (nee Smith of Aspey Brook). (Photo courtesy of Rosa and Watson Bowring)

Britannia Cove about 1860. As shown in the records of the Methodist church at Hant's Harbour, David and Ann Maria Currie had a son baptized William Cathroe in Britannia Cove on August 3, 1867. The same records show that Pierce and Lucy Currie had a son named Moses baptized in Britannia Cove on October 4, 1868. The 1935 census for Britannia Cove records that Daniel Currie was born there in 1860, and a Charles Currie was born there in 1864.

According to oral tradition, one James Hiscock was among the earliest settlers to the Lower Lance Cove area. He is reported to have been living in a tilt near Lower Lance Cove Pond when the Curries came to Britannia Cove. Probably, he was a winter man who returned to his earlier place of residence, which was likely in the Trinity area, to fish during the summer.

1860s - Harris, Hart, Ivany, Pittman and others

Indications are that the Ivanys were among the first permanent settlers to what is now known as Lower Lance Cove. One Richard Ivany of English Harbour settled in Skimmer's Cove during the late 1850s or early 1860s. His sons included William, who is reported to have been born in Skimmer's Cove in 1860, and James and John, a twin, who were born in English Harbour in 1864. It is likely that during those early days the Ivany family lived in each of these places during different times of the year. Even after he settled in Britannia Cove, Richard is reported to have made frequent visits to English Harbour. In fact, he died while travelling from English Harbour to Britannia Cove. The story is that he died on the shoreline apparently after going astray while attempting to walk from Nut Cove to Burgoynes Cove, where he had planned to get a boat ride across the sound to his home in Skimmer's Cove. There were two, and some believe, unrelated families of Ivanys in Britannia Cove during the early days. In addition to Richard and his descendants from which the present Ivanys in Lower Lance Cove are descendants, there was a George Ivany there in the 1860s. It is believed that George Ivany came to Skimmer's Cove from Ireland's Eye Island and that he returned to the Old Tilts (later renamed Ivanhoe) on that island.

Joseph Pittman of Somersetshire, England, and his wife, Grace, settled in Skimmer's Cove during the 1860s. Church records in Hant's Harbour show that Joseph and Grace Pittman had a son John baptized in Skimmer's Cove in 1868, and another son named James baptized there the following year. According to their family Bible, Joseph and Grace Pittman had thirteen children. Unlike other early settlers who established traditions of fishing and lumbering in this area, the early Pittmans in Britannia Cove were often classified as farmers.

James Ivany and his sister Mary. Their parents, Richard and Martha Ivany, were the first Ivanys to settle in Skimmer's Cove. (Photos courtesy of George Ivany)

Thomas and Sarah Harris were living in Britannia Cove in the 1860s, for in 1869 they had a son, Charles, baptized there by the Methodist Minister who was visiting from Hant's Harbour. Another church record shows that Thomas and Sarah Harris had a daughter baptized in Upper Lance Cove in 1869. Whether they are the same couple, or whatever the connection between these two couples, it is known that one Samuel Harris of New Chelsea settled in British Cove, a cove to the west of Lower Lance Cove Head, during the 1860s. Mark and Dinah Hart also settled at British Cove. Mark was born at Robin Hood (later renamed Port Rexton) in 1840 while Dinah was

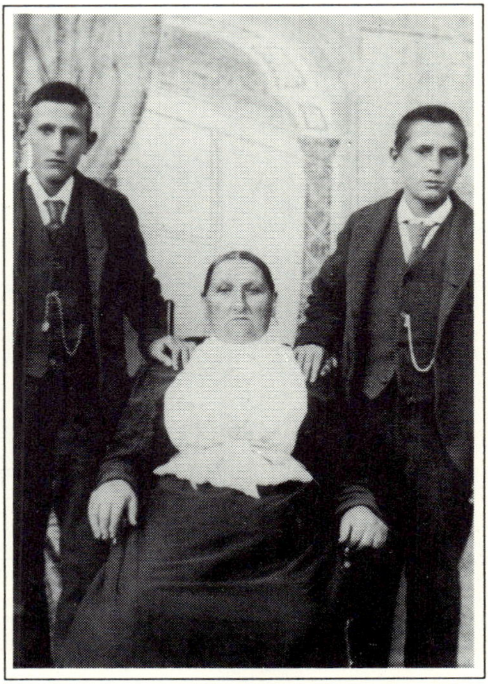

Grace Pittman. Grace and her husband Joseph started the Pittman family in Britannia. Aaron (left) and John were two of their sons. (Photo courtesy of George and Hazel Pittman)

born at Salmon Cove (later renamed Champneys) in 1838.

One John Pope had land granted in Skimmer's Cove in 1868. Also in that year, he and his wife, Martha, had daughter baptized in Britannia Cove. Records show that a Thomas W. Spry received a grant for land in Lower Lance Cove in 1868, but we have no specific record of him having taken up residency in this area.

1870s - Coish, Duffett, Eastman, Piercey and others

The Coishs (sometimes spelt "Cosh") and the Duffetts (sometimes spelt "Duffitt") came to the Britannia Cove/Lower Lance Cove area at about the same time in the 1870s. James Coish and James Duffett, both of Bay De Verde, married sisters, Julia Ann and Priscilla Pennell, respectively, of Ochre Pit Cove. They made several visits to the area to take advantage of the forest, staying over a winter or two and returning to Bay de Verde during the summer months, before James Coish felt he had enough of the moving back and forth and decided to stay on Random Island. Hence, James and Julia Ann Coish founded the Coish family in Britannia Cove.

James Coish and wife Julia Ann (nee Pennell), founders of the Coish family in Britannia Cove, are shown here with members of the Coish and Verge families around 1902. Back row (left to right) Myra Coish who later married a Bailey in Old Bonaventure, Elfredia Coish who later married Ephraim George of Britannia Cove and Lydia Coish (nee Verge). Middle row (left to right) Nance Coish who moved to the United States, James and Julia Ann Coish, and Marion Verge who later married Luther Smith (senior) of Aspey Brook. Front row (left to right) Blanche Coish who later married a Stone from Monroe, and Clara Coish who later married John Blundell of Hickman's Harbour. (Photo courtesy of Earl and Alice George)

James, the youngest son of Robert Coish, was born in Bay de Verde in 1846. Joseph, an older son of Robert, stayed in Bay de Verde where he was twice married and had at least six sons. Julia Ann was born in Orche Pit Cove in 1846. The children of James and Julia Ann included a son, Robert, born in Britannia Cove in 1876 and another son, William, born in 1885. Both Robert and William became well known boat builders in the Random Sound area. It looks as if James' mother accompanied him to Britannia Cove in that one Ann Coish passed away in Britannia Cove in 1884 at the age of 84 years. In addition to James and Julia Ann Coish, church records suggest that a John and Mary Anne Coish lived in Smith Sound during the 1870s. Specifically, the Church of England records at Bay de Verde show that they had a daughter, Mary Anne Emberly, baptized at Random in 1876. The reference to Random in those days included a large area, but is possible that John and Mary Coish were on the Random Island side of Smith Sound at that time.

James Duffett, a fisherman/lumberman in Britannia. (Photo courtesy of Ralph Duffett)

Oral tradition has it that a Thomas Duffett left England and settled in Bay de Verde during the 18th century. The story continues that he had three sons, George, James and John. One of those sons, James, married Priscilla Pennell of Orche Pit Cove and they settled in Britannia Cove, starting the Duffett family in this community. James and Priscilla Duffett had four sons, Herbert, James, John and William, all of whom settled in Britannia Cove. Their daughters included Mary Ann, Lizze (Elizabeth), Emily Sarah, Emma Jane and Myria. Because Elizabeth was born in Bay de Verde in 1864, and Herbert was born in Britannia Cove in 1875, it is suggested that this family of Duffetts settled on Random Island some time during the late 1860s or early 1870s. While James and Priscilla are considered to be the founders of the Duffett clan in Lower Lance Cove, Church of England records in Bay de Verde show a son named William was born to James and Martha Duffett at Random Sound in

John T. Duffett (Photo courtesy of Ralph Duffett)

Elizabeth Ivany (nee Duffett) (Photo courtesy of Robert Verge)

Jessie Duffett, daughter of Norman and Hannah March of Lady Cove, Married John T. Duffett of Britannia Cove. (Photo courtesy of Ralph Duffett)

1876. Perhaps James and Martha Duffett settled on the mainland side of Smith Sound rather than on Random Island.

A list of voters for the Britannia Cove area in the earlier 1870s has David Currie and Pierce Currie residing at Britannia Cove, John Currie at Lower Lance Cove, George Bowring and Robert Eastman at Ladle Cove, and John Ivany, Roland Ivany, Joseph Pittman and John Pope at Skimmer's Cove. While it is questionable whether this is a complete list of voters in the Britannia Cove/Lower Lance Cove during the 1870s, it is interesting to note the distinctions concerning the places of abode at that time.

In addition to the family names already included in this presentation on people in Britannia Cove up to and including the 1870s, the following were given as residents of Britannia Cove in Methodist Church Minutes for 1877: Mr. and Mrs. Jacob Duling, Moses LeDrew, William Palmer, James Piercey and Sarah Piercey.

1880s - Butt, Hoskins, Janes, Squires and others

Butts were among the early settlers to Britannia Cove as well as to Hickman's Harbour. While the present research did not uncover any direct link between the Butts who settled in Hickman's Harbour and those who took up residence in Britannia Cove, it is possible that they had an earlier relationship. As noted later in this chapter, the Hickman's Harbour Butts came from Blackhead and the Britannia Cove Butts from

Adam's Cove, a neighbouring settlement to Blackhead. Both families came to Random Island about the same time in the late 1870s. During that time there were three husband and wife teams of Butts residing in Britannia Cove: specifically, George and Selina Butt, John Thomas and Amelia Butt, and William and Margaret Butt.

It is known that there was at least one family of Greens in Lower Lance Cove during the 1880s. Church records show that a Thomas Green of Britannia Cove married a Mary Ann Duffett of that community in 1884. Elizabeth Green, who married David Phillips of Aspey Brook during that time, is reported to have been from Britannia Cove, but formerly of Scilly Cove (later renamed Winterton), hence the suggestion that the Greens came to Britannia Cove from Scilly Cove.

According to Seary (1976:241), there were Hoskins at Trinity and Old Perlican in the 18th century. Later there were Hoskins residing at Grates Cove. Church records show that two Hoskins, Robert and William, settled in Britannia Cove, probably during the early 1880s. William and Susannah Hoskins had a daughter baptized in Britannia in 1884.

William Hoskins and his wife Susannah (nee Janes), started the Hoskins family in Britannia Cove in the 1880s. (Photo courtesy of Gwen Hoskins)

Some believe that Robert and William Hoskins came from England to work at the slate quarries in Smith Sound. It has also been suggested that they were descendants of the earlier Hoskins at Old Perlican.

Henry Janes. Born in Broad Cove on 1867, Henry married Mary Drodge of Heart's Ease, and they started the Janes family in Britannia Cove. Their son Joseph, became known as one of the best sailing skippers in Smith Sound. (Photo courtesy of Robert and Linda Janes)

The family name of Janes appeared in Britannia Cove during the 1880s. Alfred and Sarah Janes had a child baptized Mary Isabella in Britannia Cove in 1883, and another child baptized Alfred George there in 1885. The present Janes in Britannia Cove are descendants of Henry Janes, who was born in Broad Cove, Conception Bay in 1867, and his wife, Mary Janes (nee Drodge), who was born in Heart's Ease in the same year. The Janes family of Lower Lance Cove were descendants of John Janes, who was born at Blackhead in 1869. John was a brother of Ambrose Janes, who settled in Aspen Cove. The exact relationship between the Janes family of Aspen Cove/Lower Lance Cove and the Janes family in Britannia has not been established in the present research, but it looks as if the father of one of the families accompanied his son(s) to the Britannia Cove area because one George Janes died in Britannia Cove in 1918 at the age of 70 years.

The family name of Squires was added to those already in Britannia Cove during the early 1880s. One Walter Squires received a grant for land at Brtiannia Cove in 1882. Church records show that John and Leah Squires had six children baptized there in the 1880s, while William and Mary Ann Squires had a child baptized in this community in 1893.

Records show that Richard Williams, a quarry manager, resided in Britannia Cove during the 1880s. Methodist Church records show that a Walter and Ellen Williams had a son baptized in the Methodist church in Britannia Cove in 1901. The family name of Moores is first seen church records of this community during the 1880s. One Elizabeth Bursey died in Britannia Cove in 1884 at the age of 69. No other records have been found of the Bursey or Moores families having lived in this community at that time. Written records show that Edwin McGregor lived in Britannia Cove in the 1880s.

1890s - Blundon, Pelley, Stone, Verge and others

McAlpine reported that the following were fishermen in Britannia Cove in 1898: William Butt, John Bowring, Joseph Bowring, Duncan

Blundon, Henry Blundon, Daniel Currie, Robert Currie, James Coish, Robert Coish, G. Herbert Duffett, James Duffett, William Duffett, James Ivany, John Ivany, William Ivany, George Ivany, John Janes, Robert Piercey, Joseph Pittman and John Squires. McAlpine's 1898 directory also lists four fishermen in Lower Lance Cove: Thomas Green, Samuel Harris, Martin Stone and Hubert Verge. Three quarrymen, specifically, Charles Currie, David Currie and Pierce Currie, were among the residents of Britannia Cove in 1898, and there were two general dealers, namely, John Currie and William Currie, there at that time. George Pittman was also residing in Britannia Cove during the 1890s and was a long time mail courier for the area. It should be noted that other written documents show that McAlpine's directories do not give complete listings of men in this area at the time. They omit the surnames of Bellman, Carberry, Lewis and Pelleys, all of which were also among the residents of Britannia Cove during the 1890s.

Martin and Hannah Stone. They were the first Stones to settle permanently in Lower Lance Cove. Martin was a fisherman and he also built schooners. (Photo courtesy of Georgina Howell)

Levi Bellman and his wife, Elizabeth (nee Bailey) joined the Britannia Cove inhabitants during the 1890s. As discussed in the section on Snook's Harbour later in this chapter, the surname "Bellman" probably derived from "Belbin". Henry Blundon of Bay de Verde, his wife, Eliza, and their sons Duncan, Frederick, Harvey and William were living in Ladle Cove during the 1890s. The exact time of their settling in the Britannia Cove is not known, but it is reported that they that lived in the area for only a relatively short period before returning to Bay de Verde. Church records suggest that a family of Carberrys lived in Britannia Cove during the 1890s. There is some evidence to suggest that an Edward Lewis of Wales, who married a Jemima Thorne, then of Lady Cove but earlier of Middle Lance Cove, lived in Britannia Cove during the 1890s. Norman Pelley of Robinson's Bight married Ann Ellen Currie of Britannia Cove in 1890 and settled in Britannia Cove at that time. This family later resided in Pope's Harbour before returning to Britannia Cove. There was also a family of Moores and one of Sopers living in Britannia Cove during the 1890s. Both of these families moved from this community during the early 1900s.

Stones were among the earliest settlers to Trinity Bay, but it was not until the 1890s, after living in different parts of Smith Sound, that they settled on Random Island. Martin Stone of White Rock, and his wife, Hannah (nee Hart/Long) of Salmon Cove settled in Lower Lance Cove during the 1890s. Martin was born in Bonaventure in 1854, his grandfather, Thomas Stone, a son of Henry and Mary Stone who had settled in Trinity during the 18th century, was born in Trinity in 1799. Martin and Hannah Stone had ten children, several of whom were born at White Rock before they took up residence at Lower Lance Cove.

John Verge. John's parents, Isaac and Elizabeth Verge, were the first Verges in Lower Lance Cove. (Photo courtesy of Delilah and William Walters)

The original Verges in Lower Lance Cove were Isaac and his nephew Hubert from Old Bonaventure. Isaac moved to this cove in the 1890s, at about the same time as his brother, Joseph, settled in Rexman's Harbour, a harbour on the mainland side and at the mouth of Smith Sound, at about the same time. Joseph's son, Hubert, married Mary Ann Hart, daughter of Mark and Dinah Hart referred to above, and they moved in with the Harts at British Cove during the 1890s.

In addition to listing adults in the Britannia Cove/Lower Lance Cove area prior to 1900, Table 5-2 includes date and place of birth of some of those adults as well as the maiden names of wives. This table shows that while many of the early settlers to this area came from the Trinity/Old Bonaventure areas, a considerable number came from communities on the north side of Conception Bay and a few families came from Wales to live on this part of Random Island.

TABLE 5-2

DATE AND PLACE OF BIRTH OF SOME OF THE ADULTS IN BRITANNIA/LOWER LANCE COVE PRIOR TO 1900

NAME	DATE OF BIRTH	PLACE OF BIRTH
Levi Bellman		Inglewood Forest
Rebecca Bellman (nee Bailey)		Britannia Cove
Duncan Blundon	1874	Bay de Verde
Edward Blundon	1872	Bay de Verde
Frederick Blundon	1882	Bay de Verde
Harvey Blundon	1878	Bay de Verde
Henry Blundon	1829	Bay de Verde
2nd Wife		
Eliza Augustus Blundon (nee Pack)	1840	Carbonear?
Mary Helen Blundon	1877	Bay de Verde
William Blundon	1880	Bay de Verde
Lewis Bowering	1874	
William George Bowering	1871	
Edward Bowring		
Ellen Bowring	1869	Britannia Cove
George Bowring	1822	
Henry Bowring	1846	
Ist Wife		
Emily Bowring	1853	
2nd Wife		
Martha Bowring (nee Tait/Wells)	1853	
John Bowring		
1st wife		
Tryphenia Bowring (nee Laite)		
2nd wife		
Louisa Bowring		

NAME	DATE OF BIRTH	PLACE OF BIRTH
Joseph Richard Bowring	1852	
Leah Lousia Bowring	1853	
Martin Bowring		Britannia Cove
Lydia Bowring (nee Smith)		Aspey Brook
Susannah Bowring	1848	
J.C. Wesley Bowring	1876	Britannia Cove
Helen Bowring (nee Bailey)	1878	Upper Lance Cove
Wm. George Bowring	1857	
William George Bowring		
Mary Elizabeth Bowring (nee Peckham)		Salmon Cove
William H. Browning	1857	Tavistock, Devonshire, England
Ellie Grace Browning (nee Currie)		Britannia Cove
Elizabeth Bursey	1815	
George Butt		Adam's Cove
Selina Butt		
John Thomas Butt		Adam's Cove
Amelia Butt		
William Butt	1847	Adam's Cove
Margaret Butt (nee Janes)	1854	Broad Cove
Ann Coish	1800	Bay de Verde?
Emily Jane Coish	1860	Bay de Verde
James Coish	1846	Bay de Verde
Julia Ann Coish (nee Pennell)	1846	Ochre Pit Cove
John Coish		Bay de Verde
Mary Ann Coish		
Robert Coish	1876	Britannia Cove
Lydia Coish (nee Verge)	1880	Bonaventure
Myria Coish		
William James Coish	1885	Britannia Cove
Louisa Coish (nee George)	1887	Middle Lance Cove

NAME	DATE OF BIRTH	PLACE OF BIRTH
Nathaniel Critch		
Charles Currie	1864	Britannia Cove
Sarah Currie (nee Leonard)	1870	British Harbour
Daniel Currie	1860	Britannia Cove
Tryphenia Currie	1861	Harbour Grace
David Currie	1834	Llanberias, Carnarvanshire, Wales
Anna Myria Currie (nee Pottle)	1834	Scilly Cove
David Currie		Britannia Cove?
Bertha Currie (nee Gardner)		Delby's Cove
Fenwick Currie	1884	Britannia Cove
Isabel Currie (nee Bugden)	1884	Lance Cove
John Currie		Wales
John T. Currie	1861	Britannia Cove
Alice Currie (nee Laite)		Upper Lance Cove
Moses Currie	1868	Britannia Cove
Sadie Currie (nee Whalen)	1876	Western Bay
Pierce Currie	1831	Llanberias, Carnarvanshire, Wales
Lucy Currie (nee Pelley)	1842	Hant's Harbour
Robert Currie		Britannia Cove?
Bessie Currie (nee English?)		
Thomas Currie	1881	Britannia Cove
1st wife		
Emmaline Currie (nee Whelan)	1887	Western Bay
2nd wife		
Lydia Currie (nee Pelley/Maidment)		

NAME	DATE OF BIRTH	PLACE OF BIRTH
Thomas Charles Currie	1872	Britannia Cove
William Currie	1868	Britannia Cove
Mary Currie (nee Burry)		Glovertown?
Emily Sarah Duffett	1878	-
Emma Jane Duffett	1884	Britannia Cove
Herbert Duffett	1875	Britannia Cove
Cicely Duffett (nee Vardy)	1885	Hickman's Harbour
James Duffett		
Martha Jane Duffett		
James Duffett	1842	Bay de Verde
Priscilla Duffett (nee Pennell)	1841	Ochre Pit Cove
James Allan Duffett	1880	Britannia Cove
Anne Maud Duffett (nee Mills)	1883	Thoroughfare
John T. Duffett	1887	Britannia Cove
Jessie Duffett (nee March)	1879	Lady Cove
Myria Duffett		
William Henry Duffett		Bay De Verde
Ist Wife		
Sarah Duffett (nee Pond)	1875	Foster's Point
2nd Wife		
Rachel Duffett (nee Miller/Harnum)		Foster's Point
Jacob Duling		
Theophilus Gardner		
Mary Ann Gardner	1853	
Ephraim George	1881	Middle Lance Cove
Elfredia George (nee Coish)	1882	Britannia Cove
Thomas George	1885	Middle Lance Cove
Annie George (nee Wheaton)	1886	Bradley's Cove

NAME	DATE OF BIRTH	PLACE OF BIRTH
Thomas Green	1859	Scilly Cove
Mary Ann Green (nee Duffett)	1865	Bay De Verde
Samuel Harris	1840	Seal Cove
Thomas Harris		
Sarah Harris (nee Laite)		Upper Lance Cove?
Mark Hart	1840	Robin Hood
Dinah Hart	1838	Salmon Cove
James Hiscock		
Anna Hoskins	1855	
Robert Hoskins	1855	
William Hoskins		Plymouth, England?
Susannah Hoskins (nee Janes)		Broad Cove, C. Bay
George Ivany	He was an adult in l855.	
James Ivany	1864	English Harbour
Elizabeth Ivany (nee Duffett)	1864	Bay de Verde
John Ivany	1864	English Harbour
Caroline Ivany (nee Hiscock)	1861	Scilly Cove
John Ivany	He was an adult in 1868.	
Martha Amelia Ivany	1871	
Mary Jane Ivany	1865	Skimmer's Cove
Newman Ivany		
Emma Ivany	1850s	
Richard Ivany	1824	English Harbour
Martha Ivany	1822	
Walter J. Ivany	1885	Britannia Cove
Sarah Ivany (nee Bowring)	1890	Britannia Cove
William Ivany	1860	Skimmer's Cove
lst Wife		
Lucy Ivany (nee Blundell)	1865	Hickman's Harbour

NAME	DATE OF BIRTH	PLACE OF BIRTH
2nd Wife		
Emily Ivany		Britannia Cove
(nee Bowring)		
Alfred Janes		Broad Cove, C. Bay?
Sarah Janes		
Bertha Janes	1882	
George Janes	1832	
Henry George Janes	1865	Broad Cove, C.Bay
Mary Janes	1867	Heart's Ease
(nee Drodge)		
John Charles Janes	1870	Blackhead
1st Wife		
Fanny Jane Janes	1876?	New Chelsea
(nee Harris)		
2d Wife		
Jane Janes		
(nee Verge)		
Martha Janes	1834	
Moses LeDrew		
Edward Lewis	1871	Wales
Jemima Lewis	1880	Middle Lance Cove
(nee Thorne)		
Edwin McGregor	1836	
William Moores		
Patience Moores		
William Palmer		
Norman Pelley		Robinson's Bight
Anne Ellen Pelley		Britannia Cove
(nee Currie)		
Amos Piercey		
James Piercey		
Robert Piercey		
Harriett Piercey		
Sarah Piercey		
Elizabeth Pittman	1876	Britannia Cove
George Pittman	1864	
George Pittman	1876	Britannia Cove

NAME	DATE OF BIRTH	PLACE OF BIRTH
James Pittman	1869	Britannia Cove
John Pittman	1868	Britannia Cove
Joseph Pittman Grace Pittman	1828 1842	Somersetshire, England
Lucy Pittman	1862	
Mary Ann Pittman	1870	Britannia Cove
Sarah Pittman	1860s	
John Pope Martha Pope		
William Soper Catherine Soper (nee Jones)		St. John's United States
Thomas W. Spry		
John Squires Leah Squires		
Walter Squires		
William Squires Mary Ann Squires	 1862	
Caroline Stone	1880	White Rock
Martin Stone Hannah Stone (nee Hart/Long)	1854 1856	Old Bonaventure Salmon Cove
Obed Stone Lillian Kate Stone	1880	White Rock
Walter Stone Elizabeth Stone (nee Pitcher)	1883	White Rock Bonaventure
William George Stone Susannah Stone (nee Bailey)	1882 1886	White Rock Cat Cove
John Thomas Sarah Thomas		
Hubert Verge *1st Wife* Mary Hannah Verge (nee Hart) *2nd Wife* Priscilla Verge	1873 1875 1883	Old Bonaventure Britannia Cove Upper Lance Cove

NAME	DATE OF BIRTH	PLACE OF BIRTH
(nee Laite)		
3rd Wife		
Jane Verge		
(nee Hyde)		
Isaac Verge		Old Bonaventure
Elizabeth (Bessie) Verge		
John Verge		
Leander Verge	1882	Old Bonaventure
Amy Ann Verge		Hodder's Cove
(nee Ivany)		
Richard Williams		Wales
Walter Williams		
Ellen Williams		

Source: This Table was developed from vital statistics from the Methodist Church at Blackhead, Britannia Cove, Carbonear, Hant's Harbour, Heart's Content, Lower Island Cove and Old Perlican; vital statistics from the Church of England at Bay de Verde, Heart's Delight, Trinity, Trinity East and Random Mission; 19th century lists of voters as recorded in *White's Papers* at Trinity; *Lovell's Province of Newfoundland Directory for 1871*; *McAlpine's Newfoundland Directory for 1894 to 1897*; *McAlpine's Newfoundland Directory for 1898*;*Geographical Index to Land Grants 1830 to 1930*; Minutes of the Methodist Church of Canada for 1877; nominal censuses for Britannia Cove and Lower Lance Cove for 1935 and 1945; tombstones on Random Island; and interviews with Islanders.

1900/45 - Edwards, George, Leawood, Thomas and others

Around 1900 and during the first two decades of the 20th century several families moved to the Britannia/Lower Lance Cove area. They included the George family which was started in Lower Lance Cove by two sons of Robert and Sarah George of Middle Lance Cove. One of their sons, Ephraim, married Elfredia Coish of Lower Lance Cove, and their other son, Thomas, married Annie Wheaton of Bradley's Cove. Some of the families in Brtiannia/Lower Lance Cove at that time were there because of the work provided by the slate quarry at Nut Cove. One of those was John and Sarah Thomas, who, according to Church records, resided in Britannia Cove in 1901. However, other records suggest that they also resided at the slate quarry in Nut Cove at that time. Apparently, there was a family of Bolls started in Britannia Cove in 1900 when Herade

Ephraim (left) and Thomas George. They were sons of Robert and Sarah (nee Thorne) George of Middle Lance Cove, and they established the George name in Britannia after 1900. (Photos courtesy of Earl and Alice George, and Maxwell and Sadie Ivany)

Bolls married a Mary J. Bugden, but they lived in this cove for only a few years. Church records also show Edward and Sarah Edwards residing in Britannia Cove in 1901. As described in an obituary to John Leawood in *The Monthly Greeting* of 1927, John Leawood moved to Britannia in 1902 to work as a "sub collector" with the slate quarry office in the cove. Shortly thereafter, George Leawood joined his brother in Britannia. As noted in the Bound's Mead and Weybridge sections of this book, the Leawoods came from Hant's Harbour to Bound's Mead and later to Foster's Point.

In 1930, an extended Mills family moved from Thoroughfare to Lower Lance Cove. It included Silas Mills, his wife Sarah Jane (nee

Bugden) and the families of their sons, Alphaeus and Nathaniel. Descendants of Silas and Sarah Mills are among the present population of Lower Lance Cove. The 1945 census also shows one Elias Whelan, originally from Western Bay, residing in Britannia Cove, but this family name never became established in the cove.

Vital statistics as recorded by the Methodist Church suggest the following families resided in the Britannia/Lower Lance Cove area during the early part of this century: Robert and Harriett Piercey (1903), Elihu and Laura Hiscock (1905), Selby and Bertha Noseworthy (1906), Andrew and Virtue Goldsworthy (1915), Chesley and Louise Thompson (1920), and Pierce and Annie Wells (1920).

Elliott's Cove

The first visitors to the Elliott's Cove area were attracted to it because of the lush forest extending back from the coastline over a level terrain. There were also several brooks in the area, and, although the brooks were small, the earlier settlers who planned to utilize the forest were attracted to them. The early visitors to this area included Elliotts, Evans, Chipmans, Cramms and Morrisseys, who were in the area during the 1840s and 1850s. They had winter tilts at different places along the shoreline which extends from the area east of the cove itself to Brown's Mead on the western end of Random Island. A study of the first permanent settlers at Elliott's Cove reveals that one family name, that of Smith, dominated this cove through most of its history. In fact, Smiths had established the community of Elliott's Cove before any other permanent settlers arrived. The dates of arrival of the Smiths and pioneering families to Elliott's Cove were as follows:

1860s - Smith
1880s - Cooper, Hodder, Martin, Pelley and Smith
1890s - Craven, Gallagher, Garland, Goobie and Hiscock.

1860s - Smith

Smiths were widespread in early Newfoundland settlements. While many of them were of English descent, some were Scottish. Those who came to Elliott's Cove were English, and they had earlier settled at Hant's Harbour. One report suggests that Thomas and Deborah Smith of Hant's Harbour were the first of the Smiths to settle in Elliott's Cove, arriving there in the 1860s (*The Monthly Greeting*, 1928:6). Thomas and Deborah were soon followed by Thomas' brothers, sisters and parents. Church records and interview data suggest that six Smith brothers, whose names were Aaron, Charles, Gideon, Moses, Thomas and William, along with their sisters, Jane, Mary and Elizabeth, and their parents, Thomas and Martha Smith, from Hant's Harbour, settled in

Elliott's Cove during the 1860s. Thomas Smith (senior) was born in Scilly Cove (later renamed Winterton) around 1800 and was planter in that community for many years before accompanying his children to Elliott's Cove. One report is that both his father and his grandfather were named William and their surname was Smith-Bramleigh (Broomley?). His grandmother is believed to have been Spainish. The surname Smith-Bramleigh got shortened to Smith when the family arrived in Newfoundland in the late 18th century. Thomas Smith (senior) married Martha Tilley of Hant's Harbour on December 4, 1828. Written documents suggest that most, if not all, of their children were adults and that several of them were married with families before they settled in Elliott's Cove. Records of the Methodist Church at Hant's

Aaron Smith and his wife Jane Ann (nee Reid). Aaron, one of six brothers who were pioneers at Elliott's Cove in the 1860s, started the once flourishing brickyard at Snook's Harbour. (Photo courtesy of Hazel Brown)

Allan Smith and his wife Louisa. Allan, like his father, Thomas, operated a ferry service in the Northwest Arm for many years. (Photo courtesy of Boyce and Lavenia Smith)

Attwood Smith and his wife Alice (nee Cooper). (Photo courtesy of Alice and Shirley Smith)

Norman Smith. Along with his brother, Attwood, Norman operated the brickyard in Wake's Brook for many years. (Photo courtesy of Hazel Brown)

Harbour show two married couples, namely, Thomas and Deborah Smith and William and Lydia Smith, each couple having a child baptized in the Northwest Arm of Random on October 13, 1869. It is likely that these two couples were in Elliott's Cove at the time. While five of the six Smith brothers and their wives who settled in Elliott's Cove stayed there and created the Smith clan in this community, one of the brothers, William, and his wife, Lydia, moved across Random Island to become the founding family of Aspey Brook. Jane Ann Smith, that is, one of the Smith sisters who went to Elliott's Cove with her six brothers and her parents in the 1860s, later married a John Loder of Ireland's Eye and they settled in Snook's Harbour.

1880s - Cooper, Hodder, Martin, Pelley and Smith

For a period of about fifteen years from the late 1860s to the 1880s, offspring of Thomas and Martha Smith were the only permanent settlers in Elliott's Cove. Sometime in the 1880s Henry J. Smith of Bishop's Cove settled at Elliott's Cove. He married Mary Jane, daughter of Moses Smith of Elliott's Cove. William Cooper of Ireland's Eye married Emily Smith of Elliott's Cove and lived in this cove for a short time in the 1880s before moving to Snook's Harbour. Sometime after the mid 1880s a John Hodder of Thoroughfare married a Lillian Smith of Elliott's Cove and they started the Hodder family in this community. One of their children, perhaps their first child, a daughter named Lucy, was born in Elliott's Cove in 1889.

Henry Smith and his wife Mary (nee Smith). Henry took up residence in Elliott's Cove during the 1880s. He married into the Smith family which had started this community earlier. (Photo courtesy of Murley and Madge Berkshire)

Sydney Pelley, John Martin and Thomas Smith got grants for land at Cramm's Brook in the 1880s. Other than those land records, no reference has been found to Pelleys or Martins living at Cramm's Brook or at Elliott's Cove, where those at Cramm's Brook were usually considered to be residing.

1890s - Craven, Gallagher, Garland, Goobie and Hiscock

Five family names were added to the list of people in the Elliott's Cove/Cramm's Brook area during the 1890s. One was that of James Craven, who arrived in Elliott's Cove around 1890 from London, England, to manage the Brickyard which was operated in Elliott's Cove by the Newfoundland Brick and Tile Company. Also during the 1890s, the family name of Gallagher is found among the inhabitants of this community. Church records show that a Catherine Gallagher of Cramm's Brook, Elliott's Cove, married a Malcolm Stanley of Shoal Harbour in 1897. There is also a record of Elizabeth Ann Garland of Elliott's Cove marrying Jethro Pelley of Brown's Mead. The Goobie (also spelt "Gooby" in early records) family was started at Elliott's Cove in 1892 when a John Goobie of Foster's Point married Martha Smith of Elliott's Cove. John was born at Hant's Harbour and was only a young

John Goobie. John's family went to Foster's Point from Hant's Harbour in the 1870s where John lived until he married Martha Smith of Elliott's Cove. (Photo courtesy of Randy Head)

boy when he accompanied his family to Foster's Point in the 1870s. George Hiscock, originally of Trinity, and his wife, Nellie Ann of Lee Bight (later renamed Adeytown) settled at Cramm's Brook near Elliott's Cove during the 1890s or early 1900s. Their previous place of abode was Lee Bight.

McAlpine lists the following five as fishermen of Elliott's Cove during the 1890s: John Gooby, John Hodder, Charles Smith and Henry Smith. Aaron Smith is listed as a lumberman and Gideon Smith is classified as a sawmill operator. Moses Smith is reported as a coaster. James Craven is described as a foreman living at the brickyard. The dominance of Smiths as pioneers at Elliott's Cove is seen in Table 5-3. This table also includes the date and place of birth of many of the adults in this cove prior to 1900 as well as the maiden names of the wives in this community at that time. While Hant's Harbour is the dominant settlement of origin of Elliott's Cove pioneers, a number of other places are represented in the adult population prior to 1900.

1900/45 - Aston, Berkshire, Burt, Patey, Paul and Walters

The 1911 nominal census for Elliott's Cove includes three families who apparently took up residence there around 1900 or shortly thereafter. Specifically, they were Samuel and Eliza Walters, Albert and Myrtle Berkshire and William and Mary Paul. Samuel Walters from Salmon Cove (later renamed Champneys), and his wife, Eliza (nee Berkshire) of Bay L'Argent and Spencer's Cove, settled in Elliott's Cove around 1900. It is understood that Samuel Walters came to this area to work with the railway at Clarenville. Eliza's brother, Albert Berkshire, married a Myrtle Smith of Elliott's Cove in 1911 and started the Berkshire family in this community. The Berkshires were offsprings of William Thomas Berkshire, who was born at Redan, England in 1842 and came to Newfoundland around 1854. William and Mary Paul came to Elliott's Cove from Snook's Harbour, but they also lived at other places on the

TABLE 5-3

DATE AND PLACE OF BIRTH OF SOME OF THE ADULTS IN ELLIOTT'S COVE PRIOR TO 1900

NAME	DATE OF BIRTH	PLACE OF BIRTH
William Cooper	1857	Ireland's Eye
Emily Cooper (nee Smith)	1861	Hant's Harbour
James Craven		London, England
Jane Craven (nee Cave)		Plymouth, England
Catherine Gallagher	1879	
Elizabeth Ann Garland		
John Goobie	1867	Hant's Harbour
Martha Goobie (nee Smith)	1866	Hant's Harbour
Amy A. Hiscock	1877	
Annie Hiscock	1855	
George Hiscock	1843	Trinity
Ann Hiscock		Lee Bight
William Hiscock	1876	Lee Bight
Sarah Hiscock	1886	Quirpon
John Hodder	1863	Thoroughfare
Lillian Hodder (nee Smith)	1868	Elliott's Cove
Rose Hodder	1810	Thoroughfare
John Martin		
Sydney Pelley		
Aaron Smith	1855	Hant's Harbour
1st wife Emily Smith (nee Ivany)	1861	English Harbour
2nd wife Jane Ann Smith (nee Reid)	1864	Foster's Point
Alice Smith		

NAME	DATE OF BIRTH	PLACE OF BIRTH
Allan Smith	1877	Elliott's Cove
Annie Louisa Smith (nee Taylor)	1885	Harbour Grace
Archibald Smith	1881	Elliott's Cove
Rachel Smith (nee Samson)	1882	White Rock
Charles Smith	1851	Hant's Harbour
Mahala Smith	1852	Foster's Point
Edwin Smith	1870	Elliott's Cove
Charity Smith (nee Strong)	1871	Russell's Cove
Ethel Smith		Elliott's Cove
Elizabeth Smith	1844	Hant's Harbour
Ephraim Smith	1875	Elliott's Cove
Effie Jane Smith (nee Reid)	1870	Foster's Point
Gideon Smith		Hant's Harbour
1st wife		
Hannah Smith (nee Ivany)	1846	Champneys
2nd wife		
Emily Louise Smith (nee Pynn)		St. John's
Harrison Smith	1882	Elliott's Cove
Dinah Smith	1887	Greenspond
Henry J. Smith	1855	Bishop's Cove
Mary J. Smith (nee Smith)	1871	Elliott's Cove
Moses Smith	1833	Hant's Harbour
1st wife		
Jane Smith (nee Pelley)		Hant's Harbour
2nd wife		
Susan Smith (nee Rideout)	1839	Twillingate

NAME	DATE OF BIRTH	PLACE OF BIRTH
Norman Smith	1883	Elliott's Cove
1st wife		
Emma Smith (nee Craven)	1885	Portsmouth, England
2nd wife		
Deborah Smith (nee Cooper/Mills)	1884	Elliott's Cove
Sarah Smith		Elliott's Cove
Susan Smith	1842	Hant's Harbour
Thomas Smith	1804	Scilly cove
Martha Smith (nee Tilley)	1811	Hant's Harbour
Thomas Smith	1839	Hant's Harbour
Deborah Smith (nee Hopkins)	1847	Hant's Harbour
William Smith	1834	Hant's Harbour
Lydia Smith (nee Hopkins)		Hant's Harbour
William Ivany Smith	1884	Elliott's Cove

Source: This Table was developed from vital statistics from the Methodist Church at Britannia Cove, Foster's Point, Hant's Harbour, Random North and Shoal Harbour; *McAlpine's Newfoundland Directory 1894 to 1897*; *McAlpine's Newfoundland Directory for 1898*; nominal censuses for Elliott's Cove in 1911, 1921, 1935 and 1945; tombstones in Elliott's Cove; and interviews with Random Islanders.

western portion of Random Island including Evelley's Brook. Like a few other families on Random Island at the time the Pauls often moved from one place to another.

The surname Patey appears on the Elliott's Cove census for the first time in 1921. The Patey family in this settlement at that time included Adolpheus Patey, who was born at Great Brehat, his wife, Elsie (nee Walters), who was born at Spillars Cove, and their children, who were born in Elliott's Cove. Also residing in Elliott's Cove in 1921 was a Josiah Aston (spelt "Austin" in church records), who was born in England, and his wife, Maude, who was born at Champneys. Josiah, a Methodist minister, lived in Elliott's Cove for only a short time before moving to the United States. William T. Smith of Wake's Brook and his wife, Druscilla (nee Edison) of Hay Cove, moved to Elliott's Cove in 1925. William's father settled at Wake's Brook from Bishop's Cove in the 1890s.

A Burt family made Elliott's Cove their home in the 1940s. It consisted of a William and Cecilia (nee Smith) Burt and their children. William came from Botwood and Cecilia was originally from Snook's Harbour and Elliott's Cove.

Hickman's Harbour

As noted earlier in this book, names of some of the early visitors and winter people to Hickman's Harbour and surrounding area are revealed in the names of specific geographical locations such as Beckford's Hill, Dean's Cove, Dwyer's Pond, Strong's Tickle and Taylor's Cove. While some of the transients were in the area before permanent settlers came, others were likely there after the harbour was permanently settled. The chronological order of families settling in Hickman's Harbour prior to 1900 has been identified as follows:

1840s - Blundell
1850s - Martin
1860s - Benson, Bryant, Martin and Thistle
1870s - Adey, Butt, Critch, Penney, Simmons, Vardy and others
1880s - Hiscock, Lambert and Martin
1890s - Churchill, Fagnar, Marsh, Pittman and Short.

1840s - Blundell

The first permanent settlers in Hickman's Harbour were Blundells. They were descendants of the Blundells from England, who had earlier immigrated to the Island Cove/Bay de Verde areas of Newfoundland. In Hickman's Harbour, they were sometimes known as "Blundons". However, early church records, as well as a description given by Reverend Henry Petley, a Church of England Missionary, of his visit to this place in 1859, show that they were referred to as "Blundells" when they first settled in Hickman's Harbour. Even though there has been a tradition in Newfoundland of changing the name Blundell to that of Blundon, they are different surnames (Seary 1976:38-39). Except for those in Hickman's Harbour, Blundell is a rare surname in Newfoundland. According to the tombstone of Stephen Blundell in the old Methodist cemetery in Hickman's Harbour, he was the first permanent settler to this harbour. This is contrary to the view expressed in *The Encyclopedia of Newfoundland and Labrador* (1984:939), that Hezekiah Blundell was the first permanent settler to Hickman's Harbour. Hezekiah was Stephen's son and he was only 10 or 11 years of age when his father and family came to this area. Stephen Blundell, along with his wife, Elizabeth Ann, and at least three children (Hezekiah, Alfred and Priscilla), settled permanently in Hickman's Harbour in the early 1840s. Hezekiah was born in Island Cove, Conception Bay, in 1832 and Alfred was born there in 1835. Newfoundland census for 1911 suggests that Stephen's daughter, Harriett, was born in Hickman's Harbour in 1843. It is likely that Stephen and his family made visits to the harbour, perhaps spending a winter or two there while returning to Island Cove to fish in the summer, before deciding to stay in Hickman's. During those early visits, Stephen and his family lived in a tilt which they constructed on the river emptying into the far end of the harbour. This tilt, and later

Hezekiah Blundell, his wife Sarah (nee King/Penney of Deer Harbour), and his granddaughter May Blundell, who later married Frederick Cook. Hezekiah continued the lumber tradition of his father, Stephen. (Photo courtesy of Frank Vardy and Cecil Hansford)

Heber Blundell was a longtime fisherman in Hickman's Harbour. (Photo courtesy of George and Delilah Blundell)

Asa Blundell, son of Hezekiah and Ann Blundell, is shown here with a mark of his trade — a log on his shoulder. (Photo courtesy of Ralph and Clarice Blundell)

their sawmill, was located up river from what became known as the Mill Pond.

Methodist Church records at Hant's Harbour show that Alfred Blundon of Random married a Sarah Martin of Fox Harbour in 1860. Alfred and Sarah settled on the west side of Hickman's Harbour where they made a living by lumbering and fishing. Their sons, Heber, Joseph and Stephen, also settled on this side of the harbour and continued the lumbering/fishing tradition. Hezekiah Blundell and his wife, Ann, who was from Bay de Verde, took up residence in the bottom of the harbour where Hezekiah concentrated on logging and lumbering. At one time, Hezekiah, in partnership with one William J. King of Deer Harbour, operated a sawmill in Deer Harbour. While at Deer Harbour he married his second wife, Sarah, a sister of William J. King. After a short stay in Deer Harbour, Hezekiah and his wife returned to Hickman's.

Stephen Blundell was born on the west side of Hickman's Hr. where he followed his father in the fishing industry. (Photo courtesy of Margaret Noseworthy)

Jane Martin and her half sister Mary (Polly) Pittman. They were daughters of Alfred and Sarah Blundell. (Photos courtesy of Ivy O. C. Martin and Laura Belle Marsh)

1850s - Martin

The second family to settle permanently in Hickman's Harbour was that of Benjamin and Catherine Martin of Grates Cove. They were married in the Wesleyan Chapel in Grates Cove in 1850, and had four sons (Simeon, 1851, Benjamin, 1854, Abraham, 1855 and James 1858) before taking up permanent residence at Hickman's Harbour in 1859. Like many of the early settlers to Hickman's, Benjamin made several visits to the harbour to get wood and even spent a winter there living in a tilt before deciding to settle there. Benjamin and Catherine had two sons (Alfred, 1862, and Hezekiah, 1872) and two daughters (Sarah Ann, 1867 and Susannah, 1873) born in Hickman's Harbour. All of their children married and settled in Hickman's Harbour. Starting with James around 1880, different members of this family had business establishments in this and neighbouring communities over the years. One view is that Benjamin Martin's ancestors came from England to Grates Cove in the 18th century. However, there is evidence that he was of Irish descent. More specifically, his ancestors may have been Irish Catholics who were converted to Protestantism during the mission of Reverend Lawrence Coughlan in Harbour Grace in the 1760s. Benjamin married a devoted Wesleyan and the whole family became steeped in the tradition of this Church.

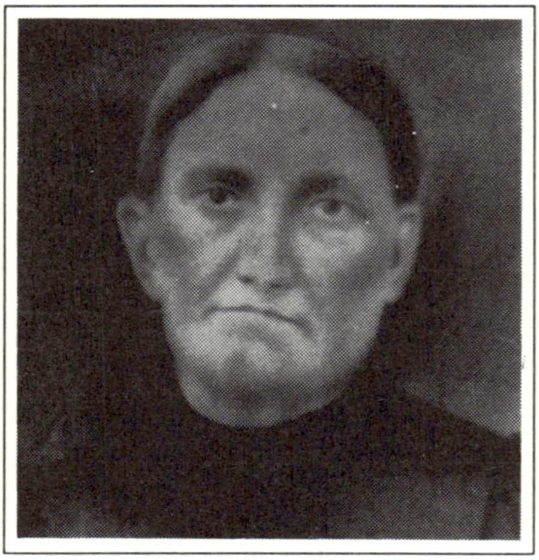

Catherine, wife of Benjamin I, and three of their six sons. This was the first Martin family to settle in Hickman's Harbour.
Top — Catherine Martin (Photo courtesy of Ivy O. C. Martin) Abraham Martin, a fisherman /sawmill operator (Photo courtesy of Hubert Martin)
Bottom—Benjamin Martin II, a fisherman (Photo courtesy of Samuel Martin) Hezekiah Martin, a quarryman (Photo courtesy of Mary Burry)

1860s - Benson, Bryant, Martin and Thistle

Shortly after the first Martins had settled in Hickman's, they were joined in the 1860s by Bensons, Bryants, Thistles and another family of Martins. Elias Martin and his wife, Sarah, arrived in Hickman's Harbour with at least one child, Uriah, who was born in Grates Cove in 1864. While Benjamin, the first Martin in Hickman's, and Elias were both from Grates Cove, they were not closely related and may have had different ancestors altogether. Apparently there were different families of Martins in Grates Cove during those early times. Given the fact that Martin was a common surname in England, Ireland, Scotland and the Channel

Islands during earlier times, it is not surprising that there were different families of Martins on the north side of Conception Bay during the settling of this area. Elias and Sarah Martin of Hickman's Harbour had six sons (Eleazer, Elias, Elisha, Heber, Joshua and Uriah) and at least two daughters (Annie and Mariah). All but one of these children settled in this harbour. Levi and Jane Benson were the first Bensons in Hickman's. They arrived in the harbour from Grates Cove about the same time as did Elias Martin. Elias had married Levi's sister, Sarah, and Levi had married Elias' sister, Jane. Hence, the connections regarding their settling in Hickman's Harbour at the same time.

Joshua Martin — Fisherman/logger and quarryman. (Photo courtesy of Evan Courtney)

Unlike others who came to Hickman's Harbour and surrounding area during those early days to take advantage of the forest, Charles Bryant came because of his interest in slate rock. Many people believe that Charles Bryant came to this harbour from Wales. However, this does not seem to be the case. Perhaps this belief came about because the Welsh were known for their interest and expertise in slate mining. The Curries came from Wales to Britannia Cove to start the slate quarries in Smith Sound, and others came from Wales to work the quarries in Smith Sound and around Hickman's Harbour. Indications are that Charles Bryant's ancestors were from Somerset, England, and they lived in other communities in Trinity and Conception Bays before Charles came to Random Island. Charles and Emily (nee Blundell) Bryant had four sons (Hanuel, Herbert, Heman and Malcolm), three of whom made their homes in Hickman's. Two of their daughters, Annie and Bertha, moved away from the harbour, married men from elsewhere

James Benson, son of Levi and Jane Benson. (Photo courtesy of Wilfred and Gertie Vardy)

Malcolm Bryant and his wife Sarah (nee Marsh). In his early years, Malcolm worked at the slate quarry. Later he, along with his brothers, operated a water-driven sawmill in Hickman's Harbour. (Photo courtesy of Hanuel Bryant)

Annie, daughter of Charles Bryant, married John King and lived in New York for several years. Their son Ralph, later returned to Hickman's Harbour and started the first King famiily there. (Photo courtesy Ralph and Myra King)

and returned to the harbour after their husbands died. Annie introduced the surname of King to the harbour and it was continued by her son, Ralph. Bertha brought the surname of Brown to the harbour, but it never became an established family name in this community. A third daughter, Harriett, married William Roberts, a Welshman. They lived in the harbour for a few years while William worked at the slate quarries.

The Thistle family was started in Hickman's Harbour by Samuel and Elizabeth Thistle, who came with their children during the 1860s. It is generally believed that the Thistles came from Mulley's Cove (now part of Broad Cove, Conception Bay). Early records show that, among others, there was a William Thistle in Mulley's Cove in 1777 and a Sarah Thistle in Broad Cove in 1821 (Seary, 1976:478). According to Newfoundland census of 1911 and 1921, the first Thistle children in the harbour, that is, Azariah, Henrietta, Reuben and Susannah, were born at Blackhead. In a later census, the grandchildren of Samuel and Elizabeth Thistle reported their ancestors were born in Mulley's Cove and Broad Cove. The Thistles settled in Hickman's a few years after Benjamin and Catherine Martin had made it their permanent home. The story is told

Reuben Thistle was noted as an excellent carpenter. (Photo courtesy of Ethel Thompson)

that Benjamin and Catherine were excited when Samuel and Elizabeth Thistle decided to move to Hickman's Harbour. It would mean that the Martin children would have more company than before. The Thistles and the Martins did indeed provide companionship for each other in that Susannah Thistle and her sister (perhaps, a half sister), Henrietta, married brothers, Abraham and Simeon Martin, respectively. Sarah Ann Martin, a sister of Abraham and Simeon, married Azariah Thistle, a brother of Susannah and Henrietta. Azariah was born in Broad Cove, and his full name was Azariah Martin Thistle, which suggests that there may have been a relationship between the Martins and the Thistles before the Martins left Grates Cove to settle at Hickman's.

1870s - Adey, Butt, Critch, Penney, Simmons, Vardy and others

During the 1870s, at least eight family names were added to those already a part of the community of Hickman's Harbour. One of those was that of Adey. A young couple, Edward and Mary Ann Adey, from Hant's Harbour took up permanent residence in Hickman's shortly after 1874. Edward Adey is said to be a descendant of a James Adey, who immigrated to Newfoundland before 1800, and was a proprietor in Hant's Harbour at that time. The surname Adey has gone through different spellings over the years. Even within the same generation, and at the same point of time, one finds different spellings for this surname in Hickman's Harbour. The 1911 census, for example, includes a Willis Addey and a Noah Eddy, whereas, in fact, these two men were brothers. There is a tombstone in the Methodist cemetery in Hickman's Harbour to Mary Ann Eddy erected by her husband, Edward, and in the same plot there is one to Edward Addy.

Ebenezer and Rosannah (nee Martin) Butt. Ebenezer and his brothers operated a water-driven sawmill at Strong's Tickle. (Photo courtesy of Hazel and George Pittman, and Susie and Ebenezer Lambert)

William and Sarah Butt and their three sons (Mark, Ebenezer and Thomas) started the Butt family in Hickman's Harbour. Butt is one of the oldest surnames in Newfoundland. It has been claimed that the Butts in this province are descendants of

Mary (Polly) Critch (nee Hopkins). Mary and her husband Samuel, were part of the extended family of Critches which settled at Hickman's Harbour in the 1870s. Photo courtesy of Samuel and Evangeline Martin)

one Roger Butt (spelt "Butts"), a planter of Crocker's Cove, Conception Bay in 1625. This claim has also been questioned (Butt, 1985:4). Whatever the origin of the Butts in Newfoundland it is known that William and Sarah and their three sons came from Blackhead to Hickman's Harbour around 1878. Their fourth and fifth sons, Walter and James, were born after they arrived in their new place of abode. At about the same time, William's brother, Joseph, settled in St. Jones Within and started the Butt family in that community.

At least four Critch brothers (Amos, Charles, Samuel and William George) from Hant's Harbour settled in Hickman's Harbour during the early 1870s. As far as can be ascertained, their father was George, perhaps William George, and he accompanied his sons to the harbour, or joined them shortly after they had settled there. One George Critch is reported to have died in Hickman's Harbour at the age of 78 in 1889. There was also a John Critch who settled in this place at the same time, but the relationship between George and John has not been discovered. John may have been George's son, which would mean that there were five Critch brothers settling in the harbour during the 1870s. John Critch died in 1891 at the age of 50 years. While Charles Critch moved to St. John's and Amos Critch set-

Five of the six daughters of Samuel and Mary Critch. Front row (l-r) Jessie (wife of Ezekiel Martin), Jane (wife of Solomon Marsh), Dorcas (wife of Tobias Whelan). Back row (l-r) Lydia (wife of Moses Martin) and Elizabeth (wife of Thomas Butt). (Photo courtesy of Welma Stead)

tled at Bald Nap, Samuel and William George Critch took up permanent residence in the Dean's Cove area of Hickman's Harbour. For some reason, Samuel Critch, who died in 1916 at the age of 70 years, was known to all, even his grandchildren, as "Connie Critch" and sometimes just "Connie".

Lucy Butt. Daughter of William George and Hannah Critch, Lucy was often consulted for medical advice, especially for cuts, bruises and broken limbs. She acted in this capacity for more than fifty years. Her husband was Walter Butt. (Photo courtesy of Samuel and Susie Butt)

A William Goudy appeared on a voters list for Hickman's Harbour around 1870. No other written record has been found of his stay in this place, but very likely he was a winterman who spent some time in a tilt built on the side of the pond near Hickman's Harbour which still bears his name; Billy Goudy's Pond.

The surname of Pelley first appeared on Random Island in the 1840s when Job and John Pelley of Hant's Harbour settled in Robinson's Bight. Other Pelleys pioneered the community of Lady Cove. The only Pelley to settle in Hickman's Harbour was Joseph Pelley, who came there from Hant's Harbour in 1874. The story is told that Joseph Pelley's first visit to Hickman's Harbour was in response to a word of mouth advertisement from Harriett Blundell for a husband. In her early days, Harriett, a daughter of Stephen Blundell, the first permanent settler to Hickman's Harbour, was selective when it came to choosing a husband, perhaps too selective. The time came when she thought age was catching up with her and she did not relish the prospects of becoming an old maid. She decided to let it be known that

Joseph Pelley, a longtime mail carrier, postmaster, businessman and operator of a passenger boat service. (Photo courtesy of Ralph and Myra King)

she wanted a man, "a well-to-do-fellow". Joseph Pelley of Hant's Harbour, thinking he could meet with the approval of Harriett, visited her in Hickman's Harbour. They were married shortly thereafter and settled in this community.

Sarah Piercey (nee Penney) daughter of the Hickman's Harbour pioneers James and Ann Penney. (Photo courtesy of Florence and David Marsh)

James and Annie Penney were the first Penneys to inhabit Hickman's Harbour. They were not descendants of the same family as the Penneys who settled in Deer Harbour during the 1860s. The Deer Harbour Penneys were from English Harbour, while the James Penney who settled in Hickman's Harbour was born in New Perlican. His wife, Annie (nee Soper), was born at Hant's Harbour. According to 1921 census their daughter, Sarah, was born in Hickman's Harbour in 1880, which suggests that they were in the harbour in the late 1870s. Their sons, John, Charles and George, were also born in Hickman's Harbour and they settled in this community.

The first Simmons (also spelt "Simmonds" and "Symonds" in early records) to make Hickman's Harbour their home were John and Mary (nee Bugden) Simmons of Trinity. Perhaps, John was an offspring of Samuel Simmonds who resided in Trinity in 1787. John came to Hickman's Harbour during the early 1870s to work in the woods with the Blundells, who were well established in the lumbering business at that time. Later in the 1870s, John and Mary Simmons settled on the west side of Hickman's Harbour. Their sons, Abner and James, also settled on the harbour's west side and raised their families there.

Mary (Polly) Simmons (nee Bugden) and her grandson Ralph Simmons around 1927. Mary, along with her husband John, founded the Simmons family in Hickman's Harbour. (Photo courtesy of Jean Mills)

James and Magdalene Vardy, founders of the Vardy family in Hickman's Harbour. Along with Simeon and Alfred Martin, James Vardy constructed a "dual" sawmill in Hickman's Harbour. This mill, with a saw bench on each side, is said to have been the largest water-driven sawmill on Random Island. It was in use for several years after James died in 1887. (Photo courtesy of Ivy Thistle and Frank Vardy.

William and Sarah (nee Martin) Vardy.

The first Vardy to settle in Hickman's Harbour was James, son of George Vardy of Claypits, Southwest Arm of Random, but earlier of Burton Green, near Christ Church, England. James and his wife, Magdalene of Grates Cove, and at least one son, John, who was born at Claypits, moved to Hickman's Harbour in the early 1870s. It is also reported that Moses Vardy, a brother of James, who married Mary Jane Blundell of Hickman's Harbour in 1879, lived at Hickman's Harbour for a short time around 1880 (Vardy, 1986:9). Moses and Mary Jane later settled in Clarenville, while James and Magdalene became the founders of the Vardy clan at Hickman's Harbour. Their sons, George,

John Vardy and his grandson Edmund Thistle. John was a sawmill operator and entrepreneur in Hickman's Harbour. (Photo courtesy of Muriel Martin and Ivy Thistle)

John and William started families in this harbour, and while George later moved from the community, John and William remained in it, as did several of their offspring, to maintain the Vardy name there.

1880s - Hiscock, Lambert and Martin

During the 1880s a family of Hiscocks, one of Lamberts, and another family of Martins moved to Hickman's Harbour. To elaborate, Matthew and Mariah Hiscock apparently left Trinity sometime during the 1880s and made their home in Hickman's Harbour. William and Amelia Hiscock were also in this harbour at the same time. Four Hiscock men died in Hickman's Harbour in the 1890s, all in their early twenties or younger. The last written record of a Hiscock living in this community is of a Mariah Hiscock listed in the 1911 census.

Hezekiah Martin and Walter Butt. Hezekiah was part of the third family of Martins to settle in Hickman's Hr. and Walter belonged to the original Butt family in this community. (Photo courtesy of Samuel and Susie Butt)

George Lambert and his wife, Elizabeth, both of Grates Cove, became residents of Hickman's Harbour during the 1880s. When Elizabeth died George married Myria Bird of Labrador. After George's death in 1907, his son moved to Corner Brook, thus ending the Lambert family name in this harbour for the time being. However, during the 1940s another family of Lamberts settled in Hickman's Harbour. Thomas and Emily Lambert came from Southport, but they also had roots in Grates Cove. In addition to the early Martins of Hickman's Harbour, that is, the families of Benjamin and Catherine who came in the 1850s, and Elias and Sarah who came in the 1860s, another family of Martins came from Grates Cove to Hickman's Harbour in the 1880s. This was a William and Mariah Martin and their sons, Hezekiah and William. Both sons married and settled in this harbour.

1890s - Churchill, Fagnar, Marsh, Pittman and Short

Several families from different Newfoundland communities made Hickman's Harbour their home during the 1890s. One of them was a family of Churchills. A Reuben Churchill from Trinity, his wife, Geraldine, from Aspey Point, and their nine children, all of whom were born in Hickman's Harbour, were listed in the 1911 census for this community. Apparently, Reuben and Geraldine settled in Hickman's Harbour during the 1890s where they had a large family, but by 1921 no Churchills were included in the census for this place.

William and Susannah Fagnar from Caplin Cove, Conception Bay, moved to Hickman's Harbour in the 1890s. It is said that they did so because Susannah was a relative of William Martin who had settled in this place during the 1880s. William Fagnar was accidentally killed in the woods at Hickman's Harbour in 1894. Shortly thereafter his widow and her six children returned to their home in Caplin Cove.

George Martin
(Photo courtesy Llewellyn Pond)

As noted above, the first Martin family settled in Hickman's Harbour during the 1850s, another family came in the 1860s, and a third family came in the 1880s. One other Martin, a George Martin of Grates Cove, came to Hickman's Harbour in the 1890s. He is believed to have been a relative of William Martin who settled in the harbour in the 1880s. George came to work as "a hired hand" with Simeon Martin, who was a son of Catherine and Benjamin Martin, the first Martins to settle here. George later married Simeon's daughter, Susannah, and they raised a family in this community. Given the large families of the earlier Martins, that is, Benjamin and Elias, the arrival of the later Martins, that is, William and his sons, and the family

Daniel Marsh. Daniel was killed near Strong's Tickle in 1924 when the supports to his woodpile collapsed taking the wood and him over a cliff. (Photo courtesy of Allan Marsh)

created by George and Susannah, Martin was the most common surname in this community for many years into the 20th century.

Also in the 1890s, James Marsh of Lee Bight married Magdalene Martin of Hickman's Harbour and they made Hickman's their home. At about the same time, he was joined in the harbour by his sister, Sarah, who married Malcolm Bryant of this place. Some time later, probably during the early 1900s, their brothers Daniel and William Marsh of Lee Bight moved to Hickman's Harbour. William married Mary Butt and Daniel married Minnie Martin. Both of these women were born in Hickman's Harbour. While James, Sarah, William and Daniel Marsh came to Hickman's Harbour from Lee Bight, their roots were actually on Random Island in that their father, Joseph, was a son of Benjamin and Abigail Marsh, who lived at Rider's Harbour in the early 1850s before settling in Deer Harbour later in that decade.

John Pittman, a son of Joseph and Grace Pittman of Britannia Cove and earlier of Somersetshire, England, married Mary (Polly) Blundell of Hickman's Harbour in 1892. They settled in Hickman's to become the only Pittman family to live in this community. Also in the 1890s, a William Bugden of Trinity and his wife, Amelia Jane (nee Simmons) of Hickman's Harbour took up residency in this harbour and lived there for several years before moving. A family of Shorts settled in Hickman's Harbour in 1899. It was a James Short of Hant's Harbour and his wife, Druscilla, from Lee Bight. Since their children died before reaching adulthood, there was no one to continue the Short name in the harbour after James passed away in 1940.

In addition to listing husband and wife together and including the maiden name of the wife, Table 5-4 identifies the date of birth and place of birth of many of the adults in Hickman's Harbour prior to 1900. By listing those born in 1880 and earlier, this table shows that the pioneers of Hickman's Harbour were mainly from communities on the south side of Trinity Bay and on the north side of Conception Bay. A relatively small number people came from Trinity to settle permanently in Hickman's Harbour. Even though Hickman's Harbour was not permanently settled until the 1840s, Table 5-4 indicates that it attracted a large number of people shortly thereafter and many of the adults in the community before 1900 were born there.

TABLE 5-4

DATE AND PLACE OF BIRTH OF SOME OF THE ADULTS IN HICKMAN'S HARBOUR PRIOR TO 1900

NAME	DATE OF BIRTH	PLACE OF BIRTH
Edward Adey	1847	Hant's Harbour
1st wife		
Mary Ann Adey (nee		
2nd wife		
Jemima Adey (nee Short/Thorne)	1846	Hant's Harbour
Henry Adey	1875	Hant's Harbour
John Adey	1875	Hant's Harbour
Jane Adey (nee Gregory)	1867	Queen's Cove
Lavina Adey	1883	Hickman's Harbour
Noah Adey	1882	Hickman's Harbour
Christina Adey (nee Burridge)	1884	Middle Lance Cove
Willis Adey	1880	Hickman's Harbour
Bertha Adey (nee Martin)	1885	Hickman's Harbour
George Benson	1870	Hickman's Harbour
1st wife		
Mary Ann Benson (nee Pond)	1872	Foster's Point
2nd wife		
Mariah Benson (nee Bird/Lambert)	1873	Sound Bay, Labrador
James Benson	1874	Hickman's Harbour
Mary Benson		Bay Roberts
Levi Benson	183?	Grates Cove
Jane Benson (nee Martin)	1835	Grates Cove

NAME	DATE OF BIRTH	PLACE OF BIRTH
Alfred Blundell	1835	Island Cove
1st wife		
Sarah Blundell		Fox Harbour
(nee Martin)		
2nd wife		
Jane Blundell	1835	Grates Cove
(nee Martin/Benson)		
A. Joseph Blundell	1871	Hickman's Harbour
Evelyn Blundell	1877	Lower Shoal Harbour
(nee Reid)		
Allan Blundell	1872	Hickman's Harbour
Annie Blundell	1880	Hickman's Harbour
(nee Martin)		
Asa Blundell	1872	Hickman's Harbour
1st wife		
Emily Blundell	1878	Lower Lance Cove
(nee Duffett)		
2nd wife		
Edith Blundell	1882	Lady Cove
(nee Soper/Eastman)		
Heber Blundell	1866	Hickman's Harbour
1st wife		
Jane Blundell	1871	Lee Bight
(nee Adey)		
2nd wife		
Elizabeth Blundell	1880	Hatchet Cove
(nee Blundon)		
Hezekiah Blundell	1833	Island Cove
1st wife		
Ann Blundell	1844	Island Cove
(nee Blundon)		
2nd wife		
Sarah Blundell	1852	Western Bay
(nee King/Penney)		
Howard Blundell	1875	Hickman's Harbour
Lizzie Blundell	1879	Lee Bight
(nee Harris)		
Priscilla Blundell	1830s	Island Cove
Sarah Blundell	1877	Hickman's Harbour

NAME	DATE OF BIRTH	PLACE OF BIRTH
Stephen Blundell	1796	Island Cove
Elizabeth Ann Blundell	1807	
Stephen Blundell	1861	Hickman's Harbour
1st wife		
Margaret Blundell (nee Penney)	1878	Deer Harbour
2nd wife		
Rachel Blundell (nee Penney)	1882	Deer Harbour
3rd wife		
Emma Blundell (nee Mercer/Gilbert/Hansford)	1871	Bay Roberts
Stephen Blundell	1865	Hickman's Harbour
Jane Blundell (nee Spurrell/Smith)		Fox Harbour
William Blundell	1866	Hickman's Harbour
Mary (Polly) Blundell (nee Soper)	1869	Hant's Harbour
Annie Amelia Bryant	1879	Hickman's Harbour
Bertha Bryant	1873	Hickman's Harbour
Charles Bryant	1846	
1st wife		
Emily Bryant (nee Blundell)	1845	Hickman's Harbour?
2nd wife		
Sarah Bryant (nee Martin/Benson)	1845	Grates Cove
Hanuel Bryant	1870	Hickman's Harbour
Susannah Bryant (nee Martin)	1873	Hickman's Harbour
Heman Bryant		Hickman's Harbour
Sarah Jane Bryant		
Herbert Bryant	1866	Hickman's Harbour
Druscilla Bryant (nee Gregory)	1869	Queen Cove
Malcolm Bryant	1879	Hickman's Harbour
Sarah Bryant (nee Marsh)	1880	Lee Bight

NAME	DATE OF BIRTH	PLACE OF BIRTH
William Bugden	1875	Trinity
Amelia Jane Bugden (nee Simmons)	1875	Hickman's Harbour
Ebenezer Butt	1867	Blackhead
Rosannah Butt (nee Martin)	1865	Grates Cove
James Butt		Blackhead
Thersia Butt (nee Jacobs)		Little Heart's Ease
Mark Butt	1867	Blackhead
Sarah Butt (nee Critch)	1868	Little Heart's Ease
Thomas Butt	1872	Blackhead
Elizabeth Ann Butt (nee Critch)	1877	Hickman's Harbour
Walter Butt	1879	Hickman's Harbour
Lucy Butt (nee Critch)	1882	Hickman's Harbour
William Butt	1839	Blackhead
1st wife		
Mary Butt	1833	
2nd wife		
Sarah Butt		
Reuben Churchill	1872	Trinity
Geraldine Churchill	1872	Aspen Cove
Charles Critch	1830s	Hant's Harbour
Christina Critch	1876	Hickman's Harbour
George Critch	1811	Hant's Harbour?
George Charles Critch	1871	
Sarah Jane Critch (nee Soper)	1854	Hant's Harbour
James K. Critch	1878	Hickman's Harbour
Alice Critch (nee Penney)	1881	Deer Harbour
John Critch	1841	Hant's Harbour
Ann Critch (nee Penney)		Hant's Harbour

NAME	DATE OF BIRTH	PLACE OF BIRTH
Samuel Critch	1846	Hant's Harbour
Mary (Polly) Critch (nee Hopkins)	1855	Hant's Harbour
Sarah Jane Critch	1844	
Sarah Jane Critch	1857	
Wm. George Critch	1845 or 1843	Hant's Harbour
1st wife		
Hannah Critch (nee Evans?)	1842	Hant's Harbour
2nd wife		
Caroline Critch (nee Sinclair)	1841	Trinity
Wm. John Critch	1874	Hickman's Harbour
1st wife		
Eliza Ann Critch (nee Marsh)	1875	Deer Harbour
2nd wife		
Lydia Critch (nee Hyde)	1881	Hillview
James Dean		
William Fagnar	1857	Caplin Cove
Susannah Fagnar (nee Martin)		Grates Cove
E. Garland		
William Goudy		
Esther Hiscock	1837	Trinity
Henry Hiscock	1871	Trinity
Matthew Hiscock		Trinity
Mariah Hiscock	1852	Trinity
Nehemiah Hiscock	1870	
Norman Hiscock	1875	
Samuel Hiscock	1873	
William Hiscock	1868	
1st wife		
Amelia Hiscock (nee Baker)	1869	Hodge's Cove
3rd? wife		
Julia Hiscock		North West Brook

NAME	DATE OF BIRTH	PLACE OF BIRTH
George Lambert	1860	Grates Cove
1st wife		
Elizabeth Lambert	1865	Blackhead
(nee Butt)		
2nd wife		
Mariah Lambert	1875	Sound Bay, Labrador
(nee Bird)		
Daniel Marsh	1879	Lee Bight
Minnie E. Marsh	1889	Hickman's Harbour
(nee Martin)		
James Marsh	1874	Lee Bight
Magdalene Jane Marsh	1881	Hickman's Harbour
(nee Martin)		
Abraham Martin	1855	Grates Cove
Susannah Martin	1864	Mulley's Cove
(nee Thistle)		
Alfred Martin	1884	Hickman's Harbour
Alfred Martin	1862	Hickman's Harbour
Mariah Martin	1870	Hickman's Harbour
(nee Martin)		
Benjamin Martin	1822	Grates Cove
Catherine Martin	1827	Caplin Cove
(nee/Bussey)		
Benjamin Martin	1854	Grates Cove
1st wife		
Rosannah Martin	1856	Old Perlican
(nee Button)		
2nd wife		
Jane Martin	1862	
(nee Baker/Seaward)		
David Martin	1882	Hickman's Harbour
1st wife		
Susannah Martin	1880	Hodges Cove
(nee Baker)		
2nd wife		
Mae Martin	1893	Hodges Cove
(nee Baker)		

NAME	DATE OF BIRTH	PLACE OF BIRTH
Eleazer Martin	1867	Hickman's Harbour
Caroline Martin	1867	Hickman's Harbour
(nee Blundell)		
Elias Martin	1836	Grates Cove
Sarah Martin	1845	Grates Cove
(nee Benson)		
George Martin	1870	Grates Cove
Susannah Martin	1881	Hickman's Harbour
(nee Martin)		
Heber Martin	1871	Hickman's Harbour
Elfredia Martin	1875	Hickman's Harbour
(nee Martin)		
Hezekiah Martin	1872	Hickman's Harbour
Susannah Martin	1876	Foster's Point
(nee Pond)		
Hezekiah Martin	1874	Grates Cove
Eliza Martin	1886	Queen's Cove
(nee Gregory)		
James Martin	1858	Grates Cove
Jane Martin	1861	Hickman's Harbour
(nee Blundell)		
James Martin	1880	Grates Cove
Joshua Martin	1879	Hickman's Harbour
Mary Ellen Martin	1879	Catalina
(nee Edwards)		
Moses Martin	1876	Hickman's Harbour
Lydia Martin	1882	Hickman's Harbour
(nee Critch)		
Simeon Martin	1851	Grates Cove
Henrietta Martin	1857	Mulley's Cove
(nee Thistle)		
Uriah Martin	1864	Grates Cove
Jane Martin	1857	Grates Cove
(nee Snelgrove)		
Wesley Martin		Hickman's Harbour
Marion Martin		Hickman's Harbour
(nee Martin)		

NAME	DATE OF BIRTH	PLACE OF BIRTH
William Martin	1859	Grates Cove
Mariah Martin (nee Brewer)		Grates Cove
James Penney	1854	New Perlican
Annie Penney (nee Soper)	1845	Hant's Harbour
John Penney	1883	Hickman's Harbour
Lilly Penney (nee Vardy)	1896	Hickman's Harbour
Joseph Pelley	1855	Hant's Harbour
Harriett Pelley (nee Blundell)	1843	Hickman's Harbour
John Pittman	1868	Britannia Cove
Mary (Polly) Pittman (nee Blundell)	1868	Hickman's Harbour
James Short	1875	Hant's Harbour
Driscilla Short (nee Adey)	1874	Lee Bight
Abner Simmons	1890	Hickman's Harbour
Pearl Simmons (nee Critch)	1903	Hickman's Harbour
James Simmons	1880	Hickman's Harbour
Ethel Simmons (nee Pittman)	1892	Hickman's Harbour
John Simmons	1839	Trinity
Mary Simmons (nee Bugden)	1845	Trinity
Azariah Thistle	1861	Broad Cove
1st wife		
Sarah Ann Thistle (nee Martin)	1867	Hickman's Harbour
2nd wife		
Myria Thistle (nee Duffett)	1872	Lower Lance Cove
Reuben Thistle	1867	Broad Cove
1st wife		
Mary Ann Thistle (nee Vardy)	1872	Claypits

NAME	DATE OF BIRTH	PLACE OF BIRTH
2nd wife		
Mary Thistle	1876	Trinity
(nee Churchill)		
Samuel Thistle	1833	Broad Cove
Elizabeth Thistle	1835	Blackhead
(nee Thistle)		
George Vardy	1887	Hickman's Harbour
Lillian Alice Vardy		Hickman's Harbour
(nee Martin)		
James Vardy	1847	Claypits
Magdalene Vardy	1845	Island Cove
(nee Bussey)		
John Vardy	1867	Claypits
Sarah Vardy	1869	Lower Shoal Harbour
(nee Reid)		
Moses Vardy	1854	Claypits
Mary Jane Vardy	1858	Hickman's Harbour
(nee Blundell)		
William Vardy	1880	Hickman's Harbour
Sarah Vardy	1884	Hickman's Harbour
(nee Martin)		

Source: This Table was developed from vital statistics from the Methodist Church at Blackhead, Britannia Cove, Hant's Harbour, Lower Island Cove and Old Perlican; vital statistics from the Church of England at Random Mission, Trinity and Trinity East; 19th century lists of voters as recorded in *White's Papers* at Trinity; *Lovell's Province of Newfoundland Directory for 1871*; Minutes of the Methodist Church of Canada for 1877; *McAlpine's Newfoundland Directory 1894 to 1897*; *McAlpine's Newfoundland Directory for 1898*; nominal censuses for Hickman's Harbour in 1911, 1921, 1935 and 1945; tombstones at Hickman's Harbour; and interviews with Random Islanders.

1900/45 - Avery, Brown, Cook, Hart, Piercey and others

A host of family names including those Avery, Brown, Cook, Hart, Hughes, King, Piercey, Pond, Reid and Roberts, were among the newcomers to Hickman's Harbour between 1900 and 1945. Detailed accounts of the backgrounds of these families are beyond the purposes of this book. However, a few notes on their settling in the harbour are in order.

Bertha Bryant, daughter of Charles Bryant of Hickman's Harbour, married a Brown from Bonavista Bay and after his death she returned with her children to live in Hickman's, bringing the Brown name to the harbour. Bertha later married Richard Avery of Deep Bight, who had come to the harbour to work in the woods. After Bertha's passing, Richard married Marion Martin of Hickman's and their offspring continued the Avery name in this community.

When his father, a Scottish seaman, passed away Frederick Cook and his brother, James, went to live at Hickman's Harbour around 1901. They were actually grandsons of Charles Critch, who was formerly a resident of the harbour but had moved to St. John's. Frederick married May Blundell and they started the Cook family in this community. Samuel Hart of Lady Cove married a Catherine Martin of Hickman's Harbour and started a family in this harbour during the early 1900s. Their two children, twin boys, died when they were only three years old, shortly thereafter Catherine passed away and Samuel left community. Richard Reid, also of Lady Cove, married Emily Critch of Hickman's, and they are listed as residents of this harbour in the 1921 census. They lived in the harbour for several years before moving to Deer Lake.

Several Welsh families lived in Hickman's Harbour during the early 1900s. They came from Wales to work at the slate quarries in the area. One family was that of Michael Hughes, who resided in the harbour for only a short period of time. Another was that of William Roberts, who married Harriett, daughter of Charles and Emily Bryant. They left the harbour a few years after the slate quarries closed in 1910.

The surname Piercey came to Hickman's when Edward Piercey of Winterton married Sarah Penney of the harbour. She was a daughter of James and Annie Penney who settled at Hickman's from New Perlican in the 1870s. Around 1910 another Penney family lived at Hickman's Harbour. Elijah Penney of Deer Harbour married Priscilla Blundell of Hickman's Harbour in 1897, and after living in Deer Harbour and Robinson's Bight they moved to Hickman's where they stayed six or seven years before returning to Deer Harbour.

The Pond family began in Hickman's when Hanuel Pond of Foster's Point married Minnie Martin of this harbour. Alexander Dean of Southport, a descendant of James Dean, who wintered in Dean's Cove during the 19th century, married Clara Pittman of Hickman's Harbour and created the Dean family in this community. Ernest Ivany of Britannia married Mildred Bryant of Hickman's in 1927 and they started the first Ivany family in this community. Cecil and Lillian Hansford started the Hansford family in Hickman's Harbour in 1929. Cecil came from Deep Bight to Hickman's in 1915 with his mother, who married Stephen Blundell. Lillian came to the harbour as a Salvation Army Officer/teacher.

In 1934, Joseph Verge of Lower Lance Cove married Viola Martin of Hickman's and created the only Verge family to live in this harbour. The census of 1935 shows Charles and Maud Brenton as residing in Hickman's Harbour, but they stayed in this place for only a couple of years. Ezra Marsh and his sons, Adam and Philip of Deer Harbour and Random Head Harbour, settled in Hickman's during the 1930s. They, like the Marshes that came to Hickman's from Lee Bight in the 1890s, were descendants of Benjamin and Abigail Marsh, who settled in Rider's Harbour from Bonaventure in the 1840s. An extended family of Greens from St. Jones Without moved to Hickman's Harbour in the 1930s. It included Charles, his wife, Rachel, their son Jasper and his wife, Susannah (nee Martin, originally from Hickman's Harbour), and Jasper's sons by a previous marriage. Ralph and Myra (nee Adey) King and their children moved to Hickman's Harbour from Clarenville in 1936. Ralph, a grandson of Charles Bryant, had lived in the harbour as a boy. He was born in New York and moved to Newfoundland with his mother after his father passed away. Also in the 1930s, Eli Hollett of Rantem came to Hickman's Harbour with William Butt and married William's sister, Emily, and thereby added the surname Hollett to the residents of Hickman's Harbour.

During the 1940s, Thomas and Emily Lambert and their family from Southport moved to Hickman's. This meant that the surname of Lambert was back in the harbour after an absence of some thirty years. The 1945 nominal census of Hickman's Harbour also includes a family of Clarks. Joseph Clark of Middle Lance Cove married Madora Critch of Hickman's Harbour and they resided in this harbour for a few years before moving to Canada. Barlett Green, of St. Jones Without, and his wife, Lydia (nee Seaward), of Gooseberry Cove, settled in Hickman's Harbour in 1949. An extended family of Seawards, actually a brother and the parents of Lydia Green, made their home in Hickman's for a few years beginning in the early 1950s. Also in the 1950s, a family of Whites was established in Hickman's Harbour. Saul White, a sea captain, from Twillingate, married Viola Butt of the harbour.

Lady Cove

While winter people probably frequented Lady Cove and March's Cove during the 1850s and 1860s, it seems as if March's Cove was the first to attract permanent settlers. Given the fact that March's Cove, which in oral tradition became known as "London" and is still know as such by local people, has generally been considered part of the community of Lady Cove, the present outline of the earliest settlers to this area makes reference to each of these places but it does not pursue a distinction between these two geographically separate identities. Even though it is difficult to give precise dates of the arrival of different families, an attempt is made to identify the decades when each of the early families settled in the Lady Cove/March's Cove area. By combining information obtained from written documents with that from interviews, the following was developed as the chronological order of the pioneering families settling in the Lady Cove/ March's Cove area:

1860s - March, Reid and Soper
1870s - Hart, March and King
1880s - Adey, George, Hiscock, Pelley and Sharpe
1890s - Burridge, Burt, Day and Eastman.

1860s - March, Reid and Soper

As far as can be ascertained, the first permanent settlers to the Lady Cove area were Marches, Reids (sometimes spelt "Reed" in early documents) and Sopers, all of whom were pioneers in this area during the 1860s. The Harts may have been in this area at that time as well, but the present writer is inclined to think that they did not settle there until the 1870s. As suggested by the name of March's Cove, which was included in a list of places in the area with eligible voters in the 1870s, Marches had visited, and perhaps spent winters in this cove, if not permanently settling it in the 1860s. It is interesting to note that there were no Marches listed as residents of March's Cove in the 1870s. Instead, it was occupied by Reids and Sopers. Church records suggest that a James Reid, who was born in Hant's Harbour in 1824, settled in March's Cove during the 1860s. They also show another James Reid as an early settler to this area in that a couple by the name of James and Mary Reid had children baptized in Lady Cove during the 1880s. The largest number of Reid offspring to settle in this area were children of Henry John Reid, who was born in Hant's Harbour in 1850, and Ester Reid (nee Ellis) of George's Brook. This family of Reids settled in the London area of Lady Cove. They had seven children living at home in 1911.

The first Soper family to settle permanently in March's Cove, was Jonas and his wife, Sophia. They were both born in Hant's Harbour, Jonas in 1820 and Sophia in 1822. We are not sure when they settled in

John and Martha Soper. The Sopers of Lady Cove became famous for their knowledge of the sea and sailing pursuits. (Photo courtesy of Gerald Martin)

March's Cove, but it was probably during the 1860s. Other early Sopers from Hant's Harbour to settle in this cove included Edward, who was born in 1841, John, who was born in 1844, and Charles, who was born in 1862. If they were not children of Jonas and Sophia Soper, they were obviously related to them, and in the case of Edward and John they were young men when they settled on Random Island. A voters list compiled during the 1870s show four Sopers at March's Cove: Edward, John, Jonas and Samuel.

Thomas Hart. All present day Harts in Lady Cove are descendents of Thomas, who was a sailor and sawmill operator. (Photo courtesy of Weldon Hart)

1870s - Hart, March and King

As noted earlier in this book, the first Hart to settle on Random Island was a Catherine Hart, wife of Richard Brennock at Rider's Harbour in 1832. One of the first Harts to settle in the

Lady Cove area was a Nathaniel Hart, who was a fisherman out of March's Cove in the 1870s. Other information suggests that Nathaniel and his brothers, George and Theophilus, all of whom were born in Hant's Harbour, settled in the Lady Cove area during the 1870s. Nathaniel Hart had one son named William, who was born in Hant's Harbour in 1869. George Hart and his wife, Janet, had a son named Thomas, who was born in Lady Cove in 1885. The present day Harts in Lady Cove are all descendants of this Thomas Hart and his wife, Ada (nee Day). As noted in Table 5-5, Lydia Hart and Lillian Hart were among the first Hart women to settle in this area.

Lothrop March, Norman March and William March of Old Perlican were the first Marches to settle permanently in Lady Cove. They were offspring of Stephen March from England, who occupied fishing rooms in Old Perlican during the early 19th century. Norman March was born at Old Perlican in 1845; William March was born there in 1846, and Lothrop March was born there in 1854. Since they did not settle permanently in Lady Cove until they were young men, the earliest they could have made it their home was in the late 1860s. It is known that William and Norman were brothers and it is possible, though we have no evidence to the effect, that Lothrop was their brother. They settled in Lady Cove at the same time and were very likely the children of earlier Marches who visited the cove and point of land near Lady Cove which

Rachel and Archibald March. Rachel came to Lady Cove as a school teacher from Cupids. She married Archibald March, son of Lothrop and Rachel March who had settled in Lady Cove earlier. (Photo courtesy of Vernon March)

Pleaman March and his son John. Pleaman, son of William and Magdalene March, was well known for his fish-splitting ability. (Photo courtesy of Austin and Blanche March)

Mary March (nee Soper), wife of Pleaman, and their son Lawrence. Although she had no formal training, Mary acted as an optometrist in that she tested peoples eyesight and supplied glasses to them. She was also a midwife. (Photo courtesy of Austin and Blanche March)

James March, son of William and Magdalene March, was a fisherman and logger in Lady Cove. (Photo courtesy of Reuben and Olive March)

Ada March (nee Stanley), wife of James March and daughter of Eli Stanley of Bald Nap. (Photo courtesy of Reuben and Olive March)

bear their surname: March's Cove and March's Point. Also in Lady Cove in the 1870s was one Sophia March, probably the mother of the March brothers. She died in 1903 at the age of 87 years. It is suspected that William March, if not Lothrop and Norman, was married before settling in Lady Cove. According to *The Methodist Monthly Greeting* (1904), William's wife was Magdalene (nee Belman), a daughter of one Robert Belman, a schoolmaster and lay reader at Seal Cove (later renamed New Chelsea). Norman's wife, Hannah, was born in Hant's Harbour. Lothrop's wife, Rachel (nee Reid), was also born in Hant's Harbour, but was probably living at Foster's Point at the time of their marriage.

Edgar and Minnie (nee Haynes) March. For a number of years Edgar had fishing/coastal schooners sailing out of Lady Cove. (Photo courtesy of Reuben and Olive March)

A Philip King was listed as a voter in Lady Cove in the 1870s. He was also given as resident of Robinson's Bight at about this time. Since no other information has been unearthed concerning this Philip King, it would seem that he resided in the Lady Cove/Robinson's Bight areas for only a short time.

1880s - Adey, George, Hiscock, Pelley and Sharpe

During the 1880s, at least five new families joined those already in Lady Cove. To elaborate, Isaac Adey and his wife, Mary, moved from Lee Bight (later renamed Adeytown) in the 1880s and settled in Lady Cove. Isaac was in all probability of the same lineage as the Adeys who settled at Foster's Point in the 1860s and those that settled at Hickman's Harbour in the 1870s. Later, after Isaac's death, Mary married William Sharpe, then of Lady Cove but formerly of Bay Roberts.

As far as can be ascertained, Richard George and his wife, Mary Jane George, started the first George family in Lady Cove. They came to this cove from Heart's Content during the early 1880s. It is known that members of the George family in Lady Cove are direct descendants of one John George, who was born in Heart's Content in 1876. This John George came to Lady Cove in the 1880s with Richard and Mary Jane George, and he was either a son or, as some local people believe, a nephew of Richard George. It has also been suggested that the Georges in Lady Cove were of the same family as Robert George, who settled in Middle Lance Cove, and John Noah George of Foster's Point.

John George and family. For a number of years John was responsible for the liver processing division of Burt's fishing operation at Lanse Aux Meadows. (Photo courtesy of Weldon Hart)

Church records show a George and Ann Hiscock in Lady Cove during the 1880s. George Hiscock was of the same family of Hiscocks that came from Trinity to the Northwest Arm of Random to live at Lee Bight and Elliott's Cove. They may have been related to the family of Hiscocks who took up residence in Hickman's Harbour in the 1880s. One Henry Hiscock, who is reported to have been born at Sound Island, married a Christina Hart of Lady Cove in the late 1890s.

Among the pioneers in the Northwest Arm part of Random Island were Job and John Pelley from Hant's Harbour, both of whom started a

Cecilia Hart (nee Pelley) of Shoal Harbour was the wife of William Hart of Lady Cove. (Photo courtesy of Effie Clench)

sawmill at Robinson's Bight around 1850. The Pelleys in Lady Cove also came from Hant's Harbour, but lived in Shoal Harbour before settling in Lady Cove. All of these Pelleys were likely descendants of the Pelleys who settled in Hant's Harbour from the West County of England during the early 19th century (Seary, 1976:379). Records suggest that a Josiah Pelley, who was born in Hant's Harbour in 1846, and his wife, Julia Ann (nee March), who was born in Old Perlican, became the first Pelleys to settle

Josiah and Julie Ann (nee March) Pelley, founders of the Pelley family in Lady Cove. Their sons prosecuted the codfishery and were among the leading lumbermen in the area. (Photos courtesy of Neta Pelley)

in Lady Cove. Apparently, they lived at Shoal Harbour before settling in Lady Cove in the 1880s. Two of their sons, Herbert and Archibald, were born in Shoal Harbour in 1876 and 1879, respectively.

William Sharpe of Bay Roberts, and his wife, Wilmott, who may have been a Hart from Lady Cove, took up residence in Lady Cove during the 1880s. They had at least three children baptized in that community prior to 1900. After the death of Wilmott, William married at least once more and probably twice. His last wife was Mary Adey, then of Lady Cove but earlier of Old Perlican and Lee Bight. William died in 1954 at the age of 100 years.

1890s - Burridge, Burt and Eastman

Methodist Church records show that John and Elizabeth Burridge were residing in Lady Cove in the early 1890s. They had earlier lived in Middle Lance Cove. Hayward Burt of Old Perlican married Sarah Reid of Foster's Point in 1893, and they started the first Burt family on Random Island. The family name of Eastman was also added to those of the pioneers in Lady Cove during the late 1890s when William Eastman from Burin married Edith Soper of Lady Cove.

Hayward Burt and his wife Sarah (nee Reid). Hayward developed fishing/lumber businesses at Lady Cove and Lanse Aux Meadows. (Photo courtesy of Neta Pelley)

By combining information gathered from vital statistics in church records, from Newfoundland directories, from early voters lists, from nominal censuses, from tombstones and from interviews, a list of some of the adults living in Lady Cove prior to 1900 has been compiled (Table 5-5). When known, maiden name and date and place of birth have been included. It is seen that, with few exceptions, Lady Cove pioneers came from Hant's Harbour and Old Perlican. Since Lady Cove was not permanently settled until the 1860s, most of the adults given in Table 5-5, which includes mainly those born prior to 1880, were not born in Lady Cove. Although incomplete, this listing is offered as starting point for those pursuing genealogical interests.

TABLE 5-5

DATE AND PLACE OF BIRTH OF SOME OF THE ADULTS IN LADY COVE PRIOR TO 1900

NAME	DATE OF BIRTH	PLACE OF BIRTH
Isaac Adey	1858	Hant's Harbour?
Mary Adey (nee Hopkins)	1870	Hant's Harbour
John Burridge		Grates Cove
Elizabeth Burridge	1856	Grates Cove
Hayward Burt	1869	Old Perlican
1st wife		
Sarah Burt (nee Reid)	1869	Foster's Point
2nd wife		
Annie Amelia Burt (nee Bryant/King)	1879	Hickman's Harbour
William Eastman	1876	Burin
Edith Eastman (nee Soper)	1882	Lady Cove
Jane Ann George	1870s	
John George	1876	Heart's Content
1st wife		
Priscilla George (nee Garland)	1877	
2nd wife		
Rachel George (nee Baker)	1884	Fox Harbour
3rd wife		
Ada George (nee Day/Hart)	1890	Hant's Harbour
Richard George	1841	Heart's Content
Mary Jane George	1853	
George Hart	1876	Hant's Harbour
Sarah George (nee Thorne)	1879	Middle Lance Cove

NAME	DATE OF BIRTH	PLACE OF BIRTH
George Hart	1854	Hant's Harbour
Janet Hart		Seal Cove
(nee Belman)		
Lillian Hart	1882	
Lydia Hart	1831	
Mary Hart	1826	
Nathaniel Hart		Hant's Harbour
Rebecca Hart	1860s	
Samuel Hart		
Selina Hart		
Theolphilus Hart	1862	Hant's Harbour
1st wife		
Amelia Hart	1861	Hant's Harbour?
(nee Reid)		
2nd wife		
Amy Hart	1878	Snook's Harbour
Thomas Hart	1885	Lady Cove
Ada Hart	1880	Hant's Harbour
(nee Day)		
William Hart	1869	Hant's Harbour
Cecilia Hart	1880	Shoal Harbour
(nee Pelley)		
George Hiscock	1843	Trinity
Ann Hiscock		Lee Bight
Henry Hiscock		Sound Island
Christina Hiscock		Lady Cove
(nee Hart)		
Archibald K. March	1882	Lady Cove
Rachel March	1884	Cupids
(nee Butler)		
Edgar March	1882	Lady Cove
Amelia March	1882	Catalina
(nee Haynes)		
James March	1876	Old Perlican
Ada March	1879	Bald Nap
(nee Stanley)		

NAME	DATE OF BIRTH	PLACE OF BIRTH
Lothrop March	1854	Old Perlican
Rachel March (nee Reid)	1858	Hant's Harbour
Lydia March		
John Norman March	1845	Old Perlican
Hannah March	1847	Hant's Harbour
Orion March	1873	Lady Cove
Bertha March	1874	Lady Cove
Pleaman March	1874	Old Perlican
Mary March (nee Soper)	1877	Lady Cove
Sophia March	1816	
William March	1846	Old Perlican
Magdalene March (nee Belman)	1851	Seal Cove?
Willis March	1881	Lady Cove
E. Maud March (nee Dalton)	1882	Harcourt
Archibald Pelley	1877	Shoal Harbour
Emily Pelley (nee Reid)	1880	Lady Cove
Herbert Pelley	1876	Shoal Harbour
Amy Pelley (nee March)	1884	Lady Cove
Josiah Pelley	1846	Hant's Harbour
Julia Ann Pelley (nee March)		Old Perlican
Stephen Pelley	1882	Shoal Harbour
Alice B. Pelley (nee Bugden/Walters)	1895	Upper Lance Cove
Dinah Reid	1829	
Esther Reid	1870	
Henry John Reid *1st wife*	1850	Hant's Harbour
Lydia Reid (nee Soper) *2nd wife*	1868	Hant's Harbour

NAME	DATE OF BIRTH	PLACE OF BIRTH
Esther Reid (nee Ellis)	1865	Hant's Harbour/ George's Brook?
James Reid	1824	
James Reid Mary Reid (nee Pelley)		
Willis Reid		
Priscilla Reid	1880	
Richard Reid Emily Sarah Reid (nee Critch)	1887 1888	Lady Cove Hickman's Harbour
Louisa Sharpe	1879	
William Sharpe *1st wife* Wilmott Sharpe (nee Hart?) *2nd wife* Selina Sharpe *3rd wife* Mary Sharpe (nee Hopkins/Adey)	1854 1863 1870	Bay Roberts Hant's Harbour? Hant's Harbour
Alfred Soper	1885	Lady Cove
Angus Soper Martha Soper (nee Burton?)	1876 1879	Lady Cove Harbour Buffett
Charles Soper Lucy Soper (nee Pittman)	1862 1862	Hant's Harbour Broad Cove, T. Bay
Edward Soper Lucy Jane Soper (nee King?)	1841 1846	Hant's Harbour Hant's Harbour
Henry Soper Sarah Martha Soper (nee Reid)	1876 1879	Lady Cove Lady Cove
James Soper	1881	Lady Cove
John Soper Martha Soper	1844 1852	Hant's Harbour Hant's Harbour

NAME	DATE OF BIRTH	PLACE OF BIRTH
Jonas Soper	1820	Hant's Harbour
Sophia Soper	1822	Hant's Harbour
Jonas Soper	1882	Lady Cove
Martha Soper	1862	
Mary Soper	1860s	
Samuel Soper		
Sarah Jane Soper		

Source: This Table was developed from vital statistics from the Methodist Church at Britannia Cove, Foster's Point, Hant's Harbour, Hearts Content, Old Perlican, Random North and Shoal Harbour; 19th century lists of voters as recorded in *White's Papers* at Trinity; *Lovell's Province of Newfoundland Directory for 1871*; *McAlpine's Newfoundland Directory 1894 to 1897*; *McAlpine's Newfoundland Directory for 1898*; nominal censuses for Lady Cove in 1911, 1921, 1935 and 1945; tombstones at Lady Cove and Weybridge; and interviews with Random Islanders.

1900/45 - Baker, Day, Green, Goobie, King and others

According to nominal censuses from 1911 to 1945, the following family names were added to those found among the permanent settlers in Lady Cove prior to 1900: Baker, Day, Butler, Garland, Green, Goobie, Keel, King, Parsons, Pike and Williams. To elaborate, Edward King, of St. Jones Within and Foster's Point, and his wife, Mary (nee Price), of Long Cove (later renamed Loreburn), started the King family at Lady Cove around 1900. In different records, this family is listed as residing at Lady Cove and at Foster's Point. Samuel Day, of Hant's Harbour, and his wife, Mary (nee Tilley) of Old Perlican, took up residence in Lady Cove in 1906. Samuel went to Lady Cove to work with Theolphilus Hart, who was building a schooner in the cove at that time. Richard Baker, who was originally from Southport, and his wife, Deborah, who was born at St. Jones, settled in Lady Cove during that time. The 1911 census shows Mathius Garland, father of Deborah Baker, residing in Lady Cove. Later, this family is listed as residing at Foster's Point. According to the 1921 census, a George Baker who was born at Southport and his wife, Anne who was born at Port Rexton, resided at Lady Cove. Herbert Goobie of Foster's Point moved to Lady Cove between 1911 and 1921. At about the same time, William and Elizabeth Butler of Cupids took up residence at Lady Cove. They came because their daughter, Rachel, who had married Archibald March, was living at Lady Cove. Enoch Green of St. Jones Without married into the Reid family of Lady Cove and his family was reported to have been living in Lady Cove in 1945. At that time, a family of Keels from Bonavista Bay lived at Lady Cove before they moved to Clarenville. There was a family of Rideouts, that of Willis and Laura, in Lady Cove in the 1950s. Vital statistics of the Methodist church suggest that Pike (1912), Parsons (Charles and Jane Parsons 1911), Parsons (John and Elizabeth Parsons, 1917), Williams (1923) and Canning (1928) were among the family names of people living in Lady Cove prior to 1945.

Middle Lance Cove

As noted in chapter 3 of this book, Middle Lance Cove does not fit exactly into either one of the settlement groupings used in this presentation on Random Island pioneers. Since it was something more than an outlying settlement as discussed in chapter 6, and since there is one family presently living at Middle Lance Cove, it was decided to include it in this discussion of present settlements on the Random Island, even though it is not generally considered as such. We are reminded of the problems, as discussed earlier, encountered in attempting to identify exact places of abode of early settlers to Britannia and Lance Cove areas. Given this caveat, the present research suggests the pioneers to Middle Lance Cove were as follows:

1860s - Bugden, Clark and Tavernor
1870s - Barrett, Burridge, Cooper and Thorne
1880s - Beer, Bent, Carberry, George and Halliday
1890s - Adams, Bowering and Rose.

1860s - Bugden, Clark and Tavernor

Indications are that Middle Lance Cove was established as a permanent settlement during the late 1850s or early 1860s. During that time at least three families (Bugdens, Clarks and Tavernors) made Middle Lance Cove their place of abode. William Bugden, one of the eight Bugden brothers who moved from Trinity to Petley (Upper Lance Cove) in the 1850s, settled in Middle Lance Cove shortly thereafter. His sons also lived in this cove where Bugden was a prominent family name until the 1920s. After many years of being absent from this place - in fact, Middle Lance was abandoned as a settlement for many years - the family name of Bugden returned to be the only family name at present in Middle Lance Cove.

William and Druscilla (nee Tavernor) Bugden, founders of the Bugden family in Middle Lance Cove. Druscilla was a midwife for many years. (Photo courtesy of Delilah and William Walters)

A Clark (sometimes spelt "Clarke") family, that of Joseph and Elizabeth Clark of Careless Harbour (later renamed Kerley's Harbour), settled in Middle Lance Cove during the 1860s. According to different

Martha Clark (nee Walters) and her husband John. Martha was an offspring of the Walters in Upper Lance Cove and John's ancestors were pioneering Clarks in Middle Lance Cove. (Photo courtesy of Allison Bugden)

William Clark. The Britannia Cove Clarks are direct descendants of this William Clark from Middle Lance Cove. (Photo courtesy of Eliol and Gladys Clark)

records, three of their sons were born in Middle Lance Cove. These sons were Joseph, who was born in 1868, Jonathan, who was born in 1874, and William, who was born in 1877. Oral tradition has it that the ancestors of the Clarks who settled in Middle Lance Cove came from Scotland in the early part of the 19th century. Church of England records in Trinity show that there was a Joseph Clark in Careless Harbour in 1827. In addition to Joseph and Elizabeth Clark, there was a John and Elizabeth Clark in Middle Lance Cove during the 1860s. The relationship between Joseph and John is not known, but it likely they were of the same lineage. *McAlpine's Newfoundland Directory for 1898* reports that there were five Clarks in Middle Lance Cove at that time: John, Joseph (senior), Joseph (junior),

Jonathan and William. The Clarks in Britannia Cove are descendants of Joseph and Elizabeth Jane Clark of Middle Lance Cove.

Tavernors (sometimes spelt "Tavenor"and "Tavener") were among the pioneers of Trinity. Records show that Jacob and William Tavernor were living there in the early 18th century. Given the fact that they were in Trinity during those early days, it is suspected that Tavernors visited the Lance Cove area on Random Island many times before they settled there. Indications are that Joshua and William Tavernor of Trinity were the first Tavernors to settle permanently in Middle Lance Cove. They took up residence there during the late 1860s. Church of England records at Trinity show that William Tavernor of Lance Cove (probably Middle Lance Cove) married Ann Good of the same place in 1865. The list of those present at the marriage ceremony included Amelia Tavernor, Joshua Tavernor, Lillah Tavernor and Priscilla Tavernor. Since the report of Ann Good of Lance Cove marrying Joshua Tavernor is the only reference to any Goods living in Lance Cove, it is suspected that she was probably working, or living with relatives, in Lance Cove at the time.

In addition to the fact that a child named James Pittman is buried in the Congregational cemetery in Middle Lance Cove, there has been a suggestion that a family of Pittmans lived in this cove during its early days. However, it is also possible that this was a child of the Pittmans who immigrated to Britannia Cove from England during the 1860s.

1870s - Barrett, Burridge, Cooper and Thorne

A voters list for the 1870s shows Caleb Barrett as a resident of Middle Lance Cove at that time. *McAlpine's Newfoundland Directory for 1898* has three Barrett fishermen of Middle Lance Cove: Caleb, George and William. There were Barretts in the Trinity area during the early 19th century. It is suspected that offspring of the Trinity Barretts settled in Middle Lance Cove in the 1870s. Burridges and Coopers came to Random Island from Grates Cove during the early 1870s. John Burridge and Absalom Cooper landed at Bluff Head Cove at that time. Absalom Cooper and his family settled at Bluff Head Cove, while John Burridge and his family moved to Middle Lance Cove. Simultaneously, a John Cooper made Middle Lance Cove his place of abode. As noted in the follow-

John Burridge, the original Burridge in Middle Lance Cove. (Photo courtesy of Stella Martin and Mabel Wiseman ing section on Petley pioneers, a family of Thornes settled in the Middle Lance Cove/Petley area during the 1870s. Some documents indicate that the Thornes were living in Middle Lance Cove in the 1880s, other records suggest that they were living in Petley at that time.

1880s - Beer, Bent, Carberry, George and Halliday

There is a story that Joseph and Mary Beer of St. John's accompanied their daughter, Elizabeth, to Middle Lance Cove around 1882 where Elizabeth taught school for nine years prior to her death in 1891. Apparently the Beers remained in the area after their daughter had passed away. According to McAlpine's directory, Joseph Beer was a farmer in Middle Lance Cove in 1898. A family of Bents and one of Eastmans also lived in the Middle Lance Cove area in the 1880s. Oral tradition has it that the Bents came there from Wales to work at the slate quarries at Nut Cove. However, the places of abode of each of these families before they settled in Middle Lance Cove is not known. As suggested by a tombstone in the Congregational cemetery in Middle Lance Cove, a George Carberry and his wife Anna, resided in this area during the 1880s. Anna was interred in this burial ground in 1886.

A Robert George from Heart's Content married a Sarah Thorne of Middle Lance Cove, where they settled and started the George family during the 1880s. Robert was related to Richard George, the first George to settled in Lady Cove. Robert and Sarah George had at least three sons (Ambrose, Ephraim and Thomas) and two daughters (Mary and Louisa). Ephraim and Thomas later settled in Lower Lance Cove, thereby establishing the George clan in that community. Louisa also settled in Britannia/Lower Lance Cove area where she married William Coish. After the death of his wife, Sarah, Robert George married Martha Phillips in 1893. Martha was a sister of David Phillips of Aspey Brook where Robert and Martha George made their home after their marriage.

The surname Halliday (sometimes spelt "Holiday" and "Holliday") appeared in the Middle Lance Cove area during the 1880s. The Hallidays originally came from the Manchester, England to Jobs Cove, Newfoundland, and then to the Middle Lance Cove area. One story is that the Hallidays came to this area to work in the slate quarry at Nut Cove. Another, and likely more accurate, story is that the Hallidays in this area were descendants of a John Halliday, who accompanied his mother in her move from Job's Cove to this area of Smith Sound after his father died. It is said that after the death of his father, John's mother went to Labrador as a cook on a fishing schooner from Job's Cove. While on the Labrador coast she met a fellow from Middle Lance Cove whom she married and joined in her new home in that community. John Halliday married Rachel Dodge of Heart's Ease and raised a family of five boys

(Abel, Bert, John, Moses and Thomas) and one daughter (Molly) in the Middle Lance Cove/Britannia Cove area.

1890s - Adams, Bowering and Rose

As far as can be ascertained from written documents, three family names, those of Adams, Bowering and Rose, appeared in Middle Lance Cove for the first time during the 1890s. They were among the McAlpine's list of fishermen in Middle Lance Cove in 1898. That list also included the following as residents of Middle Lance Cove: William Rose, Calvin Bent, Caleb Barrett, George Barrett, William Barrett, Louis Bowering, William Bowering, William Bugden, John Clark, Jonathan Clark, Joseph Clark (senior), Joseph Clark (junior), William Clark, Thomas Rose, Joshua Tavener and William Tavener. There are tombstones in the Congregational cemetery in Middle Lance Cove to Louis and William Bowering. Those "Bowerings" are likely of the "Bowring" family which settled in Britannia Cove in the 1850s.

Table 5-6 is a summary of information uncovered in the present research on the place and date of birth of the adults in Middle Lance Cove prior to 1900. When known, husband and wife are listed together and maiden name of wife is included.

1900/45 - Anderson, Davis, Jones, Leonard, Piercey and Yarn

During the 20th century at least six family names were added to those in Middle Lance Cove. One of those was a Davis family, but the present research has not obtained any information concerning it. A Benjamin and Emma Jones were living in Middle Lance Cove around 1900. Some believe that both the Davis and Jones families were from Wales and they came to this area because of the slate quarries in Nut Cove. It has also been suggested that the Jones family came from somewhere in the New England States. There was a Robert and Harriett Piercey living in Britannia Cove (perhaps, in Middle Lance Cove) in 1903, and church records show that Edward and Sarah (nee Currie) Piercey had a daughter born in Middle Lance Cove in 1907. Other information suggests that Edward and Sarah Piercey were living in Middle Lance Cove prior to 1900 and that they came to the cove from Winterton, but no written reference has been found to substantiate this. It is understood that they moved to St. John's prior to 1920. John Anderson of British Harbour married Genevia Barrett of Middle Lance Cove and they lived in this cove for several years before moving to Petley. Two men from British Harbour made Middle Lance Cove their home during the 1930s. One was Ephraim Yarn who married a woman from the area and together they had a family in Middle Lance Cove. The other was James Leonard who married Phoebe Critch from Hickman's Harbour and they lived in the Middle Lance Cove/Petley area during

TABLE 5-6

DATE AND PLACE OF BIRTH OF SOME OF THE ADULTS IN MIDDLE LANCE COVE PRIOR TO 1900

NAME	DATE OF BIRTH	PLACE OF BIRTH
William Adams	1848	
Elizabeth Adams		
Caleb Barrett	1840	
Elizabeth Barrett		
George Barrett	1871	
1st Wife		
??		
2nd Wife		
Ina Barrett (nee Bugden)	1870	
William John Barrett	1864	
Maria Barrett (nee Randell)	1866	Freshwater
Elizabeth Beer	1859	St. John's?
Joseph Beer		
Mary Beer		
Calvin M. Bent		
Margaret Bent	1860	
Louis Bowering	1874	
Wm. George Bowering	1871	
Mary Elizabeth Bowering (nee Peckham)		Salmon Cove
Frederick Bugden		Middle Lance Cove
Jesse Bugden (nee Clark)		Middle Lance Cove
Joseph Bugden		Middle Lance Cove
Grace Bugden (nee Clark)		Careless Harbour
Samuel Bugden		

NAME	DATE OF BIRTH	PLACE OF BIRTH
William Bugden	1845	Lance Cove
1st Wife		
Amelia Bugden (nee Forde)		English Harbour
2nd Wife		
Druscilla Bugden (nee Tavernor)	1871	Middle Lance Cove
John Burridge		Grates Cove
Elizabeth Burridge	1856	Grates Cove
Joseph Burridge		Middle Lance Cove
Samuel Burridge		Middle Lance Cove
Mary Burridge	1810	
John T. Butt		Adams Cove
Amelia Butt		
George Carberry		
Anna Carberry	1850	
Samuel Carberry		
John Clark	1854	
John T. Clark	1857	
John Clark		
Elizabeth Clark	1823?	
John Clark		
Martha Elizabeth Clark (nee Walters)		Upper Lance Cove
Jonathan Clark	1874	Lance Cove
Mary Jane Clark (nee Lambert)	1878	Fox Harbour
Joseph Clark	1844	Kerley's Harbour
1st Wife		
Charlotte Clark (nee Vatcher)		
2nd Wife		
Elizabeth Jane Clark (nee Baker)	1854	
Joseph Clark	1868	Middle Lance Cove
Emily Jane Clark (nee Adey)		Hickman's Harbour
Mary Elizabeth Clark	1862	Middle Lance Cove

NAME	DATE OF BIRTH	PLACE OF BIRTH
Sarah Clark		
Selina Jane Clark		
William Clark	1877	Middle Lance Cove
Mary Elizabeth Clark (nee Bowring)	1879	Britannia Cove
Absalom Cooper		
John Cooper	1832	Grates Cove
Mary Cooper	1832	Grates Cove
John Cooper	1870	
Robert Eastman	1821	
Margaret (Peggy) Eastman		
Robert George	1854	Heart's Content
1st Wife		
Sarah George (nee Thorne)		
2nd Wife		
Martha George (nee Phillips)	1859 or 1863	Scilly Cove
John Halliday	1857	Job's Cove
Rachel J. Halliday (nee Dodge)	1872	Little Heart's Ease
Thomas Halliday		
Elizabeth Halliday (nee Cooper)		Twillingate
George Harrington	1810	County Clare, Ireland
Benjamin H. Jones		United States?
Emma Jones		
Thomas Rose	1855	
Christina Rose	1853	
Joshua Tavernor	1846	
1st Wife		
Leah Tavernor (nee)	1842	
2nd Wife		
Rosanna Tavernor (nee Ivany)		

NAME	DATE OF BIRTH	PLACE OF BIRTH
William Tavernor (senior)	1842	Trinity
Mary Ann Tavernor (nee Good)	1842	Trinity
William Tavernor (junior)		

Source: This Table was developed from vital statistics from the Methodist at Britannia Cove, Hant's Harbour and Heart's Content; from the vital statistics from the Church of England at Random Mission, Trinity and Trinity East; 19th century lists of voters as recorded in *White's Papers* at Trinity; *Geographical Index to Land Grants 1830-1930*; *McAlpine's Newfoundland Directory 1894 to 1897*; *McAlpine's Newfoundland Directory for 1898*; tombstones on Random Island; and interviews with Islanders.

the 1930s/40s. Like the Thornes in this area, James Leonard's family is, in different records, listed as residing in Middle Lance Cove and Petley at the same time.

Petley and Aspen Cove

As pointed out in chapter 2 on the origin of place names on Random Island, Petley was originally referred to as Lance Cove; later it became known as Upper Lance Cove and finally was named Petley. Like the patterns of settling other harbours and coves on Random Island, it is likely that there were winter people in the Petley/Aspen Cove area for several years before it was permanently settled around 1850. The name of Whettington Point just to the south of Petley suggests the British presence in this area, perhaps as earlier as the 17th century. The chronological order of permanent settlers, as revealed by church records and other written documents, in Petley and Aspen Cove is as follows:

1840/59 - Bugden, Laite and Walters
1860s - Bailey and Harris
1870s - Thorne
1880s - Halliday and Sceviour
1890s - Carberry, Gardiner, Janes and Parrott.

1840/59 - Bugden, Laite and Walters

The first families to settle permanently in Petley were Bugdens, Laites (sometimes spelt "Late" and "Leate" in early records), and Walters. Those pioneering families were from Trinity and its vicinity, and they visited Petley and surrounding area to avail themselves of the woods before they decided to make it their home. Indications are that John Laite and his wife, Priscilla, made up the first of the three families to settle the Petley/Aspen Cove area. They had at least three sons (Charles, George and Uriah) and one daughter (Mary). One record shows that George was born in Lance

Charles Laite, son of the first Laites to settle in Petley. The Laites in Petley developed long associations with the sea. (Photo courtesy of Delilah and William Walters)

Mary Laite (nee Bugden), daughter of the first Bugden family at Petley, was born in 1849. She married Charles Laite. (Photo courtesy of Delilah and William Walters)

Cove in 1846, thus suggesting that John and Priscilla Laite started the Laite family in this cove during early or mid 1840s. John received a grant for land in this area in 1855. Mary Ann, a daughter of John and Priscilla was born in Lance Cove in 1858. Church of England records show the following people witnessed the marriage of George Laite of Lance Cove to Dinah Guy of Trinity in 1866: Abraham Bailey, William Collins, Catherine Guy, Thomas Harris, Mary Laite, William Laite, Sarah Laite and William McCarthy. It is very likely that some of those people were living in Petley at that time while others were visitors.

Deborah (nee Cooper) and her husband Uriah Laite. Deborah, born in Grates Cove, came to Bluff Head Cove on Random Island with her family. Uriah's parents were pioneers in Petley before he was born in 1854. (Photo courtesy of Berkley and Minnie Laite)

Arriana Laite (nee Long), wife of Urais, with their children Joseph and James. (Photo courtesy of Edith and John Walters)

It is believed that the Walters of Petley originally came from Devon, England, to settle in Newfoundland during the 18th century. They were among the early settlers to Trinity Bay. Church records for Trinity show one William Walters, a fisherman, residing in Trinity in 1757. The first Walters to settle on Random Island was a James Walters who apparently settled in Aspen Cove around 1850. Three of his sons (Charles, George and Robert) also settled in Aspen Cove, while a fourth son, William, took up residence in Petley. According to church records, a daughter, whom they named Mary Ann, was born to William and Catherine Walters of Lance Cove in 1858. There are five Walters (Charles, Elson, George, Robert and William) listed in McAlpine's Newfoundland directory as fishermen of Aspen Cove in 1898, and two Walters (James and William) listed as fisher-

Robert Walters, a son of Charles Walters , was a fisherman and lumberman in Aspen Cove. (Photo courtesy of William and Delilah Walters)

Japheth Walters. A grandson of the first Walters to settle in Aspen Cove, Japheth built the schooner *E. F. Walters* in 1928 at Petley for fishing and coasting. (Photo courtesy of Effie Clench)

Mary Ann Laite (nee Walters), daughter of Charles and Hannah Walters. (Photo courtesy of Delilah and William Walters)

men in Upper Lance Cove at that time.

Matthews (1971) traced the origin of Bugdens in Newfoundland to Dorset and Hamsphire in England. There were Bugdens in Trinity Bay in the late 18th century. Church records show a Sarah Bugden in Trinity in 1772, a William Bugden of the same place in 1784, and a John Bugden of English Harbour in 1799. The first record of a Bugden on Random Island is of a Joseph Bugden of Rider's Harbour in 1814. The original Bugdens in Petley belonged to the one primary family, namely, James Bugden and Elizabeth (nee Jestigan) Bugden. James and Elizabeth were married at Trinity in 1843 and they had eight sons (Arthur, Benjamin, Heber, James, Jesse, John, Walter and William) and one daughter (Mary). Some of their children were born in Trinity, while others were born in Petley after the family had settled there in the 1850s. Records show that one of their sons, James, was born in Trinity in 1857, while another son, Heber, was born in Lance Cove in 1858, and a third son, Benjamin, was born in Upper Lance Cove in 1865. At one time, a James Bugden appears in written records as residing in Middle Lance Cove. But as noted above, the Bugdens in Middle Lance Cove were descendants of a William Bugden who was earlier reported as residing in Upper Lance Cove.

Frank Bugden, born in Petley in 1879 married Mary Ann Coish of Britannia Cove. (Photo courtesy of Earl and Alice George

Arthur Bugden. One of the eight sons of James and Elizabeth (nee Jestigan) Bugden to settle in Petley. Along with some of his brothers, he had a water-driven sawmill in the Petley area. (Photo courtesy of George Bugden)

Sarah Bugden (nee Blundell/Smith of Hickman's Harbour and Aspey Brook), her husband, James Bugden, Elfredia Smith (nee Duffett of Britannia Cove) and her husband, Edward Smith. Edward was son of Sarah and Stephen Smith of Aspey Brook. (Photo courtesy of Effie Clench)

1860s - Bailey and Harris

According to church records, James and Emily Bailey started the Bailey family in Petley. They settled in Upper Lance Cove from the Trinity area during the late 1860s. One of their sons, John, was born in Trinity in 1861, and they had a daughter, Caroline, born in Upper Lance Cove in 1872. Three of their sons (George, John and Mark) settled in Petley, in this way creating the Bailey families who lived in this community through the years. As with the Baileys who lived on other parts of Random Island, that is at Rider's Harbour and Deer Harbour, those in Upper Lance Cove were sometimes recorded as "Baily", "Bayley" and "Bayly".

The family name of Harris appeared in Upper Lance Cove during the 1860s. Methodist records show that Thomas and Sarah Harris had a daughter baptized in Britannia Cove in 1869. Lovell's 1871 directory includes a Thomas Harris as a quarrymen of Upper Lance Cove. Both of these records are very likely referring to the same Thomas Harris. McAlpine's directory shows a William H. Harris as a fisherman of Upper Lance Cove in 1894. As far as can be ascertained the Harris family came to Petley from Trinity. According to Lovell, there were 40 people living in Upper Lance Cove in 1871. The following men were listed as residents of this community at that time: William Bailey, James Bugden, William Bugden, Thomas Harris, George Late, John Late, and William Walters. All but one, Thomas Harris, were fishermen.

1870s - Thorne

Church records suggest that James and Louisa Thorne, along with Richard Thorne and his wife, settled in Upper Lance Cove during the

1870s. Other records suggest these Thornes resided in Middle Lance Cove. They actually resided on the point of land between Middle Lance Cove and Upper Lance Cove which is named Whettington's Point on the land grant map of the area. As far as can be ascertained, Thorne was the only family name added to those in Petley during the 1870s.

1880s - Halliday and Sceviour

Apparently, a family of Hallidays resided at Aspen Cove during the 1880s. Methodist Church records show that a Thomas Halliday of Aspen Cove married an Elizabeth Cooper of Twillingate in 1886. According to *McAlpine's Newfoundland Directory*, Thomas H. Halliday and John Halliday were both fishermen of Aspen Cove in 1898. The Hallidays in Aspen Cove were of the same family of Hallidays that settled in Middle Lance Cove, the origin of which is described above.

The present surname of Sceviour, had various spelling in written records over the years, including "Civier", "Scevior", "Seviour", "Sevier" and "Siver". One of the earliest family names recorded for Random Island is that of Seivir. As outlined in chapter 4, there were Seviers residing at Rider's Harbour in the late 18th century. For a number of years after Rider's Harbour was abandoned there were no Seviers on the island. Their next appearance here was at Upper Lance Cove in the 1880s where Isaac and Mary Sevir had several children baptized during that decade. Isaac and Mary Sevir had previously lived in British Harbour before settling in Petley.

1890s - Carberry, Gardiner, Janes and Parrott

During the 1890s, the family names of Gardiner (sometimes spelt "Gardner") and Parrott were added to those already in Upper Lance Cove, while the Carberry and Janes families joined the Walters in Aspen Cove during that time. Edward T. Gardiner of British Harbour became a school teacher in Upper Lance Cove around 1890. Church of England records show that Edward and his wife, Mary, had several children and the Gardiner name was in this community for many years. Samuel Parrott of Bonaventure married Elizabeth Ann Laite of Upper Lance Cove in 1896 and they started the Parrott family in Petley. In 1897, William John Carberry of Burgoynes Cove married Rhoda Walters, a daughter of Robert Walters of Aspen Cove. They settled in the bride's home community and lived there for a while before moving to the United States. While some of the Carberrys moved back to Petley and lived there until they died, others did not return to this community. Ambrose Janes of Broad Cove, Conception Bay, married a Mary Ann Clarke of Kerley's Harbour in 1893 and they settled in Aspen Cove.

TABLE 5-7

DATE AND PLACE OF BIRTH OF SOME OF THE ADULTS IN PETLEY AND ASPEN COVE PRIOR TO 1900

NAME	DATE OF BIRTH	PLACE OF BIRTH
Caroline Bailey	1872	Upper Lance Cove
Eliza Bailey		Upper Lance Cove
Emma Bailey		Upper Lance Cove
George Bailey	1877	Trinity
1st Wife		
Victoria Bailey (nee Laite)	1878	Upper Lance Cove
2nd Wife		
Patience Bailey (nee Steele)	1885	Burgoynes Cove
Hannah Bailey		Upper Lance Cove
James Bailey	1857	
Emily Bailey		
John Bailey	1861	Trinity
Amelia Bailey (nee Walters)	1876	Aspen Cove
Lizzie Bailey		Upper Lance Cove
Mark Bailey (senior)		
Arthur Bugden	1852	
1st Wife		
Amelia Bugden (nee Parrott)	1851	Bonaventure
2nd Wife		
Susannah Bugden (nee Baker)	1873	Snook's Harbour
Benjamin Bugden	1865	Upper Lance Cove
Catherine Jane Bugden (nee Vardy)	1872	Hickman's Harbour
Frank Bugden	1879	Upper Lance Cove
Mary Ann Bugden (nee Coish)	1874	Britannia Cove

NAME	DATE OF BIRTH	PLACE OF BIRTH
Heber Bugden	1858	Lance Cove
Emily Bugden	1862	Pease Cove
(nee Evelly)		
James Bugden	1819	Trinity
Elizabeth Bugden	1820s	Trinity
(nee Jestigan)		
James Bugden	1857	Trinity
1st Wife		
Elizabeth Bugden		Trouty
(nee Clifford)	1858?	
2nd Wife		
Sarah Bugden		Foster's Point
(nee Reid)		
3rd Wife		
Sarah Bugden	1877	Hickman's Harbour
(nee Blundell/Smith)		
James Bugden	188l	Snook's Brook
Mary Grace Bugden	1883	Middle Lance Cove
(nee Burridge)		
James Bugden	1878	Upper Lance Cove
Susan Maud Bugden	1880	Middle Lance Cove
(nee Carberry)		
Jesse Bugden	1854	
Charity Bugden	1858	Grates Cove
(nee Cooper)		
John Bugden	1841?	Trinity
Mary Garland Bugden	1842	Trinity
(nee Piercey)		
Joseph Bugden	1832	
Walter Bugden	1868	Lance Cove
Hannah Jane Bugden	1866	Lance Cove
(nee Laite)		
William Bugden	1845	Lance Cove
1st Wife		
Amelia Bugden		English Harbour
(nee Forde)		
2nd Wife		
Druscilla Bugden	1871	Middle Lance Cove
(nee Tavernor)		

NAME	DATE OF BIRTH	PLACE OF BIRTH
William Bugden		Middle Lance Cove
Maud Bugden		
William J. Carberry	1877	Burgoynes Cove
Rhoda Carberry (nee Walters)	1877	Aspen Cove
Edward Gardiner		British Harbour
Mary Gardiner		
Thomas Halliday		Job's Cove
Elizabeth Halliday (nee Cooper)		Twillingate
Thomas Harris		
Sarah Harris (nee Laite)		
William Harris		
Ambrose Janes	1873	Broad Cove
Mary Ann Janes (nee Clarke)	1872	Kerley's Harbour
Absalom John Laite	1878	Upper Lance Cove
Charlotte Laite (nee Davis)	1883	Pinchard's Island
Albert Laite		Upper Lance Cove
Laura Laite		
Aquila Laite	1882	Lance Cove
Mary Ann Laite (nee Walters)	1884	Aspen Cove
Charles Laite	1850 (circa)	Lance Cove?
Mary Laite (nee Bugden)	1849	Trinity?
Charles Laite	1884	Upper Lance Cove
Sarah Laite (nee Stone)	1891	White Rock
Willis Laite	1891?	Upper Lance Cove
Sarah Laite (nee Ivany)	1895?	Britannia Cove
George Laite	1846	Lance Cove?
1st Wife		
Dinah Laite (nee Guy)		Trinity

NAME	DATE OF BIRTH	PLACE OF BIRTH
2nd Wife Amelia Laite (nee Pike)	1856	Bay de Verde
John Laite *1st Wife* Priscilla Laite (nee) *2nd Wife* Tryphenia Laite (nee Ivany)	1825 1856	Trinity Otter Cove
John Laite *1st Wife* Selina Laite (nee Hart) *2nd Wife* Agnes Laite (nee Smith)		 Lady Cove Aspey Brook
Joseph Laite Martha Laite (nee Piercey)		
Margaret Laite		
Noah John Laite		
Reuben Laite Emily Jane Laite (nee Cooper)		Upper Lance Cove Bluff Head Cove
Samuel Laite Elizabeth Laite		
Uriah Laite Deborah Laite (nee Cooper)	1854 1857	Upper Lance Cove Grates Cove
Urias Laite Arriana Laite (nee Long)	1872 1873	 Salmon Cove
William Thomas Laite	1875	Upper Lance Cove
Samuel Parrott *1st Wife* Elizabeth Ann Parrott (nee Laite)	1868 1877	Bonaventure Upper Lance Cove

NAME	DATE OF BIRTH	PLACE OF BIRTH
2nd Wife		
Mary Belle Parrott		Upper Lance Cove
(nee Thorne)		
Isaac Sceviour		
1st Wife		
??		
Mary Sceviour		
2nd Wife		
Betsy Sceviour		Robinson's Bight
(nee Pelley)		
Noah John Sceviour	1873	British Harbour
1st Wife		
Lucy Sceviour		Upper Lance Cove
(nee Laite)		
2nd Wife		
Joanna Sceviour		Smith Sound
(nee Loupas)		
James Thorne		
Louisa Hannah Thorne		
Mary Thorne	1858	
Richard Thorne		
1st Wife		
??		
2nd Wife		
Rebecca Thorne		Lady Cove
(nee Hart)		
William Thorne		
Catherine Walters	1874	Upper Lance Cove
Charles Walters	1841	Aspen Cove?
1st Wife		
Hannah Walters		Western Bay
(nee Davis)		
2nd Wife		
Charlotte Maria Walters	1848	
(nee Bailey/Miller)		
Edgar Walters	1881	Aspen Cove
Mary Walters	1886	Trinity
(nee Bailey)		

NAME	DATE OF BIRTH	PLACE OF BIRTH
Elson Walters		Aspen Cove
Laura Walters (nee Thorne)		Upper Lance Cove
George Walters	1838	Trinity
Matilda Walters	1830	Conception Bay?
James Walters (Senior)		Trinity
James Walters (Junior)	1873	Aspen Cove
Effie Walters (nee Bugden)		Upper Lance Cove
Japheth Walters	1882	Upper Lance Cove
Alice B. Walters (nee Bugden)	1895	Upper Lance Cove
Jasper Walters	1878	Aspen Cove
Joannah Walters	1801	
Joseph Walters		Upper Lance Cove
Eliza Walters (nee Bugden)		Upper Lance Cove
Mary Ann Walters	1866	Aspen Cove
Robert Walters		
Christina Walters (nee Langer)	1888	Thoroughfare
Robert Walters		Aspen Cove
Ruth Walters (nee Pelley)		Broad Cove, C. Bay
Seth Walters		
William Walters		
1st Wife		
Catherine Walters (nee)		
2nd Wife		
Pamelia Walters (nee Tavernor)		Middle Lance Cove?

Source: This Table was developed from vital statistics from the Church of England at Random, Trinity and Trinity East; vital statistics from the Methodists Church at Britannia Cove; 19th century lists of voters as recorded in *White's Papers* at Trinity; *Geographical Index of Land Grants 1830-1930*; *Lovell's Province of Newfoundland Directory for 1871*; *McAlpine's Newfoundland Directory 1894 to 1897*; *McAlpine's Newfoundland Directory for 1898*; nominal censuses for Petley in 1935 and 1945; tombstones in Petley and Britannia Cove; and interviews with Random Islanders.

This is the same Ambrose and Mary Janes who resided in Aspey Brook in the 1890s. Ambrose was a brother of the John Janes who started the Janes family in Lower Lance Cove.

Including people born 1880 and earlier, Table 5-7 is a list of adults in Petley and Aspen Cove prior to 1900. It is seen that the pioneers to these two places came mainly from the Trinity area, with a couple of families coming from the north side of Conception Bay. A review of the date and place of birth of adults in Petley and Aspen Cove prior to 1900 suggests that many of them were born elsewhere. When known, maiden names of wives in Petley prior to 1900 are also included in Table 5-7.

1900/45 - Anderson, Bowring, Brookings, Langer and Smith

Among the families settling in Petley after 1900 were those named Anderson, Bowring, Brookings, Langer and Smith. To elaborate, John and Genevia Anderson and their children moved to Petley from Middle Lance Cove in the 1930s. George Langer of Thoroughfare, and his wife, Beatrice, who was from Winterton, were the original Langer family in Petley in that they settled there around 1930. Sarah Smith (nee Blundell of Hickman's Harbour), wife of Stephen Smith of Aspey Brook, married James Bugden of Petley after Stephen died in 1921. Her sons by Stephen (Albert, Edward, Ingham and William) accompanied her to Petley. Ingham returned to Aspey Brook, and Edward and William settled in Petley, creating the Smith families in this settlement. Nominal census of 1945 lists Cecil and Eloise Bowring as residing in Petley. The Brookings family settled in Petley from Old Perlican in 1946. It consisted of Elias and Clara Belle Brookings, their sons John (with his wife Muriel) and Warren.

Snook's Harbour

Based on the information available, it is difficult to identify the exact locations where early people settled in the Snook's Harbour area. In addition to the harbour itself, there were at least two other relatively large settlements in this area during the 19th century. They were at Souley's Brook and Wake's Brook and there seems to have been permanent settlers in each of these places before Snook's Harbour itself was permanently settled. In written documents, Souley's Brook and Wake's Brook were sometimes considered as separate entities while at other times they were considered part of the community of Snook's Harbour. There were Bakers living at Wake's Brook and both Bakers and Ryans at Souley's Brook. From the 1870s until the 1920s, there were people living at different locations along the Smith Sound shoreline from Snook's Harbour to Grindstone Head. Focusing specifically on the Snook's Harbour, Souley's and Wake's areas, the present research revealed the following chronological order of pioneering families settling in this part of Random Island:

1870s - Baker
1880s - Belbin, Cooper, Hefford, Jacobs, Loder and Ryan
1890s - Janes, Paul, Seaward, Smith and Strong.

1870s - Baker

Baker was among one of the most common family names of early settlers in different parts of Newfoundland. As early as 1758 there was a John Baker residing in Trinity. It seems as if Bakers were among the first permanent settlers to the Snook's Harbour area. As far as can be ascertained, two brothers named James and John Baker settled at Souley's Brook during the early 1870s. Church of England records of 1896 list James Baker, one of the original Bakers to this area, as a ferryman. James and his wife, Joanna, had at least three sons (James, John and William). The previous place of residence of the Bakers who settled in Souley's Brook has not been identified with certainty from written records nor has it been gleaned from oral history. However, it is noted that Church of England records in Trinity show that James and Joanna Baker of Rider's Harbour, which was the earliest settlement on Random Island, had a son named John who was baptized at Rider's Harbour in 1864. This leads to the speculation that the James and Joanna Baker, who were among the original permanent settlers to Souley's Brook, lived at Rider's Harbour prior to that time. Also, as seen from the 1935 census, John's brother, James, was born at Heart's Ease, hence the Baker connection with these two early settlements in Trinity Bay.

William Cooper and his wife Emily (nee Smith). (Photo courtesy of Hazel Brown)

1880s - Belbin, Cooper, Hefford, Jacobs, Loder and Ryan

Different records show a William Belbin and a William Bellman in Snook's Harbour during the 1880s. These names refer to the same per-

Jessie Hefford (nee Cooper), wife of Peter Hefford, and their children, Lewis and Blanche, around 1910. (Photo courtesy of Gladys Hefford)

son, who was born in New Chelsea around 1860 and married Elizabeth Jacobs. Church records show that Jacobs were among the pioneers in the Snook's Harbour area. Esau and Emma Jacobs had a son baptized at Souley's Brook in 1884. Since Elizabeth Belbin (nee Jacobs) was born in Bay de Verde, it is speculated that the Jacobs came to Snook's Harbour from that Conception Bay community. William Cooper from Elliott's Cove, but was originally of Ireland's Eye, and Edward Cooper from Ireland's Eye settled in Snook's Harbour during the 1880s. William married Emily Smith of Elliott's Cove and they lived in Elliott's Cove before moving to Snook's Harbour. Edward's wife was Mary Ann Toope from Ireland's Eye.

The present surname of Hefford in Snook's Harbour has been spelt in different ways in early written records, including "Hefferan", "Heffers" and "Efford". Elias Hefford of New Perlican and his wife, Maria Ivany of Salmon Cove (later renamed Champneys), were the original Heffords in Snook's Harbour. It seems that Elias settled in the harbour during the late 1880s or early 1890s. He came to Snook's Harbour to sail with the Loders who operated fishing schooners out of

Peter Hefford, a longtime sailor and marine engineer. (Photo courtesy of Gladys Hefford)

Snook's Harbour at that time. Peter, a son of Elias and Maria Hefford, and their grandson, Lewis, kept the family name going in this community.

While there were permanent settlers in the general area of Snook's Harbour before the Loders moved to this part of Random Island, it is believed that the first family to take up permanent residence in the harbour itself was that of John and Jane (Mary) Ann Loder. John was a son of Silas Loder, a planter at Ireland's Eye in the mid 19th century. Another of Silas' sons, James, settled in Ireland's Eye. As noted earlier in this book, James' son, Silas, settled in Thoroughfare in 1914. John Loder's wife was Jane Ann Smith of Elliott's Cove, but formerly of Hant's Harbour. After their marriage they lived in Ireland's Eye for a short time before settling in Snook's Harbour around 1881.

Silas Loder, planter of Ireland's Eye, was the patriarch of the Snook's Harbour Loders and of the Thoroughfare Loders as well. (Photo courtesy of Marion Davis)

The Ryans of Snook's Harbour were descendants of one Roger Ryan, who had settled at Bay de Verde from Ireland some time before 1790. A William Ryan, who was born at Bay de Verde in 1877 and was in all likelihood a great-grandson of this Roger Ryan, married a Druscilla Hiscock of Lee Bight (later renamed Adeytown). William and Druscilla settled in Souley's Brook around 1900. However, William's father, who was also a William Ryan, had

George Ryan and his father William. As a boy, in the 1890s,William accompanied his father, who was also named William, to Souley's Brook. (Photo courtesy of Laverna Cook and Shirley Smith)

visited and, perhaps settled in the Snook's Harbour during the 1880s. Among the list of fishermen in Snook's Harbour in the 1890s was a William Ryan (senior) and a William Ryan (junior).

William Baker (left) and William Ryan. William Baker was a grandson of the pioneering Bakers (James and Joanna) to Wake's Brook, while William Ryan had the same relationship to the Ryans who pioneered Souley's Brook. In addition to working at the brickyard, both were logging/lumbering families. (Photo courtesy of Laverna Cook and Shirley Smith)

1890s - Janes, Paul, Seaward, Smith and Strong

The 1890s saw another five surnames in the Snook's Harbour area: Janes, Paul, Seaward, Smith and Strong. However, three of these names represent transients with only the Smith and Paul families becoming permanent settlers in the place. According to Church of

England records, William and Judiah Seaward had a son baptized in Snook's Harbour in 1890, but other than this information no other reference has been found to this family in Snook's Harbour. Similarly, these records show that during that time Ambrose and Mary Anne Jeans [sic] had a son baptized in Snook's Harbour. Even though there were both Jeans and Janes in Smith Sound during the 19th century, it is suspected that this reference to "Jeans" should have been "Janes". It is likely that it refers to the same Ambrose and Mary Janes who lived in Aspen Cove in the 1890s. There is also a reference to a family by the name of Strong residing in the Snook's Harbour area during the 1890s. However, no information has been gathered as to the identity of this family, where they came from, or how long they stayed in this place. John P. Smith from Bishop's Cove, Conception Bay, moved to Wake's Brook during the 1890s. His mother, Grace (nee Peddle?), and perhaps his father accompanied him to Wake's Brook. John P. Smith of Wake's Brook was not related to the Smiths who founded Elliott's Cove and Aspey Brook. He did, however, marry into this Smith family. His wife was a Mary Ann Smith from Aspey Brook. Indications are that a William Paul settled in Wake's Brook during the 1890s. It is speculated that he came to Snook's Harbour from Ireland's Eye Island where Pauls were among the planters of the early 19th century. His wife, Mary (nee Sugg), was born at Twillingate.

Silas Smith, son of John Smith of Bishop's Cove and his wife Mary (nee Smith), of Elliott's Cove. (Photo courtesy of Baxter, Inez and Stanley Baker)

McAlpine's Newfoundland Directory for 1898 lists the following fishermen in Snook's Harbour for that time: James Baker (senior), James Baker (junior), John Baker, William Belbin, William Cooper, Elias Heffers, Esau Jacobs, John Jacobs, Urias Jacobs, John Loder, William Loder, William Paul, William Ryan (senior), William Ryan (junior), Gideon Smith, Tobias Smith and John Smith. To comment on this list, one notes the spelling of "Heffers" instead of "Hefford". Also, while Gideon Smith may have been fishing out of Snook's Harbour at the time, his home was Elliott's Cove. It is also speculated that Tobias Smith was from Elliott's Cove or Aspey Brook rather than Snook's Harbour.

Dates and places of birth of some of the pioneers of Snook's Harbour as well as the maiden names of wives in this community prior to 1900 are given in Table 5-8. Despite the relatively small population of

TABLE 5-8

DATE AND PLACE OF BIRTH OF SOME OF THE ADULTS IN SNOOK'S HARBOUR PRIOR TO 1900

NAME	DATE OF BIRTH	PLACE OF BIRTH
James Baker Joanna Baker		
James Baker Honour Baker		
James Baker Jessie Baker (nee Hiscock)	1868 1870	Heart's Ease Salmon Cove, T.Bay
John Baker Mary Ann Baker (nee Jacobs)	1862 or 1868 1876	Rider's Harbour? Snook's Harbour?
William Baker Alice Maud Baker (nee Smith)	1878 1881	Snook's Harbour Wake's Brook
William Belbin Elizabeth Belbin (nee Jacobs)	1857 or 1860 1862	New Chelsea Bay de Verde
Edward Cooper Mary Ann Cooper (nee Toope)	1858 1866	Ireland's Eye Ireland's Eye
William Cooper Emily Cooper (nee Smith)	1857 1861	Ireland's Eye Hant's Harbour
Elias Hefford Maria Hefford (nee Ivany)	1856	New Perlican Champneys
John Hefford		Snook's Harbour
Peter Hefford Jesse Hefford (nee Cooper)	 1887	Snook's Harbour Elliott's Cove
Esau Jacobs Emma Jacobs		Bay de Verde?

NAME	DATE OF BIRTH	PLACE OF BIRTH
John Jacobs		
Urias Jacobs	1873	
Emily Jacobs (nee Laite)	1878	Lance Cove
Ambrose Janes	1873	Broad Cove, C. Bay?
Mary Anne Janes (nee Clarke)	1872	Kerley's Harbour?
Elkanah Loder	1878	Ireland's Eye
John Loder	1850	Ireland's Eye
Mary (Jane) Ann Loder (nee Smith)	1851	Scilly Cove
Thomas Loder	1879	Ireland's Eye
Leah Loder (nee Efford)	1891	Port de Grave
William J. Loder	1874	Ireland's Eye
Ella R. H. Loder (nee Reid)	1878	Foster's Point
John Mills	1884	Thoroughfare
Deborah Mills (nee Cooper)	1884	Elliott's Cove
William Paul	1861	
Mary Paul (nee Sugg/Clark)	1851	Twillingate
Robert Randell		Port Rexton
Lilly May Randell (nee Loder)		Snook's Harbour
Mary Ryan	1810	
William Ryan (junior)	1877	Bay de Verde
Druscilla Ryan (nee Hiscock)		Lee Bight
William Ryan (senior)		Bay de Verde
Edward Seaward	1809	
William Seaward		
Judiah Seaward		
Grace Smith (nee Peddle?		

NAME	DATE OF BIRTH	PLACE OF BIRTH
John P. Smith		Bishop's Cove
Mary Ann Smith (nee Smith)		Aspey Brook

Source: This Table was developed from vital statistics from the Methodist Church at Britannia Cove, Foster's Point, Random North and Shoal Harbour; vital statistics from the Church of England at Random Mission, Trinity and Trinity East; *Geographical Index to Land Grants 1830-1930*; *McAlpine's Newfoundland Directory 1894 to 1897*; *McAlpine's Newfoundland Directory for 1898*; nominal censuses for Snook's Harbour in 1935 and 1945; tombstones in Snook's Harbour, Britannia and Elliott's Cove; and interviews with Random Islanders.

Snook's Harbour, its early settlers came from a comparatively large number of places, including Bay de Verde, Bishop's Cove Champneys, Elliott's Cove, Hant's Harbour, Heart's Ease, Ireland's Eye, Lance Cove, Lee Bight, New Chelsea, New Perlican, Port de Grave, Rider's Harbour, Salmon Cove, Scilly Cove and Twillingate.

1900/45 - Bugden, Carberry, Mills, Randell and Whelan

The only family names in the 1935 census for Snook's Harbour were of families there prior to 1900. However, church records suggest that Robert Randell from Port Rexton married a Loder from Snook's Harbour and they lived in this harbour for a short time prior to 1920. John Mills from Thoroughfare married a Deborah Cooper of Snook's Harbour where the couple lived until John's death in 1907. It is also said that Richard Carberry and his wife, Mary Ann (nee Belbin), lived in this settlement during the early part of the 20th century. During the late 1930s the family name of Whelan was introduced into Snook's Harbour when Solomon Whelan of Port Blandford married Martha Ryan of Snook's Harbour. Bugdens, descendants of the Bugdens in Petley, appear in the 1945 census of Snook's Harbour. Shortly after that, the surname of Bailey appears among the residents of this place. These Baileys were descendants of the Bailey family of Petley.

Weybridge

As noted in an earlier chapter of this book, what is now Weybridge includes the places previously named Bald Nap and Foster's Point. As in other places on Random Island, there were winter people in the Foster's Point/Bald Nap area before it was permanently settled in the 1860s. Indeed, it is suspected that Foster's Point bears the name of one of those winter people. The chronological order of pioneering families settling permanently in this area during the 19th century is as follows:

1860s - Adey, Gulliford and Reid
1870s - Brown, Goobie, King, Miller and Pond
1880s - Critch, Harnum, Leawood and Stanley
1890s - Bowden and George.

1860s - Adey, Gulliford and Reid

While Adeys, Gullifords and Reids probably made visits to the Bald Nap/Foster's Point area during the 1850s, they did not settle the area until the 1860s. Written records suggest that the Reids came first, although it is generally believed that all three families came at about the same time. It is also noted that there were more Reids than people of any other name in this area at that time. A voters list for Trinity Bay suggests that in 1870 there were only four voters in Foster's Point and none in Bald Nap. Those at Foster's Point were four Reids (sometimes spelt "Reed"):

Charles, George, Richard and James. By 1873, George and James were dropped from the list and Robert Reid was added to it. Lovell's 1871 directory for Newfoundland includes George Reid, James Reid and Richard Reid as fishermen in Random Sound. It is likely that they were at Foster's Point at that time. Also residing at Foster's during those early days was a William Reid, who was born in 1805 and accompanied his sons, Charles and George, to Foster's from Hant's Harbour. According to Methodist Church records at Hant's Harbour, Robert, son of George and Martha Reid, was born at Foster's Point in 1869. In that year, Sarah, daughter of Charles and Martha Reid, was born at Foster's Point.

Front row, William Adey and his wife Elizabeth (nee Gulliford). Back row their daughters Sarah (left), who married Kesson Reid, and Mary Jane, who married Gilbert Churchill. William Adey was a longtime sawmill operator at Foster's Point. (Photo courtesy of Charles and Eleanor Reid)

While there were no Adeys on the voters list for Foster's Point during the 1870s, from church records it is known that there was a Mary Adey in this place in 1877. Records also show one Isaac Adey at Foster's Point and another, perhaps the same Isaac Adey, at Lee Bight in 1878. Unlike the Adeys in Hickman's Harbour, who changed their name to"Eddy", those in Foster's Point and Lee Bight (later renamed Adeytown) remained as Adey over the years. Lovell's Newfoundland directory for 1871 does not make reference to any Adeys in this area at that time. However, this directory has a Henry Eddy residing in Random

Ralph Reid in front of his Cooper-shop around 1930.
(Photo courtesy of Ern and Marina Reid)

Sound. Despite the fact that there was no Adey listed for Foster's Point in Lovell's 1871 directory, other documents suggest that the Adeys settled in Foster's Point during the 1860s. *The Courier,* a Harbour Grace newspaper during the 1800s, reported that a Reuben Eddie [sic] drowned while travelling from Shoal Harbour to Random Island on New Years Day 1862. It is generally believed that the Reuben Eddie referred to here had his home on Random Island at the time of this accident. The story is told that his wife, Mary, and her children, who included Richard, William and Sarah, were at Foster's Point anxiously awaiting the arrival of her husband and their father when they received the news of his drowning. Apparently, Reuben and Mary Adey had not lived at Foster's Point for very long before 1862. According to Newfoundland census for 1911, William, a son of Reuben and Mary Adey, was born in Clarenville (likely, Lower Shoal Harbour) in 1855. It also looks as if Mary returned to Hant's Harbour after the death of her husband, because her son Jacob, whom she was pregnant with at the time of her husband's drowning, was born in Hant's Harbour in 1862. Whatever the exact date and circumstance of the arrival of Reuben and Mary Adey at Foster's Point, it is known that the Adeys were well established in this place during the 1880s. The fact that there are no Adeys on the voters lists for this area in the 1870s and that they do not appear as residing in Foster's Point in Newfoundland directories until the 1890s may be explained in two ways. One reason is that women were not allowed to vote during those times, so that Mary Adey's name would not have been on any voters list or in any directory. Another reason is that William, one of the sons of Reuben and Mary Adey, was not old enough to vote until the late 1870s, and their son Jacob was not old enough to vote until well into the 1880s. Their son Richard went to live with another family in Northern Newfoundland when he was just a young boy.

Willis and Martha (nee Reid) Gulliford. They were pioneers of Bald Nap, where the Gullifords established a fishing/lumber business. (Photo courtesy of Ross Gulliford)

William Gulliford and his wife, Elizabeth, from Hant's Harbour, moved to Bald Nap during the late 1860s or early 1870s. William is listed as a resident of Bald Nap in a list of voters in Trinity Bay in the 1870s. According to one unwritten source, three, and perhaps four, Gulliford brothers came to Newfoundland from England during the early 19th century. At least two of these brothers settled in Hant's Harbour and one went to Random Island. However, since written records show that the Gullifords did not settle on Random Island before 1860, it is possible that the William Gulliford who settled on the island was a son of the William Gulliford who resided in Hant's Harbour in 1821. The Newfoundland census of 19ll includes a Willis Gulliford, who was born Foster's Point in 1871, and a George Gulliford, who was born there in 1879. Gulliford was common name in this area at that time for it is noted that eight of the fourteen names listed as contributors to the Methodist Church at Foster's Point in 1877 were Gullifords. They were Elizabeth Gulliford, Hughie Gulliford, R.J. Gulliford, William Gulliford (senior), William Gulliford (junior), and three listed as Mrs. Gulliford.

1870s - Brown, Goobie, King, Miller and Pond

Written records show that in 1870 the surnames of Brown, Goobie, Miller and Pond were added to those already in the Foster's Point/Bald Nap area. As evidenced by a voters list of 1880, there was a John Brown

Elizabeth Pond. Elizabeth, along with her husband Robert, were the first two Ponds to settle at Foster's Point. (Photo courtesy of Leslie and Betty Ivany and Mary Burry)

residing at Foster's Point at that time. Maybe this was the same John Brown that Lovell listed as fisherman of Random Sound in 1871. No other information has been obtained on him to suggest where he came from, if he had a family, or what happened to him.

The first Goobies (sometimes spelt "Gooby") to settle at Foster's Point were John and Sarah of Hant's Harbour. John was most likely a descendant of James Goobie whose name is found in the Hant's Harbour Methodist Church record of 1832. George, Herbert, John and Samuel were listed in McAlpine's directories as fishermen of Foster's Point during the 1890s. However, it is probable that they arrived in the area much earlier than that. It has been suggested that Samuel, Herbert and George were sons of John and Sarah Goobie. According to the 1911 census, Samuel was born at Hant's Harbour in 1865, George was born there in 1870, while Herbert was born at Foster's Point in 1877. From this information, it appears that the Goobies settled at Foster's Point in the early to mid 1870s. There was also a family of Millers at Foster's Point during the late 1870s. William Miller of Bonaventure married a woman from Foster's Point and they settled at the point at that time. One Edward King of St. Jones Within went to Foster's Point as a young boy in 1873 to live with his aunt Martha Reid. He later married and settled in Lady Cove.

The first family of Ponds at Foster's Point resettled there from Fox Harbour Island (later renamed Southport) during the late 1860s or early 1870s. It consisted of Robert and Elizabeth Pond and at least one of their sons, John, who was born at Fox Harbour in 1864. Another of their sons,

Joshua, was born at Foster's Point in 1874. A William Pond is also found on early records for this place. Even though the Ponds were fishermen their move from Fox Harbour to Foster's Point may have been associated with the availability of land for gardening and easy access to a forest. It is obvious that they did not select Foster's Point for any advantage it would have for fishing. There is no harbour at Foster's Point and, in fact, it is exposed to many winds. However, the availability of land and the terrain itself at Foster's were its attractive features.

1880s - Critch, Harnum, Leawood and Stanley

Amos and Christinia Jane Critch settled at Bald Nap during the early 1880s. Amos was born at Hant's Harbour and moved to Hickman's Harbour with his parents and brothers some time in the 1870s. Amos lived at Hickman's Harbour for a few years before settling in Bald Nap. He married Christinia Jane Reid from Upper Shoal Harbour. However, since there were Reids in neighbouring Foster's Point, and since the Reids and Gullifords were related, the Reid connection was perhaps a factor in their settling in Bald Nap. Also, the Gullifords, Reids and Critches lived in Hant's Harbour before they settled in Random Sound.

Senior citizens attending a birthday party at Bald Nap around 1920. Front row (left to right) Christinia, Critch (nee Reid), Lucy Soper (nee Pittman), Elizabeth Miller (nee Reid), George Reid, Aaron Smith and William Adey. Back row (left to right) Emma Adey or Martha Soper?, Sarah Stanley (nee Adey), Christinia Pelley (nee Reid), Jacob Adey, Elizabeth Adey (nee Gulliford) and Jane Ann Smith (nee Reid). (Photo courtesy of Neta Pelley)

Church of England records show a family of Horners [sic] living at Foster's Point during the late 1880s. Elias and Amelia Horner had a son baptized there in 1890. No other information has been found on this family. Given the fact that Seary (1976) does not include this name in his book on *Family Names of the Island of Newfoundland*, it is suspected that "Horner" is probably a misspelling, perhaps for "Harnum". As noted below, a family of Harnums moved from Fox Harbour to Foster's Point in the 1890s.

According to written records, two Leawoods, George and John, settled in Foster's Point in the 1880s. As far as can be ascertained they were stepbrothers and descendants of the John Leawood who spent a year at Brown's Mead in 1846 (see section on Bound's Mead in chapter 6). Writing in *The Methodist Monthly Greeting* in 1926, John Leawood (junior) reported to have remembered visiting friends at Random with his grandfather (John Leawood, senior) in 1869. Some twenty years after returning from Brown's Mead to Hant's Harbour in 1847, the senior John Leawood was apparently accompanied by his grandson John, who was eight years old at the time, as he visited his friends at Random. The grandson, John, was later to settle at Foster's Point where he lived for several years before moving to Britannia Cove around 1902 to work as a customs officer. George Leawood also lived at Foster's before making his home in Britannia Cove. After moving to Britannia Cove, George travelled from there to the United States where he worked for considerable periods of time.

Eli Stanley. Eli and his wife Sarah (nee Adey), were pioneers of Bald Nap prior to 1900. (Photo courtesy of Reuben and Olive March)

McAlpine's directories for Newfoundland in the 1890s list Eli Stanley as a fisherman of Bald Nap. As recorded in the 1911 census, Eli was born in Hant's Harbour in 1856, and his wife, Sarah (nee Adey) was born there in 1857. Church records suggest that they settled at Bald Nap in the 1880s.

1890s - Bowden and George

During the 1890s, two new surnames were added to those already at Foster's Point. One of those was that of Bowden. Apparently, a medical doctor named G.F. Bowden from St. John's, and his family, lived in this community during the 1890s and early part of the 1900s. However, this family name did not continue here. John Noah George, who was born in Heart's Content, and his wife, Elizabeth (nee Pond), who was born at Fox Harbour, made their home at Foster's Point during the 1890s. Some suggest that John Noah George was a relative of Richard George, the first George to settle in Lady Cove in the 1880s and thereby a relative of Robert George, who settled in Middle Lance Cove during that time. The family name of Harnum was also in Foster's Point during the 1890s. John and Arthur Harnum of Fox Harbour moved to Foster's sometime during that decade. They came to Foster's Point during the 1880s or 1890s, because of their relationship to the Ponds who had earlier settled there from Fox Harbour.

The foregoing presentation on the pioneers of Weybridge (Bald Nap and Foster's Point) was developed from several sources. A summary of the information used as part of the data base is outlined in Table 5-9. As suggested by the dates and places of birth of adults in Weybridge prior to 1900, as presented in this table, most of the pioneers (Adeys, Critches, Goobies, Gullifords, Leawoods and Reids) in this place were from Hant's Harbour. There was one family from Bonaventure, one from Fox Harbour, one from Heart's Content and one from St. John's.

1900/45 - Baker, Churchill, Day, Fifield, Rodgers and others

Several family names including Baker, Churchill, Day, Fifield, Gardiner, King, Parsons, Roberts, Rodgers and Sorensen were among the residents at Foster's Point/Bald Nap prior to 1945. More specifically, Richard Baker, who was born at Fox Harbour, and his wife, Deborah, who was born at St. Jones Within, were listed as residents of Foster's Point in the 1921 census. The previous census, in 1911, listed this family as residing at Lady Cove. Simeon Day is recorded in the 1921 census as single and living at Foster's Point. He was originally from Hant's Harbour, but had moved to Foster's Point from Lady Cove where he had migrated with his parents in 1906. According to the 1921 census, John Parsons, a widower, who was born at Harbour Grace, was then living at Foster's Point with his children. Church records show a Charles and Jane Parsons at Foster's Point in 1911. Also from church records, it is seen that a family of Sorrsons (perhaps, Sorenson) lived at Foster's Point in 1902. No other reference to this name has been found in any written records for this area. If the spelling of this family name is "Sorenson", it was

TABLE 5-9

DATE AND PLACE OF BIRTH OF SOME OF THE ADULTS IN WEYBRIDGE PRIOR TO 1900

NAME	DATE OF BIRTH	PLACE OF BIRTH
Jacob Adey	1862	Hant' Harbour
Emma Ann Adey	1867	Hant's Harbour
(nee Gulliford)		
Reuben Adey		Hant's Harbour
Mary Adey	1828	Hant's Harbour?
Reuben Adey	1881	Foster's Point
Mary Adey	1886	Lady Cove
(nee Adey)		
William James Adey	1854	Lower Shoal Harbour?
Elizabeth Adey	1855	Hant's Harbour
(nee Gulliford)		
G. F. Bowden		St. John's
Lizzie Bowden		
Amos Critch	1855	Hant's Harbour
Christinia Jane Critch	1862	Lower Shoal Harbour
(nee Reid)		
Ingham Critch	1884	Bald Nap
John Noah George	1866	Heart's Content
Elizabeth George	1864	Fox Harbour/
(nee Pond)		Butter Cove?
Samuel George		
George Goobie	1870	Hant's Harbour
Mary Goobie	1874	Elliott's Cove
(nee Smith)		
Herbert Goobie	1872	Foster's Point
1st Wife		
Sarah Ann Goobie	1869	English Harbour
(nee Penney)		
2nd Wife		
Isabella Goobie		Lady Cove
(nee March)		
Jane Goobie	1844	Hant's Harbour

NAME	DATE OF BIRTH	PLACE OF BIRTH
John Goobie	1838	Hant's Harbour
Sarah Goobie	1845	Hant's harbour
Samuel Goobie	1863	Hant's Harbour
Mary Goobie (nee Reid)	1867	Hant's Harbour
Arch Gulliford		
George Gulliford	1878	Foster's Point
Anna Gulliford (nee Smith)	1879	Elliott's Cove
Hughie Gulliford		
Pierce Gulliford		
R. J. Gulliford		
William H. Gulliford	1820	Hant's Harbour
Martha Gulliford	1827	Hant's Harbour?
Willis Gulliford	1871	Hant's Harbour
Martha Gulliford (nee Reid)	1872	Hant's Harbour
Arthur Harnum	1877	Fox Harbour
Rachel Harnum (nee Miller)	1877	Foster's Point
John Harnum	1871	Fox Harbour
Sarah S. Harnum	1868	Fox Harbour
Elias Horner		
Amelia Horner		
Edward King	1866	St. Jones Within
George Leawood	1865	Hant's Harbour
1st wife		
Elizabeth Leawood (nee Pond)	1871	Foster's Point
2nd wife		
Harriett Leawood (nee Reid)	1873	Foster's Point
John Leawood	1861	Hant's Harbour
1st wife		
Janet Leawood (nee Reid)	1865	Foster's Point

NAME	DATE OF BIRTH	PLACE OF BIRTH
2nd wife		
Laura Belle Leawood	1875	Elliott's Cove
(nee Smith)		
Thomas Leawood		Hant's Harbour
Abram Miller		
Nora Miller		
William Miller	1850	Bonaventure
Elizabeth Miller	1848	Hant's Harbour
W. Henry Miller	1883	
Sarah Miller	1887	
Ann Pond	1871	
John Pond	1864	Fox Harbour
Asenath Pond	1873	Foster's Point
Joshua Pond	1874	Foster's Point
Mariah Pond	1876	Bonaventure
(nee Miller)		
Robert Pond		Fox Harbour?
Elizabeth Pond	1839	Old Perlican
Robert Pond		
Mary Pond		
Sarah Pond	1815	
Thomas Pond		
Mary Eliza Pond		
William Pond		
Elizabeth Pond		
William John Pond		Fox Harbour
Mary Ann Pond	1873	Foster's Point
(nee Goobie)		
Annie Reid	1868	Foster's Point
Amy Reid		
Archibald Kesson Reid	1881	Foster's Point
1st wife		
Sarah Reid	1887	Foster's Point
(nee Adey)		
2nd wife		
Annie Reid		Old Perlican?
(nee Day)		

NAME	DATE OF BIRTH	PLACE OF BIRTH
Beatrice Reid		
Charles Reid		Hant's Harbour?
Martha Reid	1836	
Elias Reid		
Ellis Reid		Foster's Point
Elizabeth Reid	1870	
Elizabeth A. Reid	1879	
George Reid	1844	Hant's Harbour
1st wife		
Martha Reid	1834 or 1838	
2nd wife		
Emma Reid (nee Fifield)	1856	Trinity
James Reid		
John W. Reid		
Mary Reid	1870	
Ralph Reid	1879	
Richard Reid	1833	Hant's Harbour
Sarah Reid	1854	Scilly Cove
Richard Pelley Reid	1863	
Robert Reid	1870	Foster's Point
Mary Reid (nee Rose)	1873	Herring Neck, Notre Dame Bay
Susannah Reid	1873	Foster's Point
William Reid	1805	
William J. Reid	1879	Foster's Point
Alice Reid (nee Smith)		Elliott's Cove
Eli Stanley	1854	Hant's Harbour
Sarah Stanley (nee Adey)	1857	Hant's Harbour

Source: This Table was developed from vital statistics from the Methodist Church at Britannia Cove, Foster's Point, Hant's Harbour, Heart's Content, Random North and Shoal Harbour; vital statistics from the Church of England at Random; *Geographical Index of Land Grants 1830 to 1930*; *Lovell's Province of Newfoundland Directory for 1871*; *McAlpine's Newfoundland Directory 1894 to 1897*; *McAlpine's Newfoundland Directory for 1898*; nominal censuses for Foster's Point and Bald Nap in 1911, 1921, 1935 and 1945; tombstones at Weybridge and Lady Cove; interviews with Random Islanders.

probably of Swedish or Norwegian descend and obviously a transient family.

Gilbert Churchill, originally of Trinity, married Mary Jane Adey and they settled at Foster's Point during the early part of the 20th century. They, with their two children, were included in the 1921 census and they became long time residents of this place. Mark Fifield, also of Trinity, accompanied his mother, Emma, to Foster's Point where she married into the Reid family around 1906. He married Sarah Green, a school teacher originally from Hant's Harbour, and they settled at Foster's Point to become the only Fifield family to live there. A school teacher named Arthur Herbert Gardiner of British Harbour married Amy Reid of Foster's Point, and they created a Gardiner family which lived in this community for a number of years. The 1911 census lists Arthur and Emma Gardiner and their four children as residents of Foster's Point.

The King family was started at Foster's Point when Edward King from St. Jones Within and Foster's Point, and his wife, Mary, who was born at Long Cove (later renamed Loreburn) settled there around 1900. This family is also recorded in certain documents as residing at Lady Cove. Shortly after the Kings made their home at Foster's Point/Lady Cove, William Rodgers (sometimes spelt "Rogers"), also from St. Jones Within, married Selina Sharpe of Lady Cove and they settled at Foster's Point. Methodist church records suggest that a Wells family resided at Foster's Point in 1918. In that year, Isaac and Bessie Wells had a child, Ira Clouston, baptized in that community.

According to the nominal census of 1945, there was a family of Roberts (Lloyd and his sister, Ena) and a family of Greens (William and C. Bennett) living at Foster's Point. Walter Avery of Southport, his wife, Jane (nee Spurrell) of Butter Cove, and their children made their home at Foster's Point in 1952. The next year George and Maud (nee Stacey) Pitcher and their children settled at Foster's Point. They had earlier lived in St. Jones Without and Gooseberry Cove.

CHAPTER 6

PIONEERS OF OUTLYING PLACES

During the late 19th century and for the first two decades of the 20th century, many of the coves and harbours on Random Island were occupied by sawmills and dwelling houses which were used only in the winter. Such places include Brook Cove (at least three of those) Cock and Hen Cove, Salmon Cove ("Deer Cove"), Halfyard Cove, Hungry Cove, Little Harbour, Long Cove (two of those), Mill Brook (at least three of those), Strong's Tickle and Taylor's Cove. Since those places were not inhabited all year around, they were never considered as settlements in church records, census reports and other written records. However, there were nine places, not including the four earliest settlements of Deer Harbour, Rider's Harbour, Silldown and Thoroughfare, which were identified as settlements in early records and have since been abandoned. Since those nine places did not develop into well established communities on Random Island, they are referred to as outlying places. They were Bar Point, Bluff Head Cove, Bound's Mead, East Random Head, George's Cove, Random Head Harbour, Robinson's Bight, Souley's Brook and Wake's Brook. Since the populations in those outlying were reviewed in an early chapter, the present task is to identify the family names of those who settled in each of them.

Bar Point

According to Newfoundland censuses, Bar Point was a settlement onto itself from 1884 until 1911. Church records show the family names of Blundon, Champion (sometimes spelt "Champney"), Maidment and Pelley at Bar Point in the 1890s. More specifically, the families at Bar Point at that time were James and Elizabeth Blundon, Willis and Alice Jane Champion, Eli and Mary Anna (nee Lambert) Maidment, and

Richard and Mary Maidment. According to *McAlpine's Newfoundland Directory*, the following fishermen resided at the Bar Point in 1898: James Blundon, Willis Champion, Eli Maidment, Olisham Maidment, Richard Maidment, Jethro Pelley and John Pelley. As seen in the land grant index for this area, William Goddard, a medical doctor at Old Perlican, had a grant for land at Bar Point in 1894, but no record has been found of his residing on this point.

Bluff Head Cove

Bluff Head Cove, a small cove to the north of Petley and Aspen Cove, was settled in the 1870s by two families from Grates Cove. A voters list for that time shows John Burridge and Absalom Cooper residing in Bluff Head Cove. According to Methodist Church records, one of Absalom Cooper's sons, Daniel, was born at Bluff Head Cove in 1878. While John Burridge later moved to Middle Lance Cove, Absalom Cooper and his family stayed to become the only permanent settlers in Bluff Head Cove. As noted in chapter 5, there were Coopers, who were originally from Grates Cove, residing at Middle Lance Cove as early as the 1870s. They may have lived at Bluff Head Cove before moving to Middle Lance Cove. During the 1890s there were five Coopers described as fishermen in Bluff Head Cove: Absalom (senior), Absalom (junior), Albert, Charles and William. Absalom (senior) was also classified as a "millman" in Bluff Head Cove at that time.

Table 6-1 contains a summary of the information gathered concerning the Coopers of Bluff Head Cove. This place was abandoned in the early part of the 20th century when the Coopers moved to the United States and Canada.

Bound's Mead

Bound's Mead, sometimes known as Brown's Mead, is located on the western end of Random Island. It is about two miles from the Hefferton Causeway on the Northwest Arm portion of the island. According to John Leawood, writing in *The Methodist Monthly Greeting* in 1926, Brown's Mead was settled in 1846 by three families from Hant's Harbour, those of John Leawood, Aaron Tilley, and Joseph Tilley. The next year, Aaron and Joseph Tilley followed their father, John Tilley, and settled in Lower Shoal Harbour. Shortly thereafter, John Leawood returned to Hant's Harbour where he died in 1872. However, his offspring later returned to Random Island to live at Foster's Point and then Britannia Cove. Methodist Church records at Hant's Harbour include the marriage of John Laywood [sic] and Catherine Pelley in 1828. It is suspected that this is the same John Leawood who accompanied the Tilleys to Brown's Mead in 1846. It is also believed that Catherine was a

TABLE 6-1

THE COOPERS OF BLUFF HEAD COVE

NAME	ADDITIONAL INFORMATION
Absalom Cooper (senior)	Records suggest that Absalom Cooper's wife's name was Mary and she was born in 1831.
Absalom Cooper (junior) Mary Ida Cooper (nee Reid)	Absalom Cooper (junior) was born in Bluff Head Cove in 1873. He married Mary Ida Reid of Foster's Point in 1899.
Albert Cooper Lucy Cooper (nee Smith)	Albert Cooper of Bluff Head Cove married Lucy Smith of Aspey Brook in 1897.
Charles Cooper Elizabeth Cooper (nee Reid)	Charles Cooper of Bluff Head Cove married Elizabeth Reid of Foster's Point in 1897.
Charles Cooper Edith Cooper (nee Reid)	Charles and Edith Cooper had a child born in Bluff Head Cove in 1901.
Daniel S. Cooper Rachel Cooper	Daniel Cooper was born at Bluff Head Cove in 1878.
Thomas Cooper Mathilda Cooper	Thomas and Mathilda Cooper had a child born in Bluff Head Cove in 1898.
William George Cooper Sarah Jane Cooper	William and Sarah Cooper had several children born in Bluff Head Cove between 1888 and 1900.

Source: This Table was developed from vital statistics from the Methodist Church at Britannia Cove; 19th century lists of voters as recorded in *White's Papers* at Trinity; *McAlpine's Newfoundland Directory 1894 to 1897*; *McAlpine's Newfoundland Directory for 1898*; and interviews with Random Islanders.

relative, perhaps a sister, to Job and John Pelley who settled at Robinson's Bight about the same time as the Leawood and Tilley families moved to Bound's Mead. Oral tradition has it that Joseph and Hannah Strong of Old Perlican lived at Bound's Mead before moving to Broad Cove (now part of Clarenville). With the departure of John Leawood from Bound's Mead in 1847 and with the Strongs leaving around the same time, no one resided there for many years, perhaps not until the 1890s when Jethro and Elizabeth Pelley were reported to be living there.

East Random Head

East Random Head is the location of the lighthouse on Random Island. For many years there was a lighthouse keeper and his family on East Random Head, and records show that Joseph and Mary Lambert may have been the first family to hold this position. They had a daughter born at the lighthouse in 1896. Apparently, the Lambert stay at the lighthouse overlapped with that of Thomas Cooper of Englewood Forest who was appointed lighthouse keeper in 1895 (Cooper, 1982:xi). Over the years, the family name of Cooper became synonymous with the lighthouse on East Random Head. Thomas Cooper (senior) retired as lighthouse keeper in 1905 to be followed in that position by his son, George, who moved his family from Englewood Forest to the lighthouse in that year. George was succeeded as keeper of the light by his son, Thomas. These three generations of Coopers kept the light on at East Random Head until 1933.

George's Cove

According to the Newfoundland Census of 1874, there were eleven people in George's Cove. This in the only time this settlement is included in census reports. It is therefore suspected that it existed for only a short time, perhaps only for two or three years, which coincided with the 1874 enumeration. While there are no written records identifying the names of the people in George's Cove in 1874, oral tradition has it that a family of Georges lived there during those early days. It is reported that two of their children drowned in one of the neighbouring ponds which are now known as George's Cove ponds.

Random Head Harbour

Oral tradition has it that the French visited Random Head Harbour during the English/French struggles over Newfoundland in the 17th century. Deer Harbour people point to the time-worn engravings found on the moss covered granite slopes in this harbour as evidence of a French presence there. Those engravings include resemblance of a compass with several of the points indicated, parts of words and several letters which appear to have been engraved separately. Perhaps these parts of words and letters are the only remains of more extensive original engravings. Oral tradition also has it that two ships were wrecked on the rocks at the entrance to Random Head Harbour and that pirates buried money and other valuables in that harbour from those wrecks.

As indicated by names of geographical locations such as Bugden's Hole, Hurdle's Pond and Sinnex's Brook in Random Head Harbour, there were winter people and, perhaps, all year settlers in this harbour around 1840 or earlier. However, there are no written records available for settlers in this harbour until the 1890s when Ezra and Caroline Marsh of Deer Harbour moved there. Shortly thereafter a couple of other families from Deer Harbour followed suit and made Random Head Harbour their place of abode. Methodist records show that several children were born in Random Head Harbour in the 1890s, including four of Ezra and Caroline (nee Seaward) Marsh: specifically, Adam, Eliza May, Philip and Richard. As noted in Table 6-2, Adam and Philip also lived in this harbour and some of their children were born there.

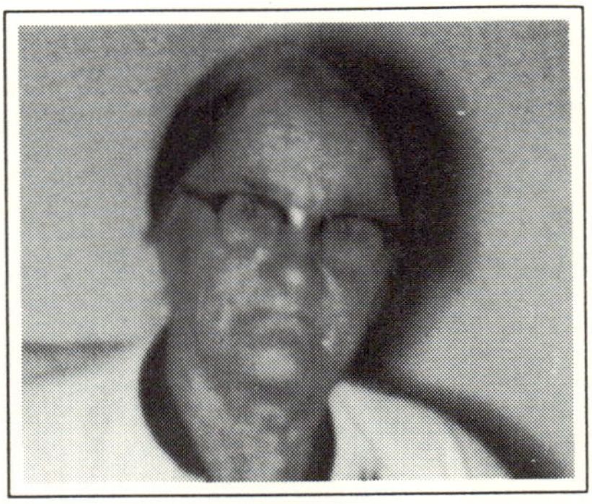

Philip and May (nee Horwood) Marsh. (Photos courtesy of William and Doreen Marsh)

Abraham and Susannah Martin and their children, of Hickman's Harbour, lived in Random Head Harbour for several winters between 1900 and 1925. Two of their sons also built dwelling houses in this harbour, but resided there only during the winter months, returning to Hickman's Harbour in late spring or early summer of each year. Table 6-2 is a summary of information on the presence of the Marshes and Martins in Random Head Harbour from 1880s to the 1930s.

James and Lillian Kelly (nee Marsh) of Deer Harbour lived in Random Head Harbour for several years in the early 1900s. Their son, Leander (Lindo) was born there in 1906.

TABLE 6-2

THE MARSHES AND MARTINS IN RANDOM HEAD HARBOUR

NAME	ADDITIONAL INFORMATION
Adam Marsh Maggie Marsh (nee Lambert)	Adam and Maggie Marsh lived in Random Head Harbour for a number of years. Their daughter Ethel Maud was born there in 1922.
Ezra Marsh Caroline Marsh (nee Seaward)	Ezra and Caroline Marsh of Deer Harbour were first permanent settlers to Random Head Harbour. They lived in Random Head Harbour from the 1880s until the 1930s.
Harry Marsh	Harry Marsh moved from Deer Harbour and built a house in The Crick at Random Head Harbour. Where he lived alone for many years.
Philip Marsh May Marsh (nee Horwood)	Philip and May Marsh lived in Random Head Harbour for a number of years and some of their children were born there before they moved to Little Harbour and then to Strong's Tickle where they resided for several years before settling in Hickman's Harbour.
Abraham Martin Susannah Martin (Thistle)	From around 1900 to the 1925 Abraham and Susannah Martin and their children spent their winters in Random Head Harbour where Abraham had a sawmill. They would return to Hickman's Harbour each spring.
Charles Martin Nora Martin (nee Peddle)	Charles Martin, son of Abraham and Susannah, built a winter house in Random Head Harbour where he and his family spent several winters. Nora was from Lady Cove.
Willis Martin Hartie Martin (nee King)	Willis Martin, son of Abraham and Susannah Martin, and his wife Hartie (nee King) of Deer Harbour spent several winters at Random Head Harbour. One of their sons, Clarence, was born in Random Head Harbour in 1916.

Source: This Table was developed from vital statistics from the Methodist Church at Britannia Cove; nominal census for Deer Harbour in 1935 and 1945; and interviews with Naomi King, Adam Marsh, Elizabeth Marsh and Charles F. Martin.

Robinson's Bight

Robinson's Bight was one of the first places to be permanently settled in the Northwest Arm of Random. Records suggest that Job and John Pelley of Hant's Harbour settled in Robinson's Bight during the late 1840s or early 1850s. One written report is that they married sisters, who were daughters of John Tilley of Hant's Harbour (Adams, 1954:54). John later moved to George's Brook and started the Pelley family in that area of Smith Sound. Job and his wife, Elizabeth, made Robinson's Bight their permanent place of abode. Charles and Hannah Clench (sometimes spelt "Clinch"), also of Hant's Harbour, lived in Robinson's Bight during those early days. It is said that the Charles and Hannah had at least two sons born in Robinson's Bight before they moved on to make Upper Shoal Harbour their permanent place of abode. Hart and Janes were also among the names of Robinson's Bight pioneers. McAlpine lists four fishermen in Robinson's Bight in 1898: Samuel Hart, Josiah Janes, German Pelley and John Pelley. Names of Robinson Bight pioneers and notes on their presence in that place are presented in Table 6-3.

Souley's Brook and Wake's Brook

Souley's Brook and Wake's Brook are located to the north west of Snook's Harbour. Both brooks were considered as settlements unto themselves in Newfoundland Censuses from 1901 to 1921, inclusive. They were settled by Bakers in the 1870s, by Coopers, Jacobs and Ryans in the 1880s, and by a family of Smiths in the 1890s. Some of the descendants of those early settlers left Random Island altogether during the 1920s, while others moved to Elliott's Cove and Snook's Harbour. Since both Souley's Brook and Wake's Brook were often considered as one settlement in written records, it is impossible to identify which families were in each of those places. Consequently, the early settlers to Souley's Brook and Wake's Brook are included in the presentation on Snook's Harbour in the previous chapter. Two family names are found on land grants for the Souley's Brook and Wake's Brook areas which have not been identified in written records as residents of those areas. One is Valentine Kelly, likely of Black Duck Cove, Ireland's Eye Island; the other is Dougal White. We do not know where White came from, nor do we know for sure if Kelly and/or White lived in the area in question. However, it is suspected that they resided there, perhaps only for short periods of time, and maybe only during winter, returning to their main places of abode for the rest of the year.

TABLE 6-3

PIONEERS OF ROBINSON'S BIGHT

NAME	ADDITIONAL INFORMATION
Richard Baker Maria Baker	Richard and Maria Baker had a child born in Robinson's Bight in 1905.
Charles Clench Hannah Clench	Charles and Hannah Clench came from Hant's Harbour to settle in Robinson's Bight during the 1840s. They resided in the Bight for a few years before settling permanently at Upper Shoal Harbour.
Samuel Hart	Samuel Hart of Robinson's Bight and Lady Cove also lived in Hickman's Harbour for a short period during the early 1900s.
Josiah Janes Lucy Ann Janes	Josiah and Lucy Ann Janes had a child born in Robinson's Bight in 1884. No other information has been found on their presence in this settlement.
Phillip King	Phillip King was listed as a voter in "Robin's Bight" in the 1870s. But no other record has been found on him.
German Pelley Amelia Ann Pelley	It is believed that German Pelley was a son of Job and Elizabeth Pelley. They had three children born in Robinson's Bight in the 1890s.
Job Pelley Elizabeth Pelley (nee Tilley)	This is first family to settle permanently in Robinson's Bight. They had a daughter born there in 1857 and son born there in 1859.
John Pelley	John Pelley and Job Pelley were brothers. After living in Robinson's Bight he moved to George's Brook in 1862.
John Pelley Amelia Jane Pelley	John and Amelia Jane Pelley had a child born in Robinson's Bight in 1883 and another one born there in 1884.

NAME	ADDITIONAL INFORMATION
Norman Pelley Anne Ellen Currie (nee Currie)	Norman Pelley of Robinson's Bight married Anne Ellen Currie of Britannia Cove in 1890s.
Elijah Penney Priscilla Penney (nee Blundell)	Elijah and Priscilla Penney moved from Deer Harbour to live in Robinson's Bight during the 1890's. After a few years in Robinson's Bight they spent a short time in Hickman's Harbour before returning to Deer Harbour.
John Robinson Cecilia Robinson	John and Cecilia Robinson, who lived in Trinity in the 18th century, are said to have spent several winters at *Pistern Mere.* After their presence this place became known as *Robinson's Bight.*
Isaac Sevier Elizabeth Sevier (nee Pelley)	Isaac Sevier of Lance Cove married Elizabeth Pelley of Robinson's Bight in 189l. They were married in Robinson's Bight.

Source: This Table was developed from vital statistics from the Methodist Church at Britannia Cove and Hant's Harbour; vital statistics from the Church of England at Trinity and Trinity East; *Geographical Index to Land Grants 1830 to 1930*; 19th century lists of voters as recorded in *White's Papers* at Trinity; *McAlpine's Newfoundland Directory 1894 to 1897*; and *McAlpine's Newfoundland Directory for 1898.*

CHAPTER 7

FOR THE RECORD

To complement the foregoing discussions on settlements and settlers on Random Island, the present chapter is a collection of facts relating to the island's population, its early industries, developments in transportation and communication on the island, commercial enterprises undertaken there, activities in connection with wildlife, and other points of interest about the island.

Physical Features

Random Island is approximately twenty-two miles long, nine miles wide on the eastern end, four miles in the middle and ten miles wide on the western end. With an area of about one hundred and twenty square miles, it is the largest island in Newfoundland.

❖ ❖ ❖

The more than two hundred and fifty ponds and numerous gullies and steadies on Random Island mean that almost one-half of the island is covered with water. The largest pond on the island is Tickle Pond, sometimes referred to as "Ivany's Pond". It is an unusual shape with numerous tickles, peninsulars and coves. From Lower Lance Cove country, it stretches southwest toward Hickman's Harbour and southeast toward Random Head Harbour.

❖ ❖ ❖

With an elevation of 843 feet (257 metres), Ginpicker Hill is the highest point of land on Random Island. It is about midway between Deer Harbour and Lower Lance Cove.

❖ ❖ ❖

Having travelled Smith Sound and anchored at the northwest corner of Random Island on July 7, 1838, J.B. Jukes, describing his excursion around Random Island, wrote:

> There is here a shallow bar connecting Random Island with the mainland, which is only passable at high water. .... The shoreline here, both on the island and main, is low and well wooded,... and its soil is of a superior fertility to that of the rest of the country, and timber is consequently better.

The next day he travelled along the Northwest Arm to Hickman's Harbour and wrote:

> The character of the scenery of Random Sound, on the south side of the island,is much the same as that of Smith's Sound on the north, wild and beautiful, and conveying, from its stillness and silence, feeling of utter solitude and seclusion (Jukes, 1942: 60-62).

Settlements

Over the years there have been at least twenty-seven settlements on Random Island. The first permanent settlement on the island was at Rider's Harbour. It was settled as such around 1770 and people lived there for over 100 years before it was abandoned in the late 1880s. The most recent settlement to be established on the island is Random Heights. It began in the 1970s, some 200 years after Rider's Harbour had its beginning.

❖ ❖ ❖

With a population of 69 people, Rider's Harbour was the largest settlement on Random Island in 1836. In fact, at that time it was larger than any settlement in Random and Smith Sounds. By 1845, Deer Harbour had the distinction of being the largest community on Random Island and larger than any place in those sounds.

❖ ❖ ❖

Outlying places on Random Island which were, at one time or another,listed as settlements in Newfoundland censuses include Bar Point, Bluff Head Cove, Brown's Mead, East Random Head, George's Cove, Random Head Harbour, Souley's Brook and Wake's Brook.

❖ ❖ ❖

The present settlements on Random Island are Aspey Brook, Aspen Cove, Britannia, Elliott's Cove, Hickman's Harbour, Lady Cove, Lower Lance Cove, Petley/Middle Lance Cove, Random Heights, Robinson's Bight, Snook's Harbour and Weybridge.

❖ ❖ ❖

During the 1860s there was considerable migration of people from Trinity and surrounding area to Random and Smith Sounds. As written in Newfoundland Census of 1869: "People appear to some extent to have left Trinity (and surrounding area) and settled in Random and Smith Sounds."

❖ ❖ ❖

While most of the pioneers to the present settlements on Random Island came from other places in Trinity Bay or from Conception Bay, the majority of those who settled in Rider's Harbour during the late 18th and early 19th centuries emigrated from England and Ireland to Rider's Harbour.

❖ ❖ ❖

What is now Weybridge was, for many years, considered as two settlements, namely, Bald Nap and Foster's Point.

❖ ❖ ❖

Petley was first called Lance Cove and then Upper Lance Cove before it was finally named Petley in honour of a Church of England minister, the Reverend Henry Petley. This Reverend Henry Petley was a son of another Reverend Henry Petley, who came to Newfoundland sometime in the 1850s as a missionary with the Society for the Propagation of the Gospel in Foreign Parts.

❖ ❖ ❖

While many people left Thoroughfare during the late 1950s, it was not fully resettled until 1960. A few families had left Deer Harbour during the late 1950s and early 1960s, but it was not officially resettled until 1967.

Demography

The first record of a marriage on Random Island is for one that took place at Rider's Harbour in 1770. It was the marriage of William Sevier of Ringwood, Hants, England, to Rachel Haddow (Hodder) of Rider's Harbour.

(From Church of England records at Trinity)

❖ ❖ ❖

The earliest record of a child born on Random Island is that of a daughter, Leah Sevier, born to William and Rachel Sevier at Rider's Harbour in 1782.

(From Church of England records at Trinity)

❖ ❖ ❖

As recorded in the King's Cove Roman Catholic Church, there were at least nine children baptized in Rider's Harbour during 1829.

❖ ❖ ❖

The first record of a child born in Hickman's Harbour was that of Harriett Blundell, daughter of Stephen and Elizabeth Ann Blundell. She was born in 1843, perhaps a year or two before her family took up permanent residence in Hickman's Harbour.

❖ ❖ ❖

The first recorded female occupation on Random Island was that of "boat keeper". Elinor Quinn of Rider's Harbour is classified as such in the record of her marriage to James Sullivan of Youghall, Ireland, in 1804. The marriage took place in Rider's Harbour.

❖ ❖ ❖

At least eight people from Random Island lived for 100 years or more. They were: Moses Brown (1826-1927) of Thoroughfare, William Sharpe (1854-1954) of Lady Cove, Keziah Marsh/nee Crocker (1867-1967) of Deer Harbour, Elfredia Martin/nee Martin (1875-1976) of Hickman's Harbour, Susannah Martin/nee Pond (1876-1976) of Foster's Point and Hickman's Harbour, Arthur Marsh (1885-1985) of Deer Harbour, Mary Adey/nee March (1886-1988) of Lady Cove and Weybridge, Lucy Ivany/nee Marsh (1889-19) of Deer Harbour and Lower Lance Cove.

❖ ❖ ❖

The last person to be buried in Thoroughfare was William Langer (1956). Beatrice King (nee Brown), formerly of Thoroughfare, was the last person to be buried in Deer Harbour (1966).

❖ ❖ ❖

Since the island was permanently settled, more than one hundred Random Islanders have died accidentally. Many of them were from drowning, some were victims of logging accidents, a few died in fires, and, in recent years, automobile accidents have claimed several lives.

Moses Brown. (Photo courtesy of Leah Mills)

William Sharp. (Photo courtesy of Weldon Hart)

Keziah Marsh. (Photo courtesy of Dorothy Oldford)

Elfredia Martin. (Photo courtesy of Betty Avery)

Susannah Martin. (Photo courtesy of Mary Burry)

Arthur Marsh. (Photo courtesy of Elizabeth Marsh)

Mary Adey. (Photo courtesy of Reuben and Olive March)

Lucy Ivany.

Fishery

The first salmon cannery in Newfoundland was on Random Island. It was located at Salmon Cove (locally known as "Deer Cove") and was in operation in the 1860s. It was owned by John Tilley, formerly of Hant's Harbour, but then of Lower Shoal Harbour. He entered a sample of his canned salmon in a fishery exhibition in Copenhagen, Denmark, in 1862 and received a bronze medal for the quality of his product. The medal included a citation which read: "Warranted to keep free from taint and to retain its purity and nutritious quality, in any climate, for many years."

(From records at the Heritage Room,
Regional Library, Clarenville.)

❖ ❖ ❖

By combining the data from each of the Random Island settlements included in the 1901 census it is found that there were eight lobster factories on Random Island at the turn of the century. It has been suggested that Thoroughfare had the first lobster factory on the island.

❖ ❖ ❖

According to Newfoundland census of 1911, there was a salmon cannery business in Thoroughfare at that time.

❖ ❖ ❖

From the 1920s until the early 1950s, there were herring factories at Britannia Cove, Deer Harbour, Hickman's Harbour and Thoroughfare. All, but one, of those places had smoke houses where kippers (smoked herring) and smoked salmon were cured for export.

❖ ❖ ❖

Benjamin Lewis Martin of Hickman's Harbour was the first person on Random Island, and probably the first in Newfoundland, to smoke caplin for export to the Canadian market. He had "smokers" for that purpose in the early 1920s. In fact, from the early 1920s to the early 1950s hanging caplin on skivers for drying and smoking was done on a larger scale in Hickman's Harbour than in any other community in Newfoundland.

❖ ❖ ❖

As reported in Newfoundland Census, forty Random Island schooners participated in the Labrador fishery in 1935.

❖ ❖ ❖

Gordon Martin's fish factory in Hickman's Harbour in the 1940s. The first floor was for cleaning and curing herring and mackerel. The second floor was used for storing twine and the third floor was used mainly for packing and drying caplin. (Photo courtesy of Welma Critch)

Gordon Martin of Hickman's Harbour was the first fisherman on Random Island, and probably the first in Trinity Bay, to use a purse seine for catching mackerel. He used such a seine in the early 1950s from his longliner-type boat the *Vera Gertrude.*

The fish factory at Thoroughfare in the 1940s. This picture is from an old postcard which had the following handwritten message on the back: "This is part of the packing room. The high part is the smoker and these little doors in the roof are for letting the smoke out. This is the view coming in through the tickle." (Photo courtesy of James Langer)

❖ ❖ ❖

A survey of Newfoundland fishing communities in 1952 reported that Deer Harbour was the only settlement in Newfoundland where codtraps were worked singlehandedly during the 1940s and early 1950s. The tradition of one man working a codtrap continued in Deer Harbour until the community was resettled in 1967.

Forestry and Related Topics

There were two major forest fires on Random Island. One of those was on the eastern end of the island in the 1830s. It started in Smith Sound and burned in a southeasterly direction until it reached Deer Harbour where several dwelling houses and fishing premises were destroyed and one man lost his life. The second major fire started September 16, 1917 in the Aspey Brook / Petley area and spread east past Britannia Cove to Tickle Pond. It destroyed the Church of England Church in Petley and several homes in the Petley / Britannia Cove area. It also burned the forest to the north of Foster's Point, Lady Cove and Robinson's Bight.

❖ ❖ ❖

Among the first water-driven sawmills on Random Island was one constructed by Job and John Pelley at Robinson's Bight in the 1850s. At about the same time Stephen Blundell and his sons built a water-driven sawmill in Hickman's Harbour. Mills of this type were constructed in the many coves and harbours with brooks emptying into them. Thoroughfare was the only settlement on Random Island that did not have a water-driven sawmill. There were forty-eight sawmills on Random Island in 1911. By 1921, the number of mills had risen to seventy.

❖ ❖ ❖

The dams which were constructed to control water for the sawmills downstream from Middle Lance Cove ponds gave way in the spring of 1910 and caused considerable loss of property. The rushing river swept away three sawmills and two log cabins used by loggers and their families.

❖ ❖ ❖

The first industrial accident on Random Island happened at Robinson's Bight around 1858. John Pelley, who had moved from Hant's Harbour to Robinson's Bight, sawed his arm nearly off while operating his mill. Since there was no other man at Robinson's Bight at the time, two women rowed a punt to Deer Cove where they got several men and a trap-skiff and continued the journey to Hant's Harbour en route to Heart's Content, the location of the nearest doctor. John kept his arm in a bag of flour to check the bleeding during the trip to Hant's Harbour. Upon arriving at Hant's Harbour, the men requested that the doctor come there to attend to Mr. Pelley's injury. Describing the scene when the doctor arrived at Hant's Harbour, Mrs. Arch Adams wrote:

> When he got to Hant's Harbour some men held Mr. Pelley by main force while the doctor sawed the bone that was hanging on with a hand saw. Then he made incisions in the flesh and drew the skin down over the remaining stump and dressed it. But by that time the patient had become mercifully unconscious. No anaesthetics, no antiseptics, no way to send word to his poor distressed wife, who had to stay behind alone with her children (Mrs. Arch Adams, 1954: 54).

❖ ❖ ❖

By combining the information given on each of the communities on Random Island in Newfoundland Census for 1901, it is seen that almost two million board feet of lumber were produced on the island in that year.

❖ ❖ ❖

One of the first engine operated sawmills on Random Island was owned by three Ivany brothers (James, John and William) of Lower Lance Cove. They purchased a stationary engine for sawing around 1910. Other engines for sawing, the first such engines in different communities, were owned by Luther Smith (senior) of Aspey Brook, William King of Deer Harbour, Reuben Adey of Foster's Point, Ellis and Kesson Reid of Foster's Point, Alexander Thistle of Hickman's Harbour, John Vardy of Hickman's Harbour, Pelleys and Marches of Lady Cove, Reuben and Aquila Laite of Petley and James Walters of Petley, and William Baker and sons of Snook's Harbour. Ralph Duffett of Lower Lance Cove had the first sawmill that could produce "dressed lumber". He got a three-sided plane in 1954.

William Ivany. William was one of the three Ivany brothers who owned one of the first stationary engine on Random Island. (Photo courtesy of Maxwell Deffett)

❖ ❖ ❖

Since the forest was one of the main reasons for settling Random Island, it is not surprising that shipbuilding was a major industry on

Random Island prior to 1900. Local fishermen built schooners for their own use, many of which were not registered. A study of ship registry prior to 1900 reveals that at least fifty schooners were built on the island during that time for merchants at St. John's and Harbour Grace, and for people in different parts of Trinity Bay. Shipbuilding continued to be a major industry on Random Island until the late 1930s.

Brickmaking

The high quality of Random Island clay with respect to brickmaking was pointed out by J.B. Jukes' geological survey of Newfoundland in 1839. The best quality is found on the western end of the island near the Bar. Early experiments in brickmaking on the island soon found that the clay at Elliott's Cove and Snook's Harbour was softer than that near the bar, and it was more suitable for pottery and building blocks than for bricks.

❖ ❖ ❖

The first brickyard on Random Island was at Elliott's Cove and was owned by Aaron and Charles Smith. This operation lasted for only a few years. The Newfoundland Brick & Tile Co. of St. John's started a brickyard to the west of Elliott's Cove at Cramm's Brook and operated it for several years with considerable success until it was burned in 1902. As reported in the Newfoundland census of 1874, some 15,000 bricks were manufactured in the Northwest Arm of Random in that year. It is likely that these bricks were made at or near Elliott's Cove. The Newfoundland census of 1891 reported that 29 men were employed in making 20,000 bricks in Elliott's Cove in that year.

Dorothy Smith of Elliott's Cove displaying flower pots made at her family's brickyard at Snook's Harbour. (Photo courtesy of Alice and Shirley Smith)

❖ ❖ ❖

John P. Smith of Wake's Brook had a small brickmaking operation at that brook for a short time during the 1890s. The brickyard which Aaron Smith of Elliott's Cove established near Snook's Harbour in 1895 became the success story in brickmaking on Random Island. The geography text used in Grade 5 in Newfoundland schools during the 1940s and 1950s included a section about brickmaking in Smith's brickyard on Random Island. It reported that flower pots and weeping tiles were manufactured at Smith's brickyard during the 1930s and 1940s, and that the flower pots were used by every florist in Newfoundland during those days (Manuel, 1960:123-124).

A news item from St. John's as reported in *The Evening Telegram* of December 10, 1941 read as follows:

> The first lot of terra cotta, made from clay, to be used as a backing for brickwork, arrived here yesterday from the plant of Aaron Smith & Sons, Smith Sound, Trinity Bay. The material will be used in the construction of a new wing at the General Hospital.

Slate Quarrying

One report is that 55,000 slates were quarried in Random Sound in 1857 (Newfoundland Census). Since neither the Hickman's Harbour nor the Dartmouth quarries were in operation at that time, it is likely the quarry in question was at Nut Cove, Smith Sound.

❖ ❖ ❖

The first slate quarry on Random Island was started near Hickman's Harbour by Charles Bryant in the 1860s.

❖ ❖ ❖

From about 1870 until 1910 there were two slate quarries on Random Island near Hickman's Harbour. One was operated by William Ellis and James Winter of St. John's and the other was owned by James Allison, a Yorkshire merchant. At that time, there was also a slate quarry at Dartmouth Cove, a cove on the mainland side of the Northwest Arm across from Hickman's Harbour. This quarry was owned by a St. John's merchant, Walter Baine Grieve.

❖ ❖ ❖

A large slate quarry was in operation in Nut Cove in Smith Sound during the latter decades of 19th century. At that time it was operated by David Currie and his brother, Pearce, both of whom came from Wales to run this quarry which was started earlier by their cousin (Martin, 1983:47). In addition to operating the slate quarries in Nut Cove, the Curries also became involved in the lumber business. In fact, they built a large water driven sawmill with a slate roof on it in Britannia Cove. This was the only slate roof sawmill ever to be built on Random Island, and perhaps the only one of its kind in Newfoundland.

❖ ❖ ❖

A commentary on the slate quarries operating in Newfoundland during the early 1900s included the following:

> In 1907 and 1908 operations were carried on with success at Hickman's Harbour which is a very fine property. All the slate taken out was sold here in St. John's and the roofs of the new St. Bonaventure College, the Salvation Army Building and several other private houses were covered with this excellent slate, which has the ideal colour of the best slate.

(From Britannia Cove file, Newfoundland Historical Society, Provincial Archives of Newfoundland and Labrador).

❖ ❖ ❖

The last shipment of slate from the Nut Cove quarry was in 1906 (Martin, 1983:47). The last shipment of slate from the Hickman's Harbour quarry was in 1910.

❖ ❖ ❖

A reminder of the importance of the slate quarries to Random Islanders during the early part of the 20th century is gleaned from the presence of slate roofs still found in different communities on the island. In 1988, there were several slate roof houses in Hickman's Harbour, at least three in Britannia Cove, one in Lady Cove and one in Petley. Earlier, several of the churches and other public buildings on the island had slate roofs, but in 1988 the last such building, the Orange Lodge in Britannia, was taken down.

Farming

Over the years there were only small numbers of fulltime farmers on Random Island. Britannia Cove and Lady Cove were the only settlements on Random Island reporting a fulltime farmer in 1891 (Newfoundland census). According to McAlpine's Newfoundland directories, there was one farmer in Middle Lance Cove in the 1890s. However, fishermen were also considered farmers of a sort in that the Newfoundland Census for 1891 and 1901 have a category of occupations called "fishermen and others who cultivate land". In 1921, there were four farmers at Foster's Point, and one each at Britannia Cove, Hickman's Harbour and Lady Cove, for a total of seven on Random Island at that time.

❖ ❖ ❖

The most important food crop grown on Random Island during early times was potato. Two hundred forty-six bushels of potatoes were grown in Rider's Harbour in 1836. There were three acres of cultivated land producing 87 bushels of potatoes in Deer Harbour in 1845. The twelve settlements on Random Island in 1884 grew almost 2,000 bushels of potatoes. The thirteen settlements on the island in 1934 reported growing close to 14,000 bushels of potatoes and 70,000 pounds of cabbage. To further illustrate the importance of farming to the livelihoods of pioneering Random Islanders, the following 1891 statistics for the island are noted: there were 235 swine and 84 milch cows on the island, 57 cattle were killed for food, more than 3,000 pounds of cabbage produced for local consumption, and about 1,500 pounds of wool produced and used to knit socks, "cuffs" and underwear.

❖ ❖ ❖

A report from the *Harbour Grace Standard* of 1891 reads as follows:

> We read with much pleasure a statement contained in an editorial paragraph in the last number of *The Trinity Record* to the effect that Mr. David Currie of Britannia Cove, Trinity Bay has raised a sheep there, the carcass of which tipped the scales at 140 pounds. The quality of the mutton, too, is said to be excellent. This is a very satisfactory showing what can be done in Newfoundland in the direction of sheep raising. There can be no doubt on that point. Will not people of this district soon bestir themselves.

(From Britannia Cove file, Newfoundland Historical Society, Provincial Archives of Newfoundland and Labrador).

Transportation

The first freight and passenger ship to give regular service to Random Island and other communities in Trinity Bay was the *Leopard*. It was operated by the Newfoundland Railway during the 1890s. The next ship to service the bay, including Random Island, was the *Ethie*. She was one of the alphabet fleet of eight steamers that the Reid Newfoundland Railway Company had constructed in Scotland around 1900. Smaller ships, specifically, the *Wren* and the *Patrol*, provided passenger and freight service to Random Island during the first World War. After that War, the *Malakoff* serviced Random Island and surrounding area for a short time. She was followed by the *Susu*, the last railway ship to provide such a service before it was discontinued in the 1920s. After that time, the government established a ferry service to all places in the Northwest Arm from Hickman's Harbour to Clarenville. This service was run for many years by Allan Smith of Elliott's Cove. Prior to Allan Smith's ferry service, his father, Thomas Smith, had a ferryboat. In fact, Thomas Smith died on board of his boat as it was making a run in 1906. Overlapping Allan Smith's ferry service in the 1920s and 1930s, and continuing until Random Island was connected by causeway to the mainland, each of the communities had one or more passenger boats for transporting people, freight and mail to and from different communities in the area. Some of the owners of these passenger boats were John W. Currie and Joseph Janes of Britannia Cove, Edgar Penney of Deer Harbour, Joseph Blundell, Charles Martin and Alexander Thistle of Hickman's Harbour, Hayward Burt of Lady Cove, and John Baker and Thomas Loder of Snook's Harbour.

❖ ❖ ❖

The *Ethie* unloading freight at Britannia Cove. She was powered by coal-burning steam engines. Note the smoke stacks. (Photo courtesy of Leslie and Betty Ivany)

The Hefferton Causeway connecting Random Island to the mainland of Newfoundland was officially opened in 1952. It was named in honour of Samuel J. Hefferton, who then represented Trinity North in the House of Assembly and was also Minister of Education at the time.

The Honourable Mr. Hefferton was Trinity North's first representative in the House of Assembly after Confederation in 1949. He was also the first Minister of Education in the Government of Newfoundland, having been appointed to that post when the interim Newfoundland Government came into office on April 1, 1949. In May of that year, he was elected to represent Random Island and the rest of Trinity North in the House of Assembly.

Encyclopedia of Newfoundland and Labrador, Volume 2, (1984:904).

❖ ❖ ❖

From the 1930s until the construction of the Hefferton Causeway, the roads connecting communities on Random Island were maintained by men using horse drawn boxcarts. A one man operation was assigned to specific areas and given the responsibility for the upkeep of the roads in that area. The men and the areas they were responsible for were as follows: George Ivany, Britannia Cove/Petley; William Cooper, Elliott's Cove; Charlie Reid, Foster's Point; Reuben March, Lady Cove; and Richard Avery (and later John Martin), Hickman's Harbour.

❖ ❖ ❖

During the 1920s, Ralph King and Graham Rodgers were among the first owners of bicycles on Random Island.

❖ ❖ ❖

The first car on Random Island was owned by Attwood and Norman Smith of Elliott's Cove. They had a cousin, George Smith, who was living in Boston, buy a car for them and ship it to Newfoundland by rail and boat around 1921. They used this car for many years to drive from their home in Elliott's Cove to their brickyard at Snook's Harbour. Later they purchased another car, but it never got the same attention as their first one which was affectionately known as "tin lizzie". Those who owned the first cars in some of the other communities on Random Island were Reuben T. Vardy (1920s) and Uriah Blundell (1930s) of Hickman's Harbour, James Walters of Petley (1930s), and Earl Pelley of Lady Cove (1940s).

❖ ❖ ❖

Esau Penney of Deer Harbour shipped his car from Boston to Newfoundland in 1930 with the intention of taking it to Deer Harbour. However, having shipped it to Clarenville by train and boat, he decided not to take it to Deer Harbour. After storing it in Clarenville for a few months he shipped it to St. John's by train, where he sold it.

The first car on Random Island belonged to Smiths in Elliott's Cove. (Photo courtesy of Hazel Brown)

James Walters had the first car in Petley. It is shown here after it was purchased by Arthur Vardy of Hickman's Harbour. (Photo courtesy of Delilah and William George Blundell)

The first car in Lady Cove, a 1947 Nash Ambassador, was owned by Earl Pelley and is shown here with Neta Pelley (left) and Ernest Pelly. Note the windcharger to the right. (Photo courtesy of Neta Pelley)

Mac Burt and his GMC truck in 1949. (Photo courtesy of Audrey Burt)

William Ryan and his car in Snook's Harbour in 1954. (Photo courtesy of Laverna Cook and Shirley Smith)

❖ ❖ ❖

While the first cars on Random Island were used to transport passengers from one place to another, the first taxi service and trucking business on the island was owned by Maxwell Burt and sons (Mac and Fred) of Lady Cove.

❖ ❖ ❖

Arthur and Doris Vardy were the first Random Islanders to drive from Random Island to St. John's after the Hefferton Causeway was opened in 1952. At that time it was an eight hour drive from Hickman's Harbour to St. John's.

❖ ❖ ❖

The first pavement was laid on Random Island roads in 1977 when the road from the Hefferton Causeway to Elliott's Cove was paved.

Communication and Technology

The only post office serving the people of Random and Smith Sounds in 1864/65 was located at Trinity. It was listed as the "forward post town" at that time. The first settlements on Random Island to receive regular mail delivery were Deer Harbour and Rider's Harbour. Since those two places were on the water route from Old Perlican to Trinity they had weekly mail delivery in 1871. However, the first post offices on Random Island were at Britannia Cove and Hickman's Harbour. The one in Hickman's Harbour was first operated by Joseph Pelley. A post office, then called a "way office", was opened in Thoroughfare in 1885 at the home of John Mills. John and his wife, Sophia, ran this office for forty-eight years then their son, Ralph and his wife, Clarice, operated it for twenty-six years. Beginning with William J. and Amelia King, the post office in Deer Harbour was always operated by the King family. Their son Jabez and daughter-in-law, Naomi, operated the post office in Deer Harbour for more than fifty years. Robinson's Bight had a post office for several years during the late 1890s and early 1900s. McAlpine described Robinson's Bight as "a post, lumbering and fishing settlement" in 1903.

❖ ❖ ❖

Before telephone connection to other parts of Newfoundland, three Random Island communities had wireless telegraph offices: Britannia Cove, Hickman's Harbour and Lady Cove.

❖ ❖ ❖

Joseph Pelley had the first telephone in Hickman's Harbour. It was installed around 1920. The first telephone in Deer Harbour was installed in the post office there in 1922 by John Leawood of Britannia Cove. Edgar T. King sent the first message over this phone. It was a message to William W. Halfyard, representative for the district of Trinity in the House Assembly.

One of the first phonographs on Random Island was brought to Foster's Point from the United States of America by Jacob Adey around 1920. (Photo courtesy of William and Jean Adey)

There is a lighthouse at East Random Head on Random Island. Three generations of Coopers were keepers of this light from around 1890 to 1933.

❖ ❖ ❖

For a few years during the late 1890s and early 1900s, there was a Customers Officer, then known as "sub collector", at Britannia Cove.

❖ ❖ ❖

The first radio on Random Island was owned by the Cooper family at the East Random Head Lighthouse. Even though that radio was audible only with the aid of earphones, it was a welcomed marvel to the keepers of the lighthouse on this sea swept head. It is said that people from East Random Head Harbour and Deer Harbour would visit the Coopers on Sunday afternoons so that they could "see" and hear the radio. Radio came to other settlements on Random Island at different times between the early 1920s and the early 1940s. Most of the early radios on Random Island were operated by large dry cell batteries, while some of them were run by wet cell ones which were periodically rejuvenated by wind chargers.

❖ ❖ ❖

Wind chargers were a familiar sight in many communities on Random Island from the 1920s until the late 1940s. They were wind driven propellers that were used to charge wet cell batteries which were used to light homes and in some cases to supply power to operate radios. One such wind charger was mounted on the "bound" in Deer Harbour to provide lights for the church in that community. After the use of wind chargers to general power, but prior to 1966 when Random Island was linked to the Newfoundland power grid, several homes and public buildings were lit with small engine driven generators.

❖ ❖ ❖

John Leawood of Foster's Point and Britannia Cove had one of the first, if not the first, camera, on Random Island. Glass negatives of pictures he took prior to 1920 are of excellent quality. He was, without a doubt, Random Island's first professional photographer. William T. Smith of Snook's Harbour and Elliott's Cove had a darkroom in Elliott's Cove in the early 1940s for developing films as a commercial venture. William's son, Harrison, who was then in the Royal Air Force, got him started in this business, the first of its kind on Random Island.

❖ ❖ ❖

During the early 1950s there were two movie theatres on Random Island, one each at Britannia Cove and Hickman's Harbour.

❖ ❖ ❖

The first television set in Hickman's Harbour, and one of the first, if not the first, on Random Island, was owned by Alexander and Ethel Thistle. They got it in 1954/55 and placed it on the highest shelf in their general store for everyone to watch. Each night it became the gathering place for many, young and old, as they came to see, but often could only hear, the news and sports events on a "snow" covered screen.

❖ ❖ ❖

The first place on Random Island to be connected to a community water system was Lower Lance Cove in 1972.

❖ ❖ ❖

During the days of the first permanent settlers on Random Island the only medical doctors in Trinity Bay were at Trinity and Heart's Content. Later in the 19th century, there was a doctor stationed at Britannia Cove from where he served Smith and Random sounds. Around 1900, there were two medical doctors stationed on Random Island. One of them was in Britannia Cove and the other was at Foster's Point. Among those who were stationed at Britannia Cove were Drs. Burr, McGregor and Packard. Dr. Bowden from St. John's was stationed at Foster's Point. In those days there was no doctor at Clarenville. In fact, Clarenville did not have a resident doctor until 1925.

❖ ❖ ❖

The Lions Club came to Random Island in 1979 when the Random Lions were granted a charter.

❖ ❖ ❖

The first fire department on Random Island was organized in 1988. In that year the Random West Volunteer Fire Department was established with its base at Elliott's Cove.

Commercial Enterprises

The Curries developed the slate quarries at Nut Cove and established a lumbering business and general store at Britannia Cove during the later part of the 19th century, thus, making Britannia Cove the first centre of commerce on Random Island. It continued to be a major commercial centre in Smith Sound until the late 1920s.

❖ ❖ ❖

The first general store, incorporating lumbering and fishing businesses, at Hickman's Harbour was established by James Martin around 1880. Later James' son, Ingham, operated a similar type of business in Hickman's Harbour. Simultaneously, during the early 1900s, John Vardy started a fish/lumber business in the harbour. From the early 1920s until the 1940s, John's sons, Edmund and Reuben, operated similar types of

James Martin. (Photo courtesy of James Wight)

businesses at Hickman's. But, as noted below, Captain Edmund Vardy developed an international operation which far exceeded any of the other businesses in the harbour, and in fact, in the whole of Trinity Bay at the time. Also in the 1930s and 1940s, one Benjamin Lewis Martin was in the fish business in this place. During the 1950s, that is after the other fish/lumber businesses in the community had ceased to be, another Benjamin Martin continued the business tradition in the harbour so that it remained a commercial centre for different communities on Random Island and in the Southwest Arm of Random until the early 1960s.

Business premises of Captain Edmund Vardy in Hickman's Harbour in the 1940s. Note the schooner, probably the *Ivy and Muriel*, docked parallel to the store. Much of the first floor was used for storing fish. While codfish was packed on part of the second floor, this floor was also used for retail trade. It contained a large department store. (Photo courtesy of Ivy Thistle)

During the 1890s, Neyle-Soper Company of St. John's had branch stores at Britannia Cove and Hickman's Harbour.

❖ ❖ ❖

The first store in Lady Cove was owned by Theophilus Hart. Hayward Burt later established a general store and fishing premises in there.

❖ ❖ ❖

Currie business premises in Britannia Cove in the 1940s or early 1950s. These buildings had slate roofs. (Photo courtesy of Provincial Archives of Newfoundland and Labrador)

Benjamin Martin of Abraham standing in front of his premises around 1954. The first floor was his cooper-shop and a sawmill. A general retail store was located on the second floor.

Willis Gulliford established a substantial fishing and lumbering business at Bald Nap during the last decades of the 19th century and it continued into the early 1900s.

❖ ❖ ❖

The first, and only, co-operative grocery store on Random Island was opened in Aspey Brook in 1940. Most of the people of that community became members of this co-op which was then managed by Rosa Bowring.

❖ ❖ ❖

In connection with the Currie business in Britannia Cove, John Currie had a fleet of schooners in the early part of the 20th century. Records of seven of those schooners are in the ship registry at the Maritime History Centre, Memorial University of Newfoundland.

❖ ❖ ❖

Several Random Island businesses had branch stores and premises elsewhere. Curries of Britannia Cove had a store at Shoal Harbour around 1900. Captain Edmund Vardy of Hickman's Harbour had a wharf, warehouse and office in Baird's Cove, St. John's, as well as fish collecting premises at different locations on the Labrador coast during the 1920s and 1930s. He had a general store at Deer Harbour in the 1940s. Ingham W. Martin of Hickman's Harbour started a general store on Broadway in Corner Brook around 1920 and operated it for a few years before returning to Hickman's in 1929. Benjamin Lewis Martin had a branch store at Clarenville from his Hickman's Harbour business. Hayward Burt of Lady Cove had a seasonally operated business including a general store and a fish business at Lanse Aux Meadows during the 1920s and 1930s. During the 1940s and early 1950s, Gordon Martin of Hickman's Harbour, in partnership with James Tucker, had a sawmill and lumbering operation on what is now Kenmount Road in St. John's. Gordon Martin also had a general store at Stanhope near Lewisporte during that time.

❖ ❖ ❖

Captain Edmund Vardy of Hickman's Harbour was a vessel owner and operated an international shipping business from Hickman's Harbour from around 1920 until the 1940s. He had at least fifteen schooners between 1920 and 1940s, and was the owner and operator of the steam-driven vessel named the *Silver City*.

The *Silver City*. Built in Scotland in 1901, this 313 ton three-mast vessel was purchased in, and brought from Belfast, Ireland by Captain Edmund Vardy of Hickman's Harbour in 1927. With local crews, he used the *Silver City* in the international trade, especially to Portugal, Spain and New England States, until 1939. (Photo copied from a painting courtesy of Ivy Thistle)

Wildlife

According to different reports, there were deer on Random Island before it was permanently settled. For example, oral tradition has it that Deer Harbour got its name because of the presence of deer in the neighbouring forest. There is also written reference to the presence of deer on the island in the 1890s. Reverend Mr. Disher, Congregational minister, Middle Lance Cove, during the 1890s reported that he shot caribou not far from his house in that cove (Disher, 1954:31).

❖ ❖ ❖

As part of the Newfoundland Government's plan to distribute the beaver population around the country, beavers were brought to Random Island in the 1930s. They were placed in ponds at Deer Harbour, Hickman's Harbour and Lady Cove. William Carberry, a wildlife officer from Aspen Cove, assisted in bringing the beavers to the island. The beaver population on the island grew rapidly. In fact, it increased so fast that within ten years certain areas of Random Island became overpopulated and they became somewhat of a nuisance. The Newfoundland

Government then decided to move beavers from the island to elsewhere in Newfoundland and to Labrador. Ralph King of Hickman's Harbour assisted in capturing beavers on Random Island in the 1940s and bringing them to Whitbourne, where they were transferred to other parts of the country.

❖ ❖ ❖

A small herd of young caribou was brought to Random Island by the Department of Wildlife of the Government of Newfoundland in 1964.

❖ ❖ ❖

Some time in the late 1930s, rainbow trout were placed in two ponds near Britannia Cove by John W. Currie. Rainbow trout were also placed in the first pond at Deer Harbour by the Department of Wildlife of the Newfoundland Government in the mid 1940s.

❖ ❖ ❖

During the 1920s and 1930s there were fox farms at Aspen Cove, Britannia Cove and Foster's Point. There were three mink ranchers on Random Island during the late 1940s and early 1950s, located at Elliott's Cove, Lower Lance Cove and Petley.

❖ ❖ ❖

APPENDIX A

CHANGES IN SETTLEMENT NAMES ON RANDOM ISLAND

As noted throughout this book, several of the settlements on Random Island, that is, the earliest, present and outlying settlements on the island, have been referred to by different names over the years. The following is a list of the previous names for each of these settlements as found in written records and as identified in oral tradition.

PRESENT NAMES	PREVIOUS NAMES
Aspey Brook	Aspen Brook
	Lower Aspey Brook
	Apsey Brook
Bound's Mead	Brown's Mead
Britannia Cove	Ladle Cove
	Porridge Cove
	Skimmer's Cove
Deer Harbour	Deer Harbour Bounds
Lower Deer Harbour	John Brown's Deer Harbour
	Dear Harbour
Hickman's Harbour	Reeke's Harbour
	Rix's Harbour
	Rixis Harbour
	Rexman's Harbour
	Rickman's Harbour
	Rixman's Harbour
Lady Cove	Lally Cove
	Lolly Cove
Lower Lance Cove	British Cove
	Lance Cove
	Skimmer's Cove
Middle Lance Cove	Caplin Cove
	Lance Cove
Petley	Lance Cove
	Upper Lance Cove
Rider's Harbour	Ridar's Harbour
	Ryder's Harbour
	Rise's Harbour

Robinson's Bight	Bistern Mere Pistern Mere Robin Bight
Silldown	Seldown Stilldown
Weybridge	Bald Nap Foster's Point

APPENDIX B

CHANGES IN NAMES OF SETTLEMENTS OF ORIGIN OF RANDOM ISLANDERS

Some of the places in Newfoundland which people left to settle on Random Island have since had their names changed. These places are referred to here as places of origin of Islanders. The following is a list of the previous names for each of these settlements as found in written records. A few of these settlements have been resettled.

PRESENT NAMES	PREVIOUS NAMES
Adeytown	Lee Bight
British Harbour	Filthy Harbour
Champneys	Salmon Cove
Clarenville	Broad Cove Brook Cove Dark Cove Lower Shoal Harbour Red Head Beach (Cliff) Russell's Cove
Dunfield	Cuckold's Cove
Elliston	Bird Island Cove
Harcourt	Broad Cove
Ivanhoe	Old Tilt
Kerley Harbour	Careless Harbour
Loreburn	Long Cove
New Chelsea	Seal Cove
Pope's Harbour	Delby's Cove
Port Rexton	Robin Hood Ship Cove
Southport	Fox Harbour
Winterton	Scilly Cove Silly Cove

APPENDIX C

ACKNOWLEDGEMENTS

We are indebted to many people for their assistance at different stages of our research on *Random Island Pioneers*. During the early part of our research, John W. Butt and Leslie Winsor directed us to valuable sources of primary data, and Grace Penney cheerfully opened the files at the Heritage Room, Clarenville Public Library, for our perusal. Burnham Gill offered needed advice. The co-operation of the staff at the Provincial Archives of Newfoundland and Labrador, at the United Church Archives, at the A. C. Hunter Library, at the Newfoundland Room, Queen Elizabeth II Library, at the Maritime History Archives, and at the General Office, Education Building, Memorial University is appreciated. Kevin and Wade Martin assisted in gathering information from tombstones in resettled places on Random Island. Maureen Kent and Ivy O.C Martin gave needed instruction on Word Perfect. The comments received from Professors Ishmael J. Baksh and Garfield Fizzard on an earlier draft were very helpful. Our gratitude goes to William Griffin, for drawing the maps in this book, to Wallace Boone, for technical advice regarding photocopying and to Trudy J. Morgan for her editorial work. The assistance of The Department of the Secretary of State is appreciated. While researching this book we talked to many people on Random Island and to many former Islanders, all of whom willingly shared information on the origins of their families and on the history of settlements on Random Island. In addition to the acknowledgements given for photos throughout this book, deep appreciation is hereby expressed to each and everyone who assisted us in gathering the information contained herein. Here is a list of these people noting the families and the communities they were particularly helpful in assisting us with:

PEOPLE	FAMILIES AND COMMUNITIES
Frederick W. Adams	Britannia Cove
Florence Adey	Weybridge
William Adey	Weybridge
Silas Avery	Avery family
Bessie Bailey	Bailey family
Edith Bailey	Deer Harbour
Harvey Bailey	Bailey family
Wilson Bailey	Bailey Family
Baxter Baker	Baker family
Colin and Leah Baker	Aspey Brook and Snook's Harbour
Willis Benson	Benson family
Murley and Madge Berkshire	Elliott's Cove and Snook's Harbour

William G. and Delilah Blundell	Hickman's Harbour
Watson and Rosa Bowring	Aspey Brook, Britannia Cove and Weybridge
Edith Bray	Smith family
Warren and Joan Brookings	Bailey and Brookings families
Hazel Brown	Elliott's Cove
Ruby Brown	Hickman's Harbour
William Brown	Thoroughfare
Hanuel Bryant	Bryant family
Allison Bugden	Middle Lance Cove
George and Ivy Bugden	Middle Lance Cove, Petley and Snook's Harbour
Cecilia Burt	Burt and Smith families
Annie Butt	Britannia Cove and Lower Lance Cove
Marion Butt	Butt and Martin families
Minnie Butt	Deer Harbour and Hickman's Harbour
Ralph Butt	Butt family
William J. Butt	Hickman's Harbour
Betty Calvert	Lady Cove
Don Churchill	Weybridge
Eliol and Gladys Clark	Middle Lance Cove
Effie Clench	Petley
Frederick and May Cook	Hickman's Harbour
Laverna Cook	Ryan family
Florence Cowan	Blundon family
Elam and Janet Critch	Hickman's Harbour
Annie Currie	Goobie family
Norman and Annie Currie	Currie family
Watkin Currie	Britannia Cove
Marion Davis	Thoroughfare
Leslie Dean	Dean family
Maxwell Duffett	Britannia Cove and Lower Lance Cove
Ralph Duffett	Duffett family
Edward Eddy	Eddy family
Earl and Alice George	Aspey Brook and Middle Lance Cove
Barlett and Lydia Green	Green family
Ross Gulliford	Weybridge
Gordon Halliday	Halliday family
Cecil and Lillian Hansford	Hickman's Harbour
Otto and Rose Hart	Lady Cove
Weldon Hart	Lady Cove
Gladys Hefford	Aspey Brook and Snook's Harbour
Lynette Hiscock and Karen Smith	Smith family
Maria Hiscock	Lady Cove and Weybridge

William and Gwen Hoskins	Hoskins family
Georgina Howell	Stone family
George Ivany	Britannia Cove and Lower Lance Cove
Maxwell and Sadie Ivany	Britannia Cove and Lower Lance Cove
Raymond Ivany	Lower Lance Cove
Ronald Ivany	Britannia Cove, Lower Lance Cove and Middle Lance Cove
David Janes	Britannia Cove, Lower Lance Cove and Middle Lance Cove
Robert and Myra Janes	Britannia Cove
Eric King	King family of Deer Harbour
Lawrence King	King family of Lady Cove
Lloyd and Myrtle King	Deer Harbour
Naomi King	Deer Harbour, Random Head Harbour and Rider's Harbour
Ralph and Myra King	Hickman's Harbour and Lady Cove
Berkley and Minnie Laite	Laite family
Sarah Laite	Lower Lance Cove, Middle Lance Cove and Petley
James Langer	Langer family
Lucy Leawood	Britannia Cove and Petley
Mary Leawood	Aspey Brook and Britannia Cove
Harold Loder	Snook's Harbour
Austin March	Lady Cove
Hector and Priscilla March	Lady Cove
Jean March	Lady Cove
Reuben and Olive March	Lady Cove
Adam Marsh	Deer Harbour, Hickman's Harbour and Random Head Harbour
Allan Marsh	Hickman's Harbour
Baxter Marsh	Deer Harbour
Elizabeth Marsh	Deer Harbour, Random Head Harbour and Rider's Harbour
John and Laura Belle Marsh	Hickman's Harbour
Maxwell Marsh	Deer Harbour
Minne C. Marsh	Deer Harbour and Hickman's Harbour
Samuel and Florence Marsh	Deer Harbour
Charles and Nora Martin	Hickman's Harbour, Lady Cove and Random Head Harbour
Harold Martin	Hickman's Harbour
John and Dorthy Martin	Hickman's Harbour
Stella Martin	Bugden and Burridge families
Chesley Mills	Thoroughfare
Cecil and Jean Mills	Mills and Simmons families
Clarice Mills	Thoroughfare

Leah Mills	Thoroughfare
Jean Orledge	King family of Lady Cove
Raymond and Marion Parrott	Thoroughfare
Earl and Marjorie Pelley	Lady Cove
Neta Pelley	Lady Cove
Blanche Penney	Butt and Penney families
Otto Pitcher	Pitcher family
George and Hazel Pittman	Britannia Cove and Lower Lance Cove
Lawrence Poole	Poole family
Charles and Eleanor Reid	Snook's Harbour and Weybridge
Fred Reid	Reid family
Isabella Reid	Lady Cove and Weybridge
Graham Rodgers	Rodgers family
Ralph Simmons	Simmons family
Alice Smith	Elliott's Cove and Snook's Harbour
Boyce and Lavenia Smith	Elliott's Cove and Weybridge
Harrison Smith	Wake's Brook
May Smith	Aspey Brook and Lower Lance Cove
Ralph and Inez Smith	Patey and Smith families
Shirley Smith	Ryan family
Clement Stone	Lower Lance Cove
Ethel Thompson	Hickman's Harbour
Ivy Thistle	Vardy family
Arthur and Phyllis Toope	Brown and Mills families
Frank and Olive Vardy	Vardy family
Lilly Belle Vardy	Marsh family
Robert Verge	Britannia Cove, Lower Lance Cove and Middle Lance Cove
Viola Verge	Verge family
William and Delilah Walters	Aspen Cove, Bluff Head Cove, Lower Lance Cove Middle Lance Cove and Petley
John and Edith Walters	Aspen Cove, Middle Lance Cove and Petley
Louise Whelan	Deer Harbour and Hickman's Harbour
Lillian Williams	Thoroughfare
Masie Williams	Butt and Critch families
Sarah Wiseman	Hickman's Harbour

APPENDIX D

PRIMARY SOURCES OF WRITTEN INFORMATION

Church Records

Vital Statistics from the following Church of England/Anglican Church records as given in the Department of Public Health and Welfare (DPHW) volumes and Archive files at the Provincial Archives of Newfoundland and Labrador:

Bay de Verde: Births/marriage 1860-91, DPHW Vol. 56.
Heart's Content: Births 1883-92, DPHW Vol. 61
_ Marriages 1879-94, DPHW Vol. 61.
Trinity: Births 1753-1823, DPHW Vol. 64A
Births 1823-60, DPHW Vol. 64
Births 1860-91, DPHW Vol. 63
Marriages 1757-1839, DPHW Vol. 64B
Marriages 1838-91, DPHW Vol. 64C.
Trinity East: Births 1869-91 DPHW Vol. 65
Marriages 1876-91 DPHW Vol. 65.
Random: Births 1880-91 DPHW Vol. 68.
Random Mission: Marriages 1886-1957, File P8/A/13.

Vital Statistics from the following Methodist/United Church of Canada records as given in the Department of Public Health and Welfare (DPHW) volumes and Archive files at the Provincial Archives of Newfoundland and Labrador:

Blackhead: Births 1816-52 DPHW Vol. 52A
Births 1852-92 DPHW Vol 52
Marriages 1916-91 DPHW Vol. 52B.
Britannia Cove: Births 1883-1930 DPHW Vol. 68.
Carbonear: Births 1793-1848 DPHW Vol. 48
Births 1848-70 DPHW Vol. 49
Births 1870-91 DPHW Vol. 50
Marriages 1794-1891 DPHW Vol. 50A.
Hant's Harbour: Births 1824-91 DPHW Vol. 59A
Births 1875-91 DPHW Vol. 59
Marriages 1825-91 DPHW Vol. 59.
Heart's Content: Births 1877-85 DPHW Vol. 60
Marriages 1878-91 DPHW Vol. 60.
Lower Island Cove: Births/Marriages 1850-91 DPHW Vol. 55.
Old Perlican: Births 1816-91 DPHW Vol. 58
Marriages 1816-91 DPHW Vol. 58A.
Random North: Marriages 1892-1921 Archive file P8/A/14.
Shoal Harbour: Births 1892-1917 Archive file P8/A/14.

Vital statistics from the following Methodist/United Church of Canada records as found in the United Church of Canada Archives, St. John's:

Britannia Cove: Births 1883-1930

Burials 1883-1956

Marriages 1888-1930.

Foster's Point: Burials 1928-1956.

Vital statistics from the following Roman Catholic Church:

King's Cove: Births 1770-1835.

Colonial Office Papers

199. 8 "Return of Possessions held in Conception Bay 1805, the 'Plantation Book'." Provincial Archives of Newfoundland and Labrador.

199. 18"An Account of the Colony and Fishery of Newfoundland and Labrador and the Present State thereof with a Map of the Whole Island, 1677." Provincial Archives of Newfoundland and Labrador.

Directories

Hutchinson's Newfoundland Directory, for 1864-65, Containing Alphabetical Directories of Each Place 1864 in the Colony, With a Post Office Directory.... St. John's: Thomas McConnan, Publisher, Bookseller & Stationer.

Lovell's Province of Newfoundland Directory for 1871: Names of Professional and Business Men, and other Inhabitants, Cities, Towns and Villages throughout the Province,.... Montreal: Printed and Published by John Lovell.

McAlpine's Maritime and Newfoundland Gazetteer.... 1903. Halifax, Nova Scotia and St. John, New Brunswick: McAlpine Publishing Co. Ltd.

McAlpine's Newfoundland Directory 1894 to 1897. Saint John, New Brunswick: McAlpine Publishing Co.

McAlpine's Newfoundland Directory for 1898. Saint John, New Brunswick: McAlpine Publishing Co.

McAlpine's Newfoundland Directory for 1904. Saint John, New Brunswick: McAlpine Publishing Co.

Geographical Index to Grants

Volume # 1, 1831-1930, Department of Forestry and Lands, Government of Newfoundland and Labrador.

Methodist Church of Canada

Minutes of the Newfoundland Conference for 1877.

Newfoundland Statistical Censuses for the following years:

1836, 1845, 1857, 1869, 1874, 1884, 1891, 1901, 1911, 1921, 1935, 1945, 1951, 1956, 1961, 1966, 1971, 1976, 1981 and 1986.

Newfoundland Nominal Censuses for following communities and years:

Aspey Brook: 1935 and 1945.

Aspen Cove: 1935.

Britannia Cove: 1935 and 1945.
Deer Harbour: 1935 and 1945.
Elliott's Cove: 1911, 1921, 1935 and 1945.
Foster's Point: 1911, 1921, 1935 and 1945.
Hickman's Harbour: 1911, 1921, 1935 and 1945.
Lady Cove: 1911, 1921, 1935 and 1945.
Lower Lance Cove: 1935 and 1945.
Petley: 1935 and 1945.
Snook's Harbour: 1935 and 1945.
Thoroughfare: 1935 and 1945.

Trinity Bay Census

"A Return of the Number of Houses, Inhabitants, Fishing Rooms, Rents of Rooms, etc. in the District of Trinity Newfoundland in the Winter of 1800 and 1801..."

White's Papers

Trinity Manuscripts/William White's Collection of sixteen items. Box #5, District of Trinity Voters. Provincial Archives of Newfoundland and Labrador.

APPENDIX E

SECONDARY REFERENCES

Adams, Mrs. Arch.—1954

"Footnotes to Hants Harbour Story." *Newfoundland Quarterly*, Volume 53, Number 3, pages 54 and 59.

Adams, Lawrence.—n.d.

"History of Brick-Making in Newofoundland." In the Heritage Room, Regional Library, Clarenville, Newfoundland.

Benson, Valerie.—1983

Benson Family Tree. St. John's: Maritime History Archives, Memorial University of Newfoundland.

Butt, W. John.—1985

The Butt Family in Newofoundland and Labrador. A paper delivered at the Newfoundland Historical Society Meeting, January 1985, St. John's.

Cooper, S.R. (Bert).—1982

Random Thoughts. St. John's: Harry Cuff Publications, Limited.

Cook, Michael.—1977

"One Man's Other Island." *The Evening Telegram,* April 23 and 30.

Department of Fisheries and Oceans.—1980

Sailing Directions: Newfoundland. (Sixth Edition). Ottawa: Department of Fisheries and Oceans, Government of Canada.

Decks Awash.—1983

"Special Issue on Random Island." *Decks Awash,* Volume 12, Number 2 (March/April), 1983.

Decks Awash.—1976

"Deer Harbour" and "Thoroughfare." *Decks Awash,* Volume 5, Number 6, pages 7-10, (October).

Disher, Rhodes, T.F.—1954

Sixty Odd Years. London: Clarke and Cockeran Publishers Ltd.

Fizzard, Garfield.—1987

Unto The Sea: A History of Grand Bank. Grand Bank: Grand Bank Historical Society.

Government of Newfoundland.—1952

Survey of Newfoundland Fishing Communities. St. John's: Government of Newfoundland.

Handcock, Gordon.—1985

"The Poole Mercantile Community and the Growth of Trinity 1700-1839." *The Newfoundland Quarterly,* Volume 80, Number 3, pages 19-30.

Harbour Grace Standard.—1891
A news report from the *Harbour Grace Standard* as found in the Britannia Cove File, Newfoundland Historical Society, Provincial Archives of Newfoundland and Labrador.

Howley, Bishop—1901
"Newfoundland Name-Lore." *The Newfoundland Quarterly*.

Howley, Most Rev. M.F.—1906
"Newfoundland Name-Lore." *The Newfoundland Quarterly*. Volume 6, Number 1, pages 1-2 and 9-10.

Jukes, J. B.—1842
Excursions in and About Newfoundland During the Years 1839 and 1846. London: John Murray.

King, Lloyd.—1963
Deer Harbour, Random Island, Trinity Bay. Deer Harbour File, Newfoundland Historical Society, Provincial Archives of Newfoundland and Labrador.

Manuel, Edith M.—1960
Newfoundland: Our Province. Exeter, England: A Wheaton & Co., Ltd., Educational Publishers.

Martin, Ruby S.B.—1942
Early Settlers of Hickman's Harbour. A Grade Eight Essay, United Church School, Hickman's Harbour.

Martin, Wendy.—1983
Once Upon a Mine: Story of Pre-Confederation Mines on the Island of Newfoundland. Montreal: The Canadian Institute of Mining and Metallurgy.

Matthews, Keith—1971
A 'Who was Who' of Families engaged in the Fishery and Settlement of Newfoundland, 1660-1840. Maritime History Archives, Memorial University of Newfoundland.

Reid, Brenda Mary.—1980
Living Conditions in Early 1900s at Weybridge and Aspen Brook, Random Island. (Paper wrote for Folklore 3420). St. John's: File # 80-319, Folklore Archives, Memorial University of Newfoundland.

Seary S.R.—1976
Family Names of the Island of Newfoundland. St. John's: Memorial Universtiy of Newfoundland.

Smallwood, Joseph R.—1981
Encyclopedia of Newfoundland and Labrador (Volume 1). St. John's: Newfoundland Publishers (1967) Limited.

Smallwood, Joseph R.—1984
Encyclopedia of Newfoundland and Labrador (Volume 2). St. John's: Newfoundland Publishers (1967) Limited.

Story, G.M., W.J. Kirwin and J.D.A. Widdowson.—1982
Dictionary of Newfoundland English. Toronto: University of Toronto Press.

The Clarenville Packet.—1975
"Historical Notes on Random Island." *The Clarenville Packet,* May 30.

The Courier—1862
A news report from *The Courier* (a Harbour Grace newspaper in the 1860s), as found in the Britannia Cove File, Newfoundland Historical Society, Provincial Archives of Newfoundland and Labrador.

The Diocesan Magazine
Reports from *Diocesan Magazine* (an offical paper of the Church of England in Newfoundland, later *The Diocesan Magazine*), 1889-1942.

The Evening Telegram—1941
A news report in *The Evening Telegram,* December 10.

The Methodist Monthly Greeting
Reports from *The Methodist Monthly Greeting* (the official Paper of the Methodist Church in Newfoundland), 1888-1925.

The Monthly Greeting
Reports from *The Monthly Greeting* (an offical paper of the United Church of Canada in Newfoundland), 1926-1935.

Tocque, Reverend Philip.—1878
Newfoundland. As it Was and As It Is In 1877. Toronto: John B. Maagury.

Vardy, R.J. (Bob)—1986
The Vardys of Trinity Bay, Newfoundland. (1st draft). St. John's: 2 Long Pond Road.

FAMILY NAME INDEX